The New Citizenship

Dilemmas in American Politics

Series Editor: **Craig A. Rimmerman**, Hobart and William Smith Colleges

If the answers to the problems facing U.S. democracy were easy, politicians would solve them, accept credit, and move on. But certain dilemmas have confronted the American political system continuously. They defy solution; they are endemic to the system. Some can best be described as institutional dilemmas: How can Congress be both a representative body and a national decision maker? How can the president communicate with more than 250 million citizens effectively? Why do we have a two-party system when many voters are disappointed with the choices presented to them? Others are policy dilemmas: How do we find compromises on issues that defy compromise, such as abortion policy? How do we incorporate racial and ethnic minorities or immigrant groups into American society, allowing them to reap the benefits of this land without losing their identity? How do we fund health care for our poorest or oldest citizens?

Dilemmas such as these are what propel students toward an interest in the study of U.S. government. Each book in the Dilemmas in American Politics series addresses a "real world" problem, raising the issues that are of most concern to students. Each is structured to cover the historical and theoretical aspects of the dilemma but also to explore the dilemma from a practical point of view and to speculate about the future. The books are designed as supplements to introductory courses in American politics or as case studies to be used in upper-level courses. The link among them is the desire to make the real issues confronting the political world come alive in students' eyes.

BOOKS IN THIS SERIES

The New Citizenship

Unconventional Politics, Activism, and Service

FOURTH EDITION

Craig A. Rimmerman
Hobart and William Smith Colleges

WESTVIEW PRESS

A Member of the Perseus Books Group

Published by Westview Press,
A Member of the Perseus Books Group

Find us on the World Wide Web at www.westviewpress.com.

Every effort has been made to secure required permissions to use all text and art
included in this volume.

Westview Press books are available at special discounts for bulk purchases
in the United States by corporations, institutions, and other organizations.
For more information, please contact the Special Markets Department at the
Perseus Books Group, 2300 Chestnut Street, Suite 200, Philadelphia, PA 19103,
or call (800) 810-4145, ext. 5000, or e-mail special.markets@perseusbooks.com.

Library of Congress Cataloging-in-Publication Data
Rimmerman, Craig A.
   The new citizenship : unconventional politics, activism, and service /
Craig A. Rimmerman.—4th ed.
      p.   cm.—(Dilemmas in American politics)
   Includes bibliographical references and index.
   ISBN 978–0-8133–4457–7 (alk. paper)
   1. Political participation—United States.   2. Citizenship—United States.   I. Title.
JK1764.R55 2010
323'.0420973—dc22

                                                                2010003214

10 9 8 7 6 5 4 3 2 1

Contents

Tables and Illustrations

Acknowledgments

This book could not have been completed without the support and inspiration of numerous people. I am grateful to series editor L. Sandy Maisel, who was enthusiastic about this project when I proposed it. Sandy is an enormously gifted teacher and scholar, and I am privileged to appear in a series of which he served as editor. For the first edition, Jennifer Knerr, then Westview's senior political science editor, offered numerous substantive suggestions along the way. Brenda Hadenfeldt, also at Westview while I was writing, made a number of thoughtful revision suggestions to the original manuscript, and I appreciate her help. Westview editors Leo Wiegman, Adina Popescu, and David Pervin entered the editorial process at a crucial stage, providing their support, dedication, and commitment to this project as well as their general good cheer. I especially want to thank Leo Wiegman for his support, encouragement, and professionalism over the years. I am indebted, as well, to three anonymous reviewers of the first edition, whose suggestions have made this a much better book. I would also like to thank Marian Safran, who did a superb job copyediting both the first and second editions; Shena Redmond, then Westview senior project editor, who guided the first edition of this book through production; and Kay Mariea, who did the same for the second edition. Steve Catalano, Westview's acquisitions editor, was the perfect editor for the third edition—supportive and enthusiastic in every way from start to finish. I have also enjoyed and benefited from my association with Michelle Mallin at Westview Press on all three editions of this book. For the third edition, copy editor Jennifer Swearingen did outstanding work, and Iris Richmond ensured that the book was published in a timely manner. In sum, I could not have asked for finer editors with whom to work.

I gratefully acknowledge the efforts of Harry Boyte and the Center for Democracy and Citizenship at the Humphrey Institute of the University of Minnesota for introducing the New Citizenship concept. I borrowed that concept and adapted it for the analysis in this book.

I first began grappling with the ideas in this book as a young graduate student at Ohio State University from 1979 to 1984. While there, I had the privilege of working with a number of supportive professors, including John Dryzek, Jim Farr, Lawrence J. R. Herson, Randall Ripley, and Goldie Shabad. I am grateful for their support and encouragement at a crucial stage in my professional development. All of them remind me by example of the important connection between quality teaching and scholarship.

I have been privileged as well to have spent the past twenty-five years teaching at Hobart and William Smith Colleges, an institution that prides itself on encouraging faculty and students to interact with one another outside traditional and narrow disciplinary boundaries. I have been fortunate to have had the chance to discuss my ideas about democracy, education, and citizenship with several colleagues through the years: Scott Brophy, Chip Capraro, Robert Gross, Chris Gunn, Steven Lee, Derek Linton, Dunbar Moodie, David Ost, Wes Perkins, and Don Spector. They have all challenged me in more ways than they will ever know. Sara Greenleaf, Joseph Chmura, and the entire Hobart and William Smith library staff have supported me with books and materials over the years. I am so grateful to teach at an institution whose library staff does everything possible to support the teaching and research interests of faculty and students. Mary Hickey helped me format the final draft so I could submit it in a readable form. Finally, Matthew Simpson, a Hobart senior honors student, did superb work in collecting Internet materials related to the third edition of the book.

The third edition also benefited enormously from the thoughtful, critical observations of three anonymous reviewers, all of whom have used this book in their courses. I am grateful not only to them but to all faculty who have chosen to share my ideas with their students. My own students in five of my courses—Introduction to American Politics; Democratic Theory; Social Policy and Community Activism; Environmental Policy; and a senior seminar titled the Civil Rights Movement and Public Policy—offered insightful responses to my arguments and reminded me of the joys of teaching.

For this fourth edition, I am once again grateful to three anonymous, external reviewers who have taught earlier editions of the book and who offered such perceptive suggestions for revision. And I continue to benefit enormously from the goodwill and thoughtfulness of my students across all of my courses at Hobart and William Smith Colleges—Democracy and Public Policy, Democratic Theory, Sexual Minority Movements and Public Policy, Social Policy and Community Activism, and Environmental Policy—who have responded with care and insight to many of the ideas that appear in this book. Thank you, as well, to Anthony "Toby" Wahl, Westview's acquisitions editor for the Dilemmas Series, who was supportive of this fourth edition from the outset. I am so lucky to be working with such an outstanding editor. I also thank Westview's outstanding production and marketing team, especially Melissa Veronesi and Kelsey Mitchell, who have been such a privilege to work with since the first edition went into production now over twelve years ago. Sharon DeJohn did a terrific job in copyediting the manuscript. And Jean Salone, Stern Hall secretary extraordinaire, has helped me in so many ways as I prepared this fourth edition for the production process.

Finally, I wish to acknowledge the many students I have taught at three different institutions—Ohio State University, the College of Charleston, and Hobart and William Smith Colleges. Through their questions, observations, and commitment, my students have encouraged me to recognize the important link that the political scientist must make between the classroom and the larger political and social scene. With gratitude, I dedicate this book to them.

Craig A. Rimmerman

Acronyms

ACORN	Association of Community Organizations for Reform Now
ACT UP	AIDS Coalition to Unleash Power
BUILD	Baltimore United in Leadership Development
COFO	Council of Federated Organizations
COOL	Campus Outreach Opportunity League
CORE	Congress of Racial Equality
DLC	Democratic Leadership Council
ELF	Earth Liberation Front
FDA	Food and Drug Administration
MFDP	Mississippi Freedom Democratic Party
NCCC	National Civilian Community Corps
NIMBY	not in my backyard
OPIC	Ohio Public Interest Campaign
SCAR	Southeast Council Against the Road
SCLC	Southern Christian Leadership Conference
SDS	Students for a Democratic Society
SECO	Southeast Baltimore Community Organization
SES	socioeconomic status
SNCC	Student Nonviolent Coordinating Committee
STARC	Student Alliance to Reform Corporations
USAS	United Students Against Sweatshops
VISTA	Volunteers in Service to America
WTO	World Trade Organization

1

···

Introduction to the Core Dilemma

Anybody had'a just told me 'fore it happened that conditions would make this much change between the white and the black in Holmes County here where I live, why I'da just said, "you're lyin'. It won't happen." I just wouldn't have believed it. I didn't dream of it. I didn't see no way. But it got to workin' just like the citizenship class teacher told us—that if we could redish' to vote and just stick with it. He says it's gon' be some difficults, gon' have troubles, folks gon' lose their lives, peoples gon' lose all their money, and just like he said, all of that happened. He didn't miss it. He hit it ka-dap on the head, and it's workin' now. It won't never go back where it was.

—Hartman Turnbow

- Ebonics? first thought.

IN HIS COLLECTION of interviews with civil rights movement participants carried out between 1974 and 1976, journalist Howell Raines includes Hartman Turnbow's reflection on the meaning of the vote for African American Mississippians in the 1960s.[1] Turnbow describes the enormous difficulties in their obtaining the right to vote. Many who participated in the civil rights movement had to embrace **unconventional politics** to open the system in a more democratic manner to those who had been excluded from the most fundamental elements of the democratic process. It is hard to believe that a mere four decades after many risked their lives to register to vote in the South, we lament the rise in civic indifference, as measured by voter-turnout rates in presidential and **off-year elections**, that is, those between presidential elections.

Recent studies also indicate that over the past fifty years there has been a decline in Americans' psychological engagement in politics and government. Citizens increasingly perceive that they cannot trust Washington government officials and that their participation in any form of conventional politics is of little consequence; in short, they are exhibiting **political alienation**. Surveys also indicate that more and more Americans have withdrawn from the affairs of their own community. Yet at the same time, the events of September 11, 2001, have been a defining moment for many Americans, especially for the current generation of college students, whose view of the future and America's role in the world have been challenged in fundamental ways. Some commentators have compared the impact of September 11 on young people to the impact of World War II and the Vietnam War on their parents and grandparents. Indeed, American civic attitudes changed suddenly in light of September 11 as many more people displayed social solidarity, a greater trust in more active federal government to heal the nation in a time of crisis, and a commitment to civic participation. In the words of social scientist Theda Skocpol, "Like the outbreak of earlier wars in U.S. history, September 11 created vast possibilities for civic renewal."[2]

Meanwhile, there has been an explosion over the past two decades in the number of talk radio and television shows that thrive in response to the citizenry's increasing alienation from the political system, talk shows that have continued to thrive in the post–September 11 landscape. Tune in to virtually any of these programs, and you will hear angry citizens decry "politics as usual" and the politicians who supposedly represent them. Various commentators have accurately reported that such programs represent a decline in civility.

In addition, there appears to be an alarming increase in factious political activity, largely on the far right, which threatens the overall stability of American society. In recent years we have witnessed the rise of right-wing hate groups, from the Posse Comitatus to Operation Rescue to the Michigan Militia, all of which have embraced violence at times as a response to particular policies their adherents oppose. With the rise of such groups, we move from a decline in civility to a threat to overall system stability. As I discuss in Chapter 2, the constitutional framers were concerned that factious activity could threaten the stability of their newly created political and economic system. The central dilemma of this book—How does a polity strike a balance among the varieties of political activities engaged in by its citizens and residents?—is related to that concern.

In this book I assess the various ways citizens do and do not participate in their communities and in American politics. Considerable attention is devoted to the attitudes and values of college students as they approach their roles as citizens within the American political system. Two questions lie at the heart of the book: What role does the citizenry play in the American political system? What role should the citizenry play? In addressing them, I evaluate the dilemma of the relationship among participation, civility, and stability from a number of vantage points. First and foremost, I examine the consequences of civic indifference for contemporary American politics. I describe the nature of civic indifference, explain why many Americans fail to vote and participate in their community's affairs, and discuss ways citizens might be empowered to reduce their distance from government. In addition, I identify alternative forms of participation (besides voting) utilized by the citizenry to register their discontent with their representatives and government. Thus the relationships between citizen participation and the broader issues of civic responsibility, community, democracy, and citizenship are clarified.

All of these important issues are interrogated in light of the extraordinary 2008 presidential election and the role that young voters played in electing

Barack Obama president of the United States. An array of commentators have pointed out that this is the first election in which what has come to be known as the **Millennial Generation** was galvanized by a candidate to organize using an array of technological developments (all of which are explored in Chapter 5) and to vote.

I also examine the broader consequences of the citizen anger with politics and politicians expressed on radio and television talk shows to see where this anger fits into the landscape of American democracy. It is indeed ironic that at the very moment that many are lamenting the civic indifference associated with low voter-turnout rates, there seems to be an upsurge in American political activity that is not associated with voting per se. This political phenomenon is evaluated from a number of different perspectives. The conservative tea party movement, which erupted in the summer of 2009, is a powerful example of citizen organizing at the grass roots.

The new facets of participation embraced by the citizenry, all of which go beyond merely voting, form the basis of the New Citizenship. The New Citizenship is rooted in the notion that people are not born as citizens; they need to be educated and trained. This training emphasizes the importance of understanding civic rights and encourages regular participation. Civic efforts need to be placed within a context broader than that of individual volunteering. The New Citizenship attempts to enhance the quality of democracy by bringing together people from different backgrounds, in a spirit of toleration, respect, trust, and social and political engagement.

I examine various manifestations of the New Citizenship, including grassroots mobilization and community participation, service learning, and the Internet, as potential vehicles for enabling the citizenry to act in a more participatory manner. These are the central elements of the New Citizenship, a concept that extends the participatory democratic vision articulated in the 1960s. It is argued here that the New Citizenship will enable the polity to confront the breakdown of civility in American politics in meaningful ways. The New Citizenship is also an important means for bridging the ever-increasing gap between the **public sphere** (the arena of intersection between an individual's interests and those of the larger community) and the **private sphere** (the locus of the individual's own interests).

The New Citizenship goes well beyond the traditional model of political participation. In his classic text, *Political Participation,* political scientist Lester Milbrath sketches the "hierarchy of political involvement." This hierarchy forms the basis of the traditional model of political participation.

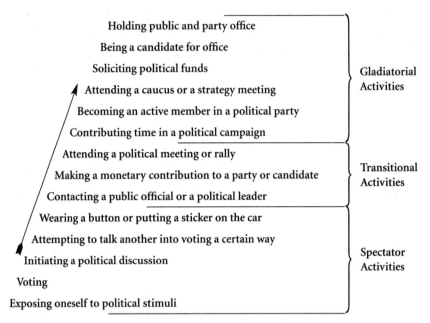

Holding public and party office
Being a candidate for office
Soliciting political funds
Attending a caucus or a strategy meeting
Becoming an active member in a political party
Contributing time in a political campaign

Gladiatorial Activities

Attending a political meeting or rally
Making a monetary contribution to a party or candidate
Contacting a public official or a political leader

Transitional Activities

Wearing a button or putting a sticker on the car
Attempting to talk another into voting a certain way
Initiating a political discussion
Voting
Exposing oneself to political stimuli

Spectator Activities

FIGURE 1.1   Hierarchy of Political Involvement

As Figure 1.1 illustrates, Milbrath's division of political participation is based on an active-inactive dimension. Those engaging in spectator activities participate passively in the political process and fail to engage in any of the political acts identified in the two other levels of the hierarchy. A second group participates in transitional activities and is "minimally involved in some or all of the first five activities shown in the hierarchy: seeking information, voting, discussion, proselytizing, and displaying preference."[3] A third, quite small group participates in the political activities of the other two groups and is involved in additional forms of participation, including holding public and party office, being a candidate for office, soliciting political funds, attending a caucus or a strategy meeting, becoming an active member in a political party, and contributing time in a political campaign. This book explores various aspects of the hierarchy of political involvement and examines forms of political participation that are associated with the New Citizenship.

Chapter 2 provides a theoretical hook for the book by outlining the varied conceptions of the role that the citizenry should play in the American political system. The intentions and consequences of the constitutional framers' efforts are described in some detail. The goal here is for students to understand the framers' thoughts on what role the citizenry should play in the newly created political system; the chapter makes the connection between the framers' efforts and the current barriers to the realization of a more participatory conception of citizenship. Considerable attention is devoted to the framers' concern for balancing citizen participation with overall system stability.

Chapter 2 also outlines two theoretical perspectives on the role that the citizenry should play in the American political system. These two visions have existed in a state of tension throughout American development. The first is the **democratic theory of elitism**, which favors a limited role for the citizenry, one in which citizens participate in periodic elections and elect well-educated and well-trained elites to represent them in the public policy process. This view of the limited role played by citizens, also called electoral-representative democracy, emphasizes the importance of elections. Interest groups lobby at the national, state, and local levels, and the decision-making process is characterized by bargaining and compromise. Citizen participation is equated with voter participation. This conception of citizenship is reinforced by Milbrath's hierarchy of political participation.

A second conception of democratic citizenship outlined in Chapter 2 is **participatory democracy**. Underlying this conception is a belief that the central means for turning a collection of people into a public is deliberation. For participatory democrats, increased citizen participation in community and workplace decision making at the local level is important if people are to realize their roles and responsibilities within the larger community. In addition, participatory democrats emphasize grassroots organizing and mobilization rooted in community building, cooperation, alliance formation, and self-help. This book examines the kind of citizen politics associated with participatory democracy and the New Citizenship in considerable detail. Indeed, such an active and vital conception of participation is the central challenge to the torpor and malaise associated with civic indifference.

Finally, Chapter 2 explores the specific ways in which the **political socialization** process, by which citizens acquire their attitudes and beliefs regarding the political system, serves as a central barrier to developing and enhancing the participatory democratic tradition and the New Citizenship. From the vantage point of participatory democrats, the political socialization process impedes meaningful and effective citizen participation because citizens are socialized to embrace the values of self-interested "economic man and woman," which are rooted in **liberal democracy**. Such values are generally associated with the constitutional framers, the constitutional structure, and the democratic theory of elitism.

Having set out the theoretical and constitutional context for discussing civic indifference, political participation, system stability, and the New Citizenship in Chapter 2, I explore the empirical literature on political participation in Chapter 3. A central argument growing out of this chapter is that if voter-turnout figures are used as indicators of citizen participation and interest in politics, then these figures reveal a detached and apathetic citizenry, one with a significant amount of civic indifference. In Chapter 3, I argue as well that the declining voter-turnout rates reflect increased citizen anger toward "politics as usual" and politicians, an anger and heightened alienation that are more clearly manifested in two additional trends: (1) the number of incumbents who have chosen to leave office voluntarily for fear of losing their seats as a result of a citizenry increasingly frustrated with professional politicians; and (2) the increased popularity of television and radio call-in talk shows, which are often devoted to discussions of politics and which allow unhappy citizens to voice their frustration and anger with America's political process.

The analysis is cast broadly in an effort to identify structural and individual explanations for civic indifference as measured by low voter turnout, at the same time as we are witnessing an increase in citizen activism. In addition, Chapter 3 explores qualitative surveys of voters' attitudes toward politics and political participation. The surveys generally find that those who have participated in **focus group** discussions, that is, people brought together to respond to a candidate's or officeholder's policies, have a sense of powerlessness and exclusion from government decisions. The surveys also indicate that a portion of the American electorate continues to be frustrated by the normal operation of politics and desires more meaningful opportunities to participate in decisions that affect the quality and direction of their lives. This theme is developed more fully in Chapter 5 when I examine alternative forms of participation, largely at the grassroots level.

Considerable attention is also devoted to the attitudes of college students and America's youth toward political participation and citizenship. Many studies throughout the years have provided considerable evidence that young people are largely apathetic, uninterested, and indifferent when it comes to politics. Indeed, recent studies of the political lives of youth provide even more support for this claim. Why are young people so indifferent to politics? One possible explanation is that this generation of youth is more preoccupied with career goals and financial security than were previous generations. Today's students perceive that they face enormous economic pressures, which are heightened by a changing and more unfriendly economy, one that simply does not provide the opportunities that were available for college graduates in years past. Indeed, one recent analysis of the human cost of the 2008–2009 recession indicates that "young people have lost 2.5 million jobs to the crisis, making them the hardest hit age group."[4] Given this negative economic climate, who can blame students for focusing on career goals rather than political concerns? A second possible explanation for their civic indifference is that college students are so convinced that politics does not solve real problems that they see no reason to participate. Yet on a more optimistic note, they can imagine a different kind of politics, one that would take their concerns more seriously than the current "politics as usual." It is this latter possibility that is embodied in the New Citizenship, which is examined in more detail in the remainder of the book. Chapter 3 also explores the possible impact of September 11, 2001, on how citizens, including college students, engage the political system. In addition, it examines the broader meaning of the Obama 2008 presidential campaign for his young supporters and why the young were galvanized on his behalf. One possible explanation is that they perceived Obama as the most likely candidate to challenge "politics as usual."

Chapter 4 explores the historical foundations of the New Citizenship by examining **unconventional politics**, that is, a politics that goes outside of the normative system and engages in protest and mass mobilization, as the African American civil rights movement did. Connections are drawn between the movement's embrace of such politics in the 1960s and the broader dilemma of engaging in political activities without losing stability and balance. I argue in Chapter 4 that the civil rights movement provides a concrete and useful example of how a renewal of democratic citizenship at both the local and national levels might be achieved. What is most impressive about the civil rights movement, as it pertains to the arguments of this book, is that it was sufficiently powerful to mobilize widespread political action, particularly among college students, for political and social reform. The movement, then, challenged civic indifference by stressing the importance of eradicating social injustice and discrimination at all levels of American society, but particularly in communities throughout the South, where that injustice prevented African Americans from exercising the right to vote.

Considerable attention is devoted to the sector of the civil rights movement associated with the development of the New Citizenship and the specific role played by students in the **Crusade for Citizenship program**. The goal of the **citizenship schools**, in which many illiterate rural African Americans in the South learned to read and write, was to empower them to overcome obstacles such as **literacy tests**—that is, voter-qualification tests designed to prevent African Americans from voting—and to recognize the importance of registering to vote and of exercising that right to vote. Given the social and political mores of the time, that was considered radical political activity. By today's political standards, however, registering people to vote is hardly deemed radical. Indeed, political organizers across the ideological spectrum recognize that registering people to vote is a central mechanism for overcoming the civic indifference often associated with low voter-turnout rates.

Chapter 4 also presents the argument that the New Citizenship is a realization and extension of the aspirations for participatory democracy expressed in the 1960s. By its very nature, the New Citizenship embraces a form of politics that is essential for overcoming the breakdown of civility in American politics. This incivility is seen on both the left and the right in organizations that threaten the balance that the framers hoped would result from their Madisonian framework of government. These organizations include ACT UP (AIDS Coalition to Unleash Power), Earth First!, the Environmental Liberation Front, Operation Rescue, and the various militia groups.

Many critics of the student culture of the 1970s and 1980s have characterized the age group as the "Me Generation." Unfortunately, most commentators fail to explore the sources of the values associated with the Me Generation and neglect to examine the intersection between the broader political and economic framework and the political socialization process that surely affects the development of American values. As I explain in Chapter 5, many young people who have come of age during the past thirty-five years reject the values associated with the Me Generation, despite their prevalence in the larger society. Some who have rejected Me Generation values have embraced grassroots political organizing activity in communities throughout the United States.

Chapter 5 explores several organizations that are examples of the New Citizenship in practice, including ACORN (Association of Community Organizations for Reform Now), the Labor/Community Strategy Center, and the Center for Health, Environment, and Justice. The goal is to see how these organizations promote change generated from the grass roots, an important component of the New Citizenship. In addition, the chapter examines student organizations of the left, including Public Allies, the Campus Outreach Opportunity League, Campus Green Vote, United Students Against Sweatshops, and the United States Student Association. Finally, the Internet is treated as a component of the New Citizenship, as it has greatly affected social and political action. Student organizations have already used the Internet as a strategy for **political mobilization,** that is, the process by which citizens are galvanized to participate in politics. In sum, in Chapter 5 I grapple with the central dilemma of civility, stability, and balance and show how organizations help to promote system stability and civility in American politics.

The final component of the New Citizenship is service-based learning and community service. Chapter 6 offers a brief overview of service on college campuses as well as a discussion of the background for the development of President Bill Clinton's national service plan, adopted by Congress in a limited form and modified by President George W. Bush. President Barack Obama's support for AmeriCorps is also discussed. The case against service is outlined in considerable detail and responded to in light of a course called Social Policy and Community Activism, which I have taught at Hobart and William Smith Colleges. Various models of citizen education are explored within the broader context of **critical education for citizenship**, an approach to education rooted in the participatory democratic vision. I maintain that students should have an opportunity to tackle important citizenship issues within the broader context of several different courses. There is little doubt that courses on citizenship are limited to the extent that they do not connect students directly with politics and the policymaking process. But that does not mean that such courses should be abolished. Indeed, students should be able to take courses in which they confront their roles as citizens within the American political system. Courses in community politics, organizing, and service-based learning can accomplish these important goals at the same time as they challenge and engage students who are alienated from the larger political system. Such courses can encourage them to overcome their own civic indifference and recognize the vital forms of participation already available under the rubric of the New Citizenship.

To the extent that we can begin to ask new questions about the role the citizenry should play in the American political system, we will have made progress in developing a more mature sense of what citizens can and should do in a democracy at all levels of government. Ultimately, that is the central goal of this book.

2

....

Theoretical Perspectives on the New Citizenship

The theory of participatory democracy is built round the central assertion that individuals and their institutions cannot be considered in isolation from one another. . . . The major function of participation in the theory of participatory democracy is therefore an educative one, educative in the very widest sense, including both the psychological aspect and the gaining of practice in democratic skills and procedures.

–Carole Pateman, *Participation and Democratic Theory*

．．

WHAT ROLE SHOULD the citizenry play in the American political system? This normative question lies at the heart of debates over issues of democracy, citizenship, and participation. To be sure, democracy is and has been a contested idea throughout history and in political theory. As we will see, the framers of the Constitution devoted considerable attention to the precise role that citizens should play in the newly created political system. There is a link between the framers' efforts and existing barriers to achieving a more participatory form of citizenship. In retrospect, one can see that the framers' constitutional design helped to foster relative system stability. Can this stability be maintained in the future?

In this chapter I identify the various ways that balance and stability are maintained while citizens are engaging in political activities. I examine two traditions in democratic political theory: participatory democracy and the democratic theory of elitism. Underlying this analysis are two additional questions: (1) What does it mean to be a "citizen"? and (2) What do we mean by "democracy"? My goal in this chapter is to provide the appropriate theoretical framework for understanding civic indifference and participation and balance and stability in contemporary American politics, and also to show relevant connections to the New Citizenship. But first I must outline some of the practical barriers facing those who call for a more expansive democratic vision and a new conception of citizenship. One such obstacle is the structure of the government designed by the constitutional framers. A second is the hero worship attached to the framers of the Constitution, which is reinforced by the political socialization process. It is to these barriers that we now turn.

The Constitutional Context for Citizen Participation

To the constitutional framers, the stability of the political system was of great concern.[1] The delegates to the Constitutional Convention confronted two major questions, First, how can a political system be created that allows the individual the freedom and equality of opportunity needed to acquire private property?[2] In modern terms, what kind of political system will allow capitalism to survive? Second, can a stable political and economic system be created when human beings are inherently bad?

Many of the men who gathered in Philadelphia in 1786–1787 had a **Hobbesian**, or negative, conception of human nature. Alexander Hamilton argued in the "Federalist No. 6" that "men are ambitious, vindictive, and rapacious." Edmund Randolph warned that the stability of the political system would be threatened due to "the turbulence and follies of our constitutions." This argument led Elbridge Gerry to conclude that democracy was "the worst of all political evils," whereas Roger Sherman argued that "the people (should) have as little to do as may be about the government," and William Livingston said that "the people have been and ever will be unfit to retain the exercise of power in their own hands."[3] Madison himself argued in the "Federalist No. 51" that "if men were angels, no government would be necessary. If angels were to govern men, neither external or internal controls on government would be necessary."

The framers' worst fears had been confirmed in fall 1786, when Daniel Shays, a former Continental Army officer, led a group of western Massachusetts farmers in protesting mortgage foreclosures. The response to Shays's Rebellion illustrates how perceived threats to system stability influenced the framers as they prepared for the Constitutional Convention in Philadelphia. Madison and the other framers recognized that for the republic to survive, the increasing political pressure generated by small propertied interests would have to be controlled. These interests challenged the existing distribution of property, and the framers fully expected such challenges to resurface time and again. The framers feared that system stability was at stake. Responding to Shays's Rebellion, George Washington expressed many of the framers' concerns in a letter to James Madison: "What gracious god, is man! That there should be such inconsistency and perfidiousness in his conduct? It is but the other day, that we were shedding our blood to obtain the state constitutions of our own choice and making; and now we are unsheathing the sword to overturn them."[4] Washington wrote further that if the newly created government could not control these disorders, "what security has a man for life, liberty, or property?"[5] It is no surprise, then, that the constitutional framers devised a Madisonian system that attempted to insulate the governmental process from the exigencies of public opinion.

Concern for stability is also expressed in Madison's brilliant "Federalist No. 10," which serves as a compelling defense of republican government. He begins with a negative conception of human nature and argues that "the latent causes of faction are sown in the nature of man." In addition, he contends that "the most common and durable source of factions has been the various and unequal distribution of property." John Diggins argues that Madison's negative view of human nature is connected directly to his vision of government:

> Madison trusted neither the people nor their representatives because he believed that no faction or individual could act disinterestedly. Madison traced the problem of man's invirtuous conduct to the origin of factions in unequal property relations, the "natural" conditions that led man to be envious, interested, passionate, and aggressive. Convinced that the human condition was unalterable, Madison advised Americans that the Constitution's "auxiliary" precautions were essential, that the Republic would be preserved by the "machinery of government," not the morality of man.[6]

Given these assumptions, the problem, according to Madison, was how to control the factional struggles that came from inequalities in wealth. Writing well before Marx, Madison recognized that inequalities in the distribution of property could lead to the instability of the political system. Because the causes of faction were inherent in man, it would be unrealistic to try to remove them. Instead, the government devised by the framers would try to control the effects of factions. Thus the framers adopted majority rule, established a system of separate institutions that shared powers and had checks and balances, created federalism, and allowed for only limited participation by the citizenry in periodic elections. Women and slaves were excluded from the franchise; only property holders could vote for members of the House of Representatives. Until the Seventeenth Amendment was adopted in 1913, U.S. senators were elected by state legislatures. The cumbersome Electoral College reflects the framers' distrust of human nature and their desire to limit popular participation by the masses.

The framers understood that the republican principle would grant legitimacy and stability to their newly created political system. They recognized that it would be unwise and impractical to extend democracy too broadly. To the framers, the representative was to play two key roles: to represent sectional and other interests in the national decision-making process by mediating

Constitutional founders = unequal representation?

competing claims, and to mediate and moderate the passions of the mob. Accountability would be provided for by establishing a system of periodic elections in which qualified citizens could choose their representatives. Benjamin Barber concludes that representative government promised the possibility of system stability by emphasizing "popular control and wise government, self-government, accountability, and centripetal efficiency."[7]

In the end, the government was created "to guard against what were thought to be the weaknesses of popular democracy."[8] The goal of the framers was to "permit political participation but prevent democracy in the United States."[9] Indeed, much of the current criticism voiced by participatory democrats is rooted in their frustration that the framers provided too limited a role for the citizenry in the political system. This view was represented over two hundred years ago by the Anti-Federalists, who warned that a governmental apparatus was being devised wherein "the bulk of the people can have nothing to say to [the government]."[10]

It is not just the structure of the framers' government that is a source of concern for those who embrace the participatory democratic tradition. They are also concerned about the radical notion of individualism embraced by the framers. This notion, which came to be known as **classical liberalism** and serves as the basis for liberal democracy, grew out of the writings of theorists John Locke, J. S. Mill, and Adam Smith. Radical individualism, which Tocqueville ultimately believed would undermine community and "the habits of the heart," has been a part of the American creed for more than two centuries. In addition to individualism, the American creed includes a fervent belief in equality of opportunity, liberty and freedom, the rule of law, and limited government.[11]

This set of values is noteworthy in that it does not include "community" or "participation in politics." To be sure, the United States was born a political economy, stressing the right of individuals to pursue private property and their individualistic impulses in the private economic sphere. In *Habits of the Heart,* Robert Bellah and his coauthors underscore the connection between American individualism and the free market: "Hence, the liberal individualist idealizing of the free market is understandable, given this cultural context, since, in theory, the economic position of each person is believed to derive from his or her own competitive effort in an open market."[12] The authors conclude that "the rules of the competitive market, not the practices of the town meeting or the fellowship of the church, are the real arbiters of living."[13] Bellah and like-minded scholars follow Tocqueville's analysis and lament the negative consequences of the American radical individualistic impulse. The central concern articulated by these social commentators is that as the people pursue "the American dream" as personified by the acquisition of private property and other material pleasures, they fail to devote the time and energy to engaging in the kind of public politics required by advocates of the participatory democratic vision. In this sense, the basic elements of liberal democracy are inimical to the fundamental values associated with participatory democracy, values that are discussed later in this chapter.

Indeed, Sheldon Wolin accurately points out that students of democratic theory and practice must devote considerable attention to examining the republican form, with the ultimate goal of evaluating "the tensions between republicanism, with its strong historical attraction to elitism, and democracy."[14] As it is, the emphases on acquiring private property and on voting in periodic elections are the central elements of American democracy, and these elements are also crucial tenets of the democratic theory of elitism. This perspective continues to be reinforced at all levels of society. Seymour Martin Lipset echoed the concerns of the framers and embraced the central elements of the democratic theory of elitism when he wrote that it was still necessary to "sustain the separation of the political system from the excesses inherent in the populist assumptions of democracy."[15] As we will soon see, it is this view, rather than the participatory democratic perspective, that forms the basis of the political socialization process. The political socialization process in America, then, is a central barrier to developing the kind of critical citizenry that is at the core of the New Citizenship and the participatory democratic tradition. I next explore that political socialization process.

Political Socialization and Citizenship in American Politics

Political socialization is the process by which citizens acquire their attitudes and beliefs about the political system in which they live and their roles within that system. Political scientists have identified several key agents of political socialization—the family, schools, peers, the media, religious institutions, and the workplace.

From the vantage point of participatory democrats, the political socialization process impedes meaningful and effective participation because citizens are socialized to embrace the values of privatism and radical individualism that are rooted in liberal democracy. Indeed, participatory democrats claim that the thrust of political socialization in America reinforces the underlying tenets of the democratic theory of elitism, tenets that highlight the passivity of the citizenry and that allow elites in power to make the crucial decisions that affect the quality and direction of the people's lives. From this vantage point, citizens are to be involved in politics only in ways that might hold elites accountable—voting, joining an interest group, working within a political party, or working for a specific candidate. In this way, then, citizens abdicate any meaningful responsibility for what happens in the public sphere to a small group of elite decision makers who will supposedly make decisions in the larger public interest. According to the elitist view, citizens do not have the time, energy, or education to make informed decisions about the direction of American public policy at all levels of government.

It should come as no surprise, then, that a study conducted by People for the American Way, titled "Democracy's Next Generation," states that many young people have an incomplete definition of politics, though they bear little responsibility for their limited conception of what it means to be a citizen. The report concludes that the "institutions with the best opportunity to teach young people citizenship—family, school, and government—have let them down."[16] This conclusion surely would not surprise others who have found that the American political socialization process reinforces a limited conception of citizenship, one that lauds participation in the private rather than the public sphere. For example, in their study of the conflict between individualism and community in American life, the authors of *Habits of the Heart* conclude:

> What would probably perplex and disturb Tocqueville most today is the fact that the family is no longer an integral part of a larger moral ecology tying the individual to community, church, and nation. The family is the core of the private sphere, whose aim is not to link individuals to the public world but to avoid it as far as possible. In our commercial culture, consumerism, with its temptations, and television, with its examples, augment that tendency.[17]

In his analysis of what motivates people to avoid participation in politics, sociologist Richard Flacks devotes considerable attention to political socialization. He argues that "Americans do not simply avoid politics; their avoidance tends to be a feature of their political consciousness. People on the average believe that they are politically inactive, that history is being made by actors other than themselves; and they are prone to accept and even welcome this situation."[18] Many citizens embrace this situation because they are merely trying to live their daily lives, which means maintaining their jobs, putting food on their tables, and providing the basic necessities of life for themselves and their families.

It is indeed the case that Americans are socialized to "equate democracy with our own constitutional structure."[19] Americans revere the Constitution and the principles underlying the document without having a basic understanding of their full meaning and the consequences of those principles for their daily lives.[20] This hero worship of the framers and the Constitution has contributed to overall system stability through the years, has reinforced the underlying tenets of the democratic theory of elitism, and has served as a major barrier to the development of participatory democracy on a widespread scale in the United States.

The Participatory Democratic Tradition

The participatory democratic model came to the fore during the political turmoil of the 1960s, though many of its underlying ideas grew out of the classic works of Jean-Jacques Rousseau and J. S. Mill and have been evident in New England town meetings for almost two centuries. Indeed, the New England town meeting is a model of the participatory democratic tradition. Tocqueville recognized that when he concluded that New England small towns were ideal settings for participatory democracy, because it was in those settings that citizens "take part in every occurrence" pertaining to government.[21]

Student political activists in the 1960s embraced participatory democratic principles when they created organizations such as the Students for a Democratic Society (SDS) and the Student Nonviolent Coordinating Committee (SNCC). In 1962 core SDS members gathered in Port Huron, Michigan, and wrote a set of principles that came to be known as the "Port Huron Statement," "which included a call for 'a democracy of individual participation'."[22]

The problem of defining what is meant by meaningful and effective citizen participation pervades the literature of participatory democracy[23] and was a central concern of those who wrote the Port Huron Statement (see Box 2.1). A thorough examination of participatory democratic arguments reveals that three elements must be present if meaningful and effective citizen participation is to be achieved: (1) a sense of community identity; (2) education and the development of citizenship; and (3) self-determination by those participating.[24]

BOX 2.1   The Participatory Democratic Ideal

We would replace power rooted in possession, privilege, or circumstance by power and uniqueness rooted in love, reflectiveness, reason, and creativity. As a social system we seek the establishment of a democracy of individual participation, governed by two central aims: that the individual share in those social decisions determining the quality and direction of his life; that society be organized to encourage independence in men and provide the media for their common participation.

In a participatory democracy, the political life would be based in several root principles:

that decision-making of basic social consequence be carried on by public groupings;

that politics be seen positively, as the art of collectively creating an acceptable pattern of social relations;

that politics has the function of bringing people out of isolation and into community, thus being a necessary, though not sufficient, means of finding meaning in personal life;

that the political order should serve to clarify problems in a way instrumental to their solution. It should provide outlets for the expression of personal grievance and aspiration; opposing views should be organized so as to illuminate choices and facilitate the attainment of goals; channels should be commonly available to relate men to knowledge and to power so that private problems— from bad recreation facilities to personal alienation—are formulated as general issues.

The economic sphere would have as its basis the principles:

that work should involve incentives worthier than money or survival. It should be educative, not stultifying; creative, not mechanical; self-directed, not manipulated, encouraging independence, a respect for others, a sense of dignity, and a willingness to accept social responsibility, since it is this experience that has crucial influence on habits, perceptions, and individual ethics;

that the economic experience is so personally decisive that the individual must share in its full determination;

that the economy itself is of such social importance that its major resources and means of production should be open to democratic participation and subject to democratic social regulation.

Source: "The Port Huron Statement," as reprinted in James Miller, *Democracy Is in the Streets: From Port Huron to the Siege of Chicago* (New York: Simon and Schuster, 1987), p. 333.

Proponents of participatory democracy argue that increased citizen participation in community and workplace decision making is important if people are to recognize their roles and responsibilities as citizens within the larger community. Community meetings, for example, afford citizens knowledge regarding other citizens' needs. In a true participatory setting, citizens do not merely act as autonomous individuals pursuing their own interests, but instead, through a process of decision, debate, and compromise, they ultimately link their concerns with the needs of the community.

The arguments for participatory democracy are based on two additional tenets: (1) a belief that increased citizen participation will contribute both to the development of the individual and to the individual's realization of citizenship; and (2) a belief that individuals should participate in community and workplace decisions that will affect the quality and direction of their lives. Each of these tenets is grounded in a positive conception of liberty.[25]

Proponents of participatory democracy extend the Rousseauian notion that citizen participation in decision making has a favorable psychological effect on those participating. Carole Pateman argues that through participation in political decision making, the individual learns to be a public as well as a private citizen.[26]

Besides developing the individual's creative capacities, participation in decision making encourages the individual to become more informed about the political process. Citizen participation theorists such as Benjamin Barber emphasize the beneficial learning process that is afforded to all those who participate with and talk to one another in community decision making.[27] From this perspective, the political education, rather than the socialization, of the individual will be benefited wherever increased citizen participation is encouraged.

From the vantage point of participatory democrats, citizens "have to become a public in order to sustain a democracy." What will enable citizens to become a public? According to David Mathews, president of the Kettering Foundation, a nonprofit organization dedicated to infusing participatory democratic principles into all levels of society, the central means for turning a collection of people into a public is through deliberation. Mathews defines deliberation in the following way: "To deliberate means to weigh carefully both the consequences of various options for action and the views of others."[28] To Mathews, deliberation is at the core of the participatory democratic tradition because "without becoming public citizens capable of giving common direction to government, people are capable of being little more than consumers of government services."[29]

This third component of the participatory democratic model is based on the notion that individuals from all classes in society must share in the decisions that determine the quality and direction of their lives. From this vantage point, important community decisions should not be made solely by bureaucrats and elected officials. Participatory democrats are particularly concerned that "so many socially and politically relevant decisions are in the hands of people who are not democratically accountable."[30] That is certainly true of corporate officials who have the unilateral power to close a factory, a decision that has negative consequences for the workers and the surrounding community. Indeed, participatory democrats contend that citizens should participate more vigorously in their workplaces, where they spend many hours of their day.

Participatory democracy proponents also believe that if the multiple perspectives of those involved are to be consulted, the group decision process is essential (see Box 2.2). Individuals who participate in the local decision-making process will be afforded a sense of participation and commitment that is nonexistent in a system where elites rule the policymaking and implementation process. Participatory democracy, besides contributing to the self-development of individuals and giving them practice in citizenship, ideally wrests the policy implementation process away from the elite and allows citizens to have a say in the decisions affecting their lives. In so doing, participatory democracy challenges the fundamental assumptions of leadership and followership associated with the political system.

Participatory democrats have identified several forces that drive individuals to participate more actively in decisions that affect the quality and direction of their lives. One such force "is the desire for greater control over an uncertain future."[31] A second is the desire of individuals to improve public policy decision making and make the world and their communities better places in which to live. The third force is the citizens' recognition of the importance of addressing deteriorating civic relationships and the wish to develop the means and ability to work together more effectively.[32]

In the end, participatory citizen politics can be distinguished from conventional politics in a number of different ways. Whereas "conventional politics concentrates more on getting to solutions quickly, citizen politics concentrates on carefully defining and, if need be, redefining problems before moving to solutions." At the heart of conventional politics is a belief

BOX 2.2 Three Types of Participatory Situations

Full Participation: Each member of a decision-making body has equal power to determine the outcome of decisions.

Partial Participation: The worker does not have equal power to decide the outcome of decisions but can only influence them.

Pseudo Participation: No real participation in decision making takes place (e.g. the supervisor, instead of telling the employees of a decision, allows them to question her/him about it and discuss it).

Source: Adapted from Carole Pateman, *Participation and Democratic Theory* (Cambridge: Cambridge University Press, 1970), pp. 68–71.

that leaders who will create solutions are needed, whereas at its core, "citizen politics stresses the importance of citizens claiming their own responsibility and becoming solutions themselves." Those who support a new kind of participatory citizen politics emphasize "creating new forms of power at all levels of a community," whereas conventional politics proponents advocate "using existing power wisely and empowering the powerless." The resources associated with conventional politics are generally more financial and legislative; "citizen politics uses public will as its primary political capital." Conventional politics devotes considerable time to assessing people's needs, whereas citizen politics focuses its attention on assessing their capacities. The language associated with conventional politics is rooted in "advocacy and winning," whereas citizen politics embraces a "language of practical problem solving and relationship building." A central goal of conventional politics is to attain more diversity, whereas citizen politics uses diversity to get diverse groups to work together. For advocates of conventional politics, the public is a source of accountability, whereas advocates of citizen politics look "to the public for direction." Conventional politics attempts to teach "the skills of effective public action." The creation of public events is crucial to conventional politics, whereas citizen politics emphasizes the creation of public space.[33]

This book examines the kind of citizen politics associated with participatory democracy and the New Citizenship in considerable detail. But before that, we must look at the democratic theory of elitism as a basis for understanding conventional politics.

PARTICIPATORY DEMONOCRACY

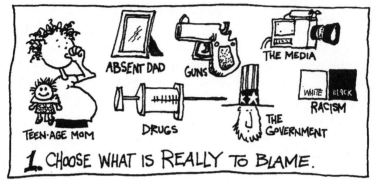

ABSENT DAD

THE MEDIA

GUNS

TEEN-AGE MOM

DRUGS

THE GOVERNMENT

WHITE BLACK RACISM

1. CHOOSE WHAT IS REALLY TO BLAME.

2. CALL A RADIO TALK SHOW.

3. DENOUNCE LOUDLY.

4. GO ON WITH YOUR DAY KNOWING YOU'VE DONE YOUR BIT.

SIGNE
PHILADELPHIA DAILY NEWS
Philadelphia
USA

The Critique of the Democratic Theory of Elitism

What role should the citizenry play in the American political system? According to those who subscribe to the democratic theory of elitism, it should be a limited one. Critics of participatory democracy base their arguments on five key beliefs: (1) the role expected of the citizen in a participatory setting is unrealistic; (2) widespread citizen participation in decision making is not feasible in a society of more than 280 million people; (3) studies confirm that participatory democrats have an unrealistic conception of the capability of ordinary citizens to participate actively in politics in their communities and in the workplace; (4) too much participation will contribute to the instability of the political and economic system; and (5) increased citizen participation impedes clear legislative goals and fosters fragmentation throughout the policymaking and implementation process.

Those who subscribe to the democratic theory of elitism attack the notion of individual self-development through citizen participation because "to continue to advocate such a theory in today's world is bound to foster cynicism toward democracy as it becomes evident that the gap between the reality and the ideal cannot be closed."[34] Other political scientists agree that participatory democracy is based on a utopian conception of human nature. One opponent contends that most individuals will not be able to transcend their own private interests and consider the concerns of the larger community in a participatory setting. Daniel Kramer, in his analysis of the failure of works councils and the War on Poverty, concludes that citizens "are more interested in their own advancement than in aiding their constituents."[35]

A second set of criticisms of the call for increased citizen participation emanates from the tenet that participatory democracy is too cumbersome and cannot be achieved in a country of more than 300 million people. Martin Oppenheimer challenges proponents of increased participation with this difficult question: "In a large-scale society, how much decentralization will be possible and necessary to promote real democracy? The concrete problem of where to draw the line has still to be faced."[36]

In *Beyond Adversary Democracy,* Jane Mansbridge responds that democracies as large as the modern nation-state must be primarily adversarial in nature. To those calling for increased citizen participation, that is clearly a depressing conclusion. Yet Mansbridge also points out that "preserving unitary virtues requires a mixed polity—part adversary, part unitary—in which citizens understand their interests well enough to participate effectively in both forms at once."[37] Mansbridge's conclusions are based on her empirical study of citizen participation in a New England town meeting (Selby, Vermont) and an urban crisis center (Helpline). Her analyses of Selby and Helpline reveal that "face-to-face meetings on the whole encourage members to identify with one another and with the group as a whole" in developing common interests.[38] She finds that certain individuals—the educated, the wealthy, and the middle class—are more likely to participate in the town meetings because they feel less inhibited about expressing their views than the uneducated. With its concentration on procedure, or form, rather than outcome, citizen participation might serve only to preserve the status quo. To be sure, the participation process does not ensure equality of results. Citizen participation might be a ritual that merely stabilizes and legitimizes "the prevailing political and economic order."[39]

Critics of participatory democracy are quick to point to the existing gap between what might be called "the democratic ideal" and the reality of citizen participation in America.[40] In addition, they argue that for participatory democracy to occur on a widespread scale, an inordinate time commitment on the part of those participating would be required. Empirical evidence for these views is found in *Voting*, a book published in 1954 by Bernard Berelson, Paul Lazarsfeld, and William McPhee. The authors conducted a survey of citizens in Elmira, New York, during the 1948 presidential election and found that "the behavior of Elmira's citizens differed significantly from the democratic ideal" that had been espoused by those committed to participatory democratic principles.[41] Citizens interviewed had little basic knowledge of the election. In addition, they differed in their attitudes toward participation; some respondents were quite interested and involved, others were only mildly interested, and some were profoundly apathetic. For Berelson, Lazarsfeld, and McPhee, this evidence supported their view that civic indifference contributes to system stability in a democracy:

> How could mass democracy work if all the people were involved in politics? Lack of interest by some people is not without its benefits, too. . . . Extreme interest goes with extreme partisanship and might culminate in rigid fanaticism that could destroy democratic processes if generalized throughout the community. Low affect toward the election . . . underlies the resolution of many political problems; votes can be resolved into a two party split instead of fragmented into many parties. . . . Low interest provides maneuvering

room for political shifts necessary for a complex society. . . . Some people are and should be highly interested in politics, but not everyone is or needs to be.[42]

The concern for system stability and fear of instability leads to a fourth set of arguments by those opposed to the participatory democratic vision. The concern for stability runs through much of the literature supporting the notion that democracy should be a political method or mechanism for choosing elite leaders. Writing in the 1940s, Joseph Schumpeter offered his conception of democracy, one that lies at the core of conventional politics and the democratic theory of elitism: "The democratic method is that institutional arrangement for arriving at political decisions in which individuals acquire the power to decide by means of a competitive struggle for the people's vote."[43] Schumpeter warned that the masses were capable of an electoral stampede that might threaten the stability of the political and economic system. More recent theorists have extended Schumpeter's arguments. Reflecting on the tumult of the 1960s, Samuel Huntington laments the "democratic distemper" that threatened "the governability of democracy" in the United States. To Huntington, the excesses of democracy "overloaded" the system from all sides and through a variety of competing interests in ways that made it increasingly difficult for the American policy process to respond effectively. As a result, Huntington, calls for "a greater degree of moderation in democracy."[44] Like others who subscribe to the democratic theory of elitism, Huntington has serious problems with the participatory democratic vision.

A final set of arguments raised by those opposed to increased citizen participation in community decision making and participatory democracy is expressed forcefully by Theodore Lowi in *The End of Liberalism*. Lowi laments the lack of goal clarity in federal legislation that accompanies the delegation of power and argues that the new bureaucratic fiefdoms are even more powerful than the old urban machines. These functional feudalities garner much of their power from the discretion they are afforded in implementing federal programs at the local level. Lowi rejects citizen participation as a solution for bureaucratic accountability, because "the requirement of standards has been replaced by the requirement of participation,"[45] and this participation leads to increased fragmentation throughout the policymaking and implementation process. Lowi calls instead for legislation that issues "clear orders along with powers" to ensure bureaucratic accountability.[46]

My book is a response to those who contend that the citizenry has little interest in American politics and in participating in decisions that affect the quality and direction of their lives. I next explore the connection between the New Citizenship and overall system stability.

The Theoretical Basis for the New Citizenship

In many ways, the New Citizenship is an extension of participatory democratic ideas that arose in the 1960s. For example, many of the core values associated with the New Citizenship are also central to participatory democratic theory. These values include civic engagement, political equality, solidarity, trust, tolerance for diverse views and people, and encouragement of civic organizations and associations.[47] If conflict occurs among citizens, it occurs within the broader context of these agreed-upon values, all of which indicate support for a larger community interest rooted in participation and the development of citizenship. The goal of the New Citizenship is to reengage political theory with practical politics. The conception of citizenship that emerges is an active, engaged, and informed citizenry, one that embraces a positive conception of liberty.[48]

Proponents of the New Citizenship also address some of the concerns of the democratic theory of elitism. For example, the proponents tend to eschew protest politics in favor of creating structures that will enable diverse people with often-competing interests to come together and, through spirited debate and discussion, to understand one another's perspectives and to identify sources for common ground. In this way, by avoiding factionalized conflicts of the kind that concerned the constitutional framers, proponents of the New Citizenship foster overall system stability. However, New Citizenship theorists also recognize that protest politics is necessary and invaluable for promoting change, especially for those who have been structurally excluded from the political decision-making process at all levels of government. As we will see in Chapter 4, many useful connections can be made between the African American civil rights movement of the 1950s and 1960s and the New Citizenship of today. The ultimate goal of the New Citizenship is for citizens to bridge the gap between the public and the private spheres through active participation in politics and/or community service. Then citizens will help shape a culture of civic engagement, one in which they are central participants in promoting political and social change.

Conclusion

This book is designed to provide readers with a more expansive and comprehensive conception of democracy and citizenship than the constitutional framers embraced. One way that the traditional political socialization process and the democratic theory of elitism can surely be challenged is through education. Yet education at all levels of society has failed to play this role effectively. David Mathews has particularly harsh words for college education: "Unfortunately, most campuses seem to reinforce, perhaps unwittingly and certainly not alone, society's worst attitudes about politics."[49] In Chapter 6 I devote considerable attention to educational models for creating more actively engaged and involved citizens in the public sphere. But before we explore the important connection between education and citizenship, we need to examine the empirical evidence on democracy, participation, and civic indifference.

3

....

Civic Indifference in Contemporary American Politics

Not only does the community gain when citizens take part but individuals grow and learn through their activity. Political participation builds individual capacities in several ways: those who take part learn about community and society; they develop civic skills that can be carried throughout their lives; and they can come to have a greater appreciation of the needs and interests of others and of society as a whole.

—Nancy Burns, Kay Lehman Schlozman, and Sidney Verba, *The Private Roots of Public Action: Gender, Equality, and Political Participation*

We have a long-term disengagement problem that will not solved by a singular election.

—Curtis B. Gans

．．．

IT IS INDEED IRONIC that at a time when young Iranians are facing arrest or even death to bring Western-style liberal democracy to their country, we in the United States are becoming increasingly critical of our own. Two important books, William Greider's *Who Will Tell the People?* and E. J. Dionne's *Why Americans Hate Politics,* examine what Greider calls the betrayal of American democracy, albeit from different perspectives. Written by popular journalists, these books are important not only because of the substance of their arguments but also because of the attention they have received in the press. Dionne laments the polarization of elections around highly charged social issues such as abortion, school prayer, and affirmative action. A focus on these issues presents the electorate with a set of "false choices" that fail to connect with practical problems faced by the citizenry. This polarization fosters an environment in which citizens distrust politicians, "hate politics," and fail to vote in elections.[1] In sum, they display the civic indifference or civic disengagement that has been a central characteristic of American politics.

Greider's analysis focuses more on structural explanations for the betrayal of American democracy. To Greider, the explanations for civic indifference largely emanate from "the politics of governing, not the politics of winning elections."[2] Citizens fail to participate in the electoral arena because they do not see the link between their vote and the decisions made by those who hold power in the American policy process. Yet Greider accurately points out that although many Americans eschew voting, they participate in politics through a variety of alternative channels, such as town meetings and protest politics. It is the latter that potentially threatens overall system stability and raises the question germane to the core dilemma of this book: How does a polity strike a balance between the varieties of political participation engaged in by its citizens and residents?

One answer to that question is that if people had a greater chance to participate in meaningful ways, then perhaps they would not turn to the alternative forms of political participation that threaten to disrupt overall system stability. A second possible explanation is offered by President Barack Obama, who underscores the pettiness of our politics in recent years, a pettiness that has consistently frustrated many citizens: "No, what's troubling is the gap between the magnitude of our challenges and the smallness of our politics—the ease with which we are distracted by the petty and trivial, our chronic avoidance of tough decisions, our seeming inability to build a working consensus to tackle any big problem."[3] Another possible response is offered by the democratic theory of elitism, which we examined in Chapter 2: Civic indifference is functional for overall system stability to the extent that citizens do not participate at all in the American political system. This chapter examines the implications of these two explanations within the broader context of the empirical literature on political participation.

The chapter also explores the empirical evidence for the claim that Americans are increasingly displaying civic indifference. I will evaluate both individual and structural explanations for that civic indifference, largely measured by voter-turnout figures in presidential and off-year elections. At the same time, I provide alternative explanations for civic indifference by considering the explosion of citizen activism that has occurred in the United States in recent years. After exploring how civic indifference is manifested, I examine both college students' attitudes toward politics and their political behavior as measured by various studies. Political participation in America cannot be adequately explained by merely focusing on the individual characteristics of the participants and nonparticipants. The analysis must be broad enough to encompass many structural and individual explanations, as we attempt to explain the decline in voting at the same time that there is an increase in citizen activism. Generally, the discussion of civic indifference focuses on voter-turnout figures, but we Americans "have multiple avenues for expressing our views and exercising our rights—contacting local and national officials, working for political parties and other political organizations, discussing politics with our neighbors, attending public meetings, joining in election campaigns, wearing buttons, signing petitions, speaking out on talk radio, and many more."[4]

It is indeed true that compared to citizens in most other democracies, Americans are more active in these avenues of political participation. At the same time, an array of studies have shown that the young typically are less involved in these forms of political participation when compared to their parents and their grandparents. But we also know that more citizens, especially young people (the so-called Millennial Generation, who were born after 1985[5]) are using Internet technology as a vehicle to engage politics and political organizing in interesting and sophisticated ways. Indeed, as two analysts of youth participation point out, "the Millennials bring with them a facility and comfort with cutting-edge communication and computing technologies that is creating the same kind of bewilderment and bemusement that parents of television-addicted Baby Boomers felt in the 1950s and 1960s."[6] We explore this trend in this chapter and in Chapter 5, especially as it manifested itself in the extraordinary 2008 presidential election. As one thoughtful analyst has astutely suggested, the challenge is for us to gain a better understanding of young people's "changing values and norms and respond in ways that integrate them into the political process—and potentially change the process to better match this new electorate."[7] This chapter has been written with this laudable goal in mind.

Measuring Civic Indifference

The most traditional means for measuring civic indifference is voter turnout in elections. Fortunately, however, voting in elections is not the only criterion for measuring the health of a democratic society. If it were, the United States would be in big trouble, given voter-turnout rates in presidential and off-year elections.[8] The United States ranks in the lower tier among the world's wealthiest democracies in average voter turnout in recent elections (see Table 3.1). Participation is disappointing even in U.S. presidential elections, despite the fact that they generate the most attention and excitement among the voting public. Only 51.5 percent of all eligible voters actually turned out to vote in the 1996 election. This meager figure was the lowest voter turnout since the 1924 presidential election.[9] As Table 3.2 indicates, there was a gradual decline in presidential election turnout between 1960 and 1988, with a small increase in the 1984 presidential contest between Ronald Reagan and Walter Mondale. In 1992 there was a fairly substantial increase in voter turnout, though the turnout rate of 55.2 percent was still considerably lower than the average voter turnout in other industrial democracies. But in 1996 the turnout figure declined to an embarrassing low of 51.5 percent. Nearly one out of every two eligible voters chose to stay home rather than cast his or her ballot in the 1996 presidential election. In the contested presidential election of 2000, the voter-turnout figure improved only slightly, to 51.2 percent. Some analysts have suggested that 1996 and 2000 were aberrations and that we should expect continued improvement in voter-turnout figures

TABLE 3.1 Voter Participation Rates in the World's
Wealthiest Democracies

	Percent
Austria	81.7
Belgium	91.1
Canada	59.5
Denmark	86.6
France	60.4
Germany	77.7
Italy	80.5
Switzerland	48.3
United Kingdom	61.4
United States	61.5

Sources: For all figures except for the United States,
www.idea.int/vt/country-view.cfm? For the United States, the
Study of the American Electorate at American University, as
reported in Stuart Comstock-Gay and Joe Goldman, "More
than the Vote," *The American Prospect*, January/February
2009, p. A8. The most recent elections are used here.

in subsequent presidential elections. Indeed, one might have surmised that
the turnout rate would be especially high in the 2008 presidential election
given the increase in voter-turnout rates in many primary states for the
highly competitive race between Hillary Clinton and Barack Obama to secure the Democratic nomination. As the data in Table 3.1 indicate, this was
not the case.

But what might this "improvement" mean in practice? Even in 1992,
when voter turnout was 55.2 percent, President Clinton's 44 percent plu-
rality of the voters translated into the support of merely 24 percent of the
citizenry.[10] And although voters in the 2000 presidential elections turned
out at a 54.3 percent rate in a very close election, they elected a candidate
in the popular vote (Al Gore) who ultimately "lost" the election to George
W. Bush, when the United States Supreme Court ruled on December 11,
2000, in *Bush v. Gore*, that hand counting of ballots in Florida could not
continue. As a result, George Bush was handed the presidency with a 271–
266 (with one abstention) electoral vote margin, which immediately raised
serious questions about his legitimacy as president and the meaning of the
vote in America, especially given election irregularities in Florida. An array
of analysts understandably worried, too, that the manner in which the 2000
election was ultimately decided could foster even more cynicism and frus-

TABLE 3.2 Voting Turnout in U.S. Presidential
Elections, 1932–2008 (in percentages)

	Percent
1932	52.4
1936	56.0
1940	58.9
1944	56.0
1948	51.1
1952	61.6
1956	59.3
1960	62.8
1964	61.9
1968	60.9
1972	55.2
1976	53.5
1980	52.6
1984	53.1
1988	50.1
1992	55.2
1996	51.5
2000	54.3
2004	60.7
2008	61.5

Sources: 1932–1992 data from U.S. Department of
Commerce, Bureau of the Census, *Statistical Abstract of
the United States* (Washington, D.C.: Government
Printing Office, 1993), p. 284; 1996–2008 data from the
Study of the American Electorate at American
University as reported in Stuart Comstock-Gay and Joe
Goldman, "More Than the Vote," *The American
Prospect*, January/Februrary 2009, p. A8

tration on the part of the voting electorate. The result could be even lower
voter turnout in future elections, despite the claims of some that voters will
now perceive that "their vote does make a difference."

Voter turnout in midterm elections is even lower. As Table 3.3 indicates,
voter participation in statewide midterm elections reached a high of 48.4
percent in 1966 before declining. Even in 1974, the first time that eighteen-
to twenty-year-olds participated in an off-year election, turnout in statewide
elections was only 38.3 percent. After 1974, turnout continued falling slowly,
declining from the 1974 percentage in every year but 1982. In 1990 just over
one-third of the eligible voting electorate voted in statewide elections.[11] And
in 1998 voter turnout reached an abysmal low of 36.1 percent, with little

TABLE 3.3   Voting Turnout in Off-Year Elections, 1962–2006

	U.S. Total*
1962	47.5
1966	48.4
1970	46.8
1974	38.3
1978	37.3
1982	40.5
1986	36.3
1990	36.4
1994	38.8
1998	36.1
2002	36.2
2006	40.3

*Average of state turnout percentages in statewide or congressional elections.
Sources: Compiled from Ruy Teixeira, *The Disappearing American Voter* (Washington, D.C.: Brookings Institution, 1992), p. 6; *New York Times* and the Committee for the Study of the American Electorate, personal communication, December 2000.

improvement in 2002 (36.2 percent). In sum, if we use voter turnout as an indicator of citizen participation and citizen interest in American politics, then these figures reveal a detached and apathetic citizenry, one that displays a remarkable amount of civic indifference.

What factors account for this low voter turnout in presidential and off-year elections? In answering this question, we are constrained by the kinds of information that pollsters and social scientists have gathered over the past fifty years.[12] Political scientists have offered both individual and structural explanations.

At the individual level, a number of explanations have been suggested. All emanate from the belief that "the key to the puzzle of why so many people do not vote lies in one or another of their attitudes and preferences, or their lack of necessary resources."[13] One explanation is that people fail to vote because of a sense of political ineffectiveness, which is measured by a decline in **political efficacy**. Political efficacy refers to "both a sense of personal competence in one's ability to understand politics and to participate in politics, as well as a sense that one's political activities can influence what the government actually does."[14] A second explanation is that people lack the required sense of civic obligation. The decline in political parties and the concomitant decrease in **partisan attachment**, a strong relationship to political parties, is a third explanation. The lack of educational resources is a fourth reason for the decline in voter turnout. Those who are more highly educated are more likely to vote in elections because "education imparts information about politics and cognate fields and about a variety of skills, some of which facilitate political learning. . . . Schooling increases one's capacity for understanding and working with complex, abstract and intangible subjects, that is, subjects like politics."[15] Political mobilization by elites can also enhance voting turnout. Some scholars contend that in recent years we have seen a decline in political mobilization, fostering lower voter turnout in elections.[16] Perhaps the most important factor is the socioeconomic status (SES) of individual voters. Individuals with high SES, which is generally measured by education level, occupational status, and income, are more likely to vote than those with lower SES. One political scientist believes that "virtually all the long-run decline in turnout is due to the gradual replacement of voters who came of age before or during the New Deal and World War II by the generations who came of age later."[17] In other words, the young vote much less often than their parents and their grandparents did. Some believe that the citizenry is provided with too many opportunities to vote in elections and that many are overwhelmed by the large number of choices on the ballot, many of which are quite complex. For example, a political scientist claims that "the practice of democracy can, indeed, be taken too far, asking for more participation than many citizens care to dedicate themselves to."[18] Finally, political scientists argue that the electorate exhibits some combination of the above factors that prevents them from participating in elections.[19]

Voter-turnout rates, however, cannot be explained entirely by the characteristics or beliefs of individual citizens. A number of political, institutional, and structural factors deserve serious consideration as well. For example, scholars contend that legal and administrative barriers to voting depress voter-turnout rates. These legal and administrative barriers, such as complicated voter registration forms, are important because they impede the well-off and well-educated much less than they do the poor and the undereducated.[20] Therefore, there is a bias that favors more highly educated and wealthy voters. Historically, the political parties in power have supported antiquated voter registration procedures as a way to protect incumbent members of their own parties. Voter registration laws supported by the Democratic and Republican parties do impede challengers who would seek the support of voters whose views are perceived to be unrepresented in the American policy process. This obstruction occurs at all levels of government.

In 1983 a number of political activists formed Human Serve as a way to reform voter registration laws in the United States. The goal was to "enlist public and private nonprofit agencies to register their clients to vote." Under the Human Serve plan, citizens would be able to register to vote at hospitals and public health centers, motor vehicle bureaus and departments of taxation, unemployment and welfare offices, senior citizen centers and agencies for the disabled, day-care centers and family-planning clinics, settlement houses and family service agencies, housing projects and agricultural extension offices, and libraries and municipal recreation programs. With this program, the founders of Human Serve hoped to make access to voter registration virtually universal.[21] Despite the political and legal obstacles, Human Serve claims to have registered a considerable number of previously unregistered voters, many of whom have little education, have never participated before in elections, and are living in or near poverty.[22]

In 1993, with the support of President Bill Clinton, Democrats in Congress were able to pass the National Voter Registration Act, despite strenuous opposition from the Republican Party. This legislation enables potential voters to register as they stand in line to get their driver's licenses. The "Motor Voter" legislation requires all states to simplify their procedures for voter registration; requires states to allow potential voters to register when they renew or apply for licenses at any state department of motor vehicles office; permits voters to register at military recruitment, social service, and other public agencies; and allows voters to register by mail.[23] Piven and Cloward's analysis suggests that since the National Voter Registration Act went into effect in January 1995, "people have been registering or updating their voting addresses at the rate of nearly one million per month in 42 states." Early estimates were that the voter registration rolls would increase by 20 million before the 1996 election and 20 million more by the 1998 midterm election.[24]

In their most recent study of voter registration and turnout, Piven and Cloward point out that "more people registered between 1995 and 1998 . . . than ever before in American history."[25] And in his magisterial study of the meaning of the vote in America, historian Alexander Keyssar astutely claims that the National Voter Registration Act "was the final act of the drama that had begun in the 1960s: it completed a lurching yet immensely important forty-year process of nationalizing the voting laws and removing obstacles to the ballot box."[26] Yet registration continues to be a serious obstacle for many Americans. Moreover, despite the increased number of registered voters due to the Motor Voter law, voter turnout has declined since the law was adopted in 1993. In his study of "the vanishing voter," Harvard political scientist Thomas Patterson concludes that "evidence indicates that the decline would have been steeper without the Motor Voter Act, but the legislation has not been the magic bullet that its optimistic supporters expected it to be."[27] Other structural barriers to voting include limits on voting hours, which restrict many Americans who work and commute long hours. Some have suggested that our elections should be held on weekends or on a national "election holiday," structural changes that would allow greater access to the voting booth. Finally, we cannot underestimate the impact of negative campaigning on potential voters. Patterson's study concludes that "it is not the largest barrier to greater involvement, but it is a significant one."[28]

In sum, the attributes most likely to be associated with a willingness on the part of individuals to vote—"from education to positive feelings about politics—are more likely to be present among the more affluent."[29] For these reasons, then, the electorate is hardly representative of the citizenry.

Political scientist Robert Putnam addressed the broader implications of civic indifference for the quality of American public life and overall system stability. To Putnam, the vitality of **civil society**—networks of civic associations and social trust that contribute to high levels of voluntary cooperation and participation—in the United States has declined considerably over the past twenty-five years or so. In his analysis, Putnam incorporates the work of the French diplomat Alexis de Tocqueville, who visited the United States in the 1830s and reported that Americans' participation in civic associations was a central element of their democratic experience. In *Democracy in America,* Tocqueville wrote:

> Americans of all ages, all stations in life, and all types of disposition are forever forming associations. There are not only commercial and industrial associations in which all take part, but others of a thousand different types—religious, moral, serious, futile, very general and very limited, immensely large and very minute. . . . Nothing in my view, deserves more attention than the intellectual and moral associations in America.[30]

Putnam asserts that since the 1970s Americans have witnessed a decline in civic engagement. The metaphor that he employs to describe this trend toward greater isolation is that more Americans are "bowling alone."[31] Reports that millions of Americans have withdrawn from community affairs support Putnam's claim that there has been a decline in civic engagement. Additional factors include the decline in voter turnout, a reduction in the number of Americans working for political parties and signing petitions, a decline in the number of Americans attending a political rally or speech, and a drop in the number of Americans running for office.[32] To Putnam, these trends are disturbing because they lead to a decline in what he calls "social capital—networks, norms, and trust—that enable participants to act together more effectively to pursue shared objectives."[33] At the core of social capital are "connections among individuals—social networks and the norms of reciprocity and trustworthiness that arise from them."[34]

Putnam believes that technological developments, such as television and perhaps computers, have contributed considerably to the decline in civic engagement. He worries that television and the computer revolution have served to isolate individuals from their communities to the point where technology might be "driving a wedge between our individual interests and our collective interests."[35] Putnam is particularly critical of television in this regard, because watching TV is often a private activity. He claims that "dependence on television for entertainment is not merely a significant predictor of civic disengagement. It is the most consistent predictor that I have discovered."[36] These technological developments have had particularly deleterious consequences for the typical college-aged student of today, who most likely has spent a considerable amount of time watching television and interacting with computers in virtual isolation from others. Putnam warns that "high on America's agenda should be the question of how to reverse these adverse trends in social connectedness, thus restoring civic engagement and civic trust."[37] How this might be accomplished is a central theme of this book. But any attempt to restore civic engagement and civic trust must also be placed within the broader dilemma of this book: how to foster a more meaningful and participatory democracy, one that also promotes overall civility.

Some analysts, including Putnam, believe that the country's response to the September 11 attacks has provided an avenue for rebuilding American civic life. Writing in October 2001, Putnam claimed that "since September 11 we Americans have surprised ourselves in our solidarity."[38] He cites the willingness of many Americans to give blood and lend financial assistance to the victims and their rescuers, a generosity that reveals Americans' true public-minded spirit. But in the immediate aftermath of the September 11 attacks, President George W. Bush encouraged the American people to continue spending and to think patriotic thoughts and sing patriotic songs, while the government did its business in responding to the threat of terrorism. Two political scientists have pointed out accurately that "tens of millions Americans displayed flags and clearly wanted to do something for their country, but their country seemed to have nothing for them to do."[39] President Bush's call for Americans to do more community service in his 2002 State of the Union address also seemed vague and insipid in light of the gravity of the attacks and the willingness of people to do so much more. He could have used the opportunity to embrace a more activist role for the federal government by developing policies that responded to the economic hardship in the form of "new domestic social security programs to aid the unemployed and spread the sacrifices caused by the coincidence of terrorism and national economic recession."[40] Of course, this would have required that the federal government shift some of its spending priorities, something that neither Bush's administration nor his conservative supporters in Congress were willing to do. Instead, they expected localities to create programs that would respond to specific needs in their communities.

And what do qualitative surveys of voters' attitudes about politics and political participation suggest regarding civic indifference prior to and after September 11, 2001? One such study, conducted in 1990–1991 by the Harwood Group for the Kettering Foundation, found empirical support for David Mathews's claim that people think that "the political arena today is too large and distant for individual actions to have an impact."[41] The Kettering study, titled *Citizens and Politics: A View from Main Street America*, gathered citizen groups in ten cities in an effort to understand what Americans think about their roles as citizens in the political system at large. For many of the participants in these focus group discussions, a sense of powerlessness and exclusion from government decisions translated into a feeling that they had a limited role in the political system. The Kettering study also identified the usual "popular dissatisfaction with government and politicians."[42] It found that participants believed that they were "pushed out" of a political process dominated by special-interest lobbyists and politicians and that negative attacks and sound bites dominated public discourse in ways that turned citizens off from politics. People perceived that debate on the issues of the day offered little opportunity for citizen participation and was generally remote from their concerns. One participant concluded, "I'm never aware of an opportunity to go somewhere and express my opinion and have someone hear what I have to say."[43]

Despite this dissatisfaction, many of the citizens in the focus groups were far from apathetic. Indeed, they had a clear sense of their civic responsibilities and wished to have more meaningful opportunities to participate in the political system.[44] But at the same time, they displayed frustration, anger, cynicism, and alienation toward politics in America. They were particularly worried about passing on their cynicism and alienation to their children. To these Americans, a professional political class of incumbent politicians, powerful lobbyists, the media elite, and campaign managers kept them from participating in the broader political system in a meaningful way. People in the study perceived that the system was dominated by money and that voting in elections simply would not make a difference because the overall system is closed to the average citizen.[45]

A more recent study of civic engagement, commissioned by the Pew Partnership for Civic Change, challenges "the popular myth that Americans are isolated in their homes and offices—shunning civic activities and unwilling to get involved." Their poll of 1,830 Americans found that "people have a profound sense of connectivity to their communities and their neighbors, are volunteering in record numbers, are helping neighbors to solve problems, and are optimistic about the future." The Pew study reveals that 77 percent of Americans are connected to their communities in meaningful ways and that "almost ninety percent of Americans of all ages have not given up and believe that working together is the best way to solve community problems."[46] This is good news, especially for those who believe that Putnam's analysis overlooks the variety of ways that citizens are participating in the larger public sphere. It also points to possible connections between the impact of September 11 and how citizens now think of community engagement. In addition, it challenges the view that citizens display far too much civic indifference. But the study fails to explore why citizens are engaged in working with others in their respective communities and does not make linkages to the political arena. Why are many of these same citizens apparently so turned off by politics that they cannot even be bothered to vote in periodic elections?

There are additional signs of this citizen anger toward politics besides low voter turnout. As political scientist Susan Tolchin reports in *The Angry*

American, "Political leaders from both parties worry about the absence of civility, the decline of intelligent dialogue, and the rising decibels of hate."[47] In the 1990s and early in the twenty-first century, there was an increase in the number of incumbents who chose to leave office voluntarily for fear of losing their seats. The losses stemmed from the votes of a citizenry increasingly frustrated with professional politicians. Some of these politicians chose to leave office because they were concerned about the rise of incivility in American politics and that the U.S. Senate had become too partisan and ultimately uncivil. For example, Senators Bill Bradley (D-New Jersey), Hank Brown (R-Colorado), James Exon (D-Nebraska), Peter Fitzgerald (R-Illinois), Nancy Landon Kassebaum (R-Kansas), Tim Wirth (D-Colorado), and Evan Bayh (D-Indiana) all declined to seek reelection at the height of their political careers. In addition, laws to limit terms at all levels of government have been passed by large margins in several states.

Citizens have also embraced the **initiative** and **referendum** as vehicles for addressing the problems that the political system at large has neglected. Through the initiative and referendum, citizens enact or reject laws directly rather than relying on elected officials to solve problems. An initiative, a proposed new law initiated by citizens, is placed on the ballot through a petition signed by a specified number of voters. Through a referendum, a law approved by elected officials is referred to the ballot either by the officials or by citizen petition.[48] The initiative and referendum process most closely approximates direct democracy in the United States. California's Proposition 13, which was ratified in the late 1970s, ushered in an era in which the referendum has been increasingly used. For example, in Long Beach, California, citizens called for a referendum on zoning ordinances. In Olympia, Washington, citizens decided state legislators' salaries by referendum. In Chicago, citizens proposed a referendum to limit school taxing power. Citizens in California's San Gabriel Valley attempted to block a controversial redevelopment project through the use of the referendum. The message of all these referendum efforts is that representative government has failed to tackle the policy issues under question, thus contributing to a more angry, alienated, and frustrated citizenry, which will bypass the normal policy process to achieve its goals.[49]

Ross Perot clearly capitalized on the citizenry's frustration with "politics as usual" in his quixotic 1992 campaign for the White House. Perot, running on the Independent Party ticket, presented himself as an antipolitician, an outsider who truly understood the frustrations of mainstream America, who could provide the leadership required to pass timely and meaningful public policies in response to the major issues of the day. To Perot, lobbyists, political action committees, and the elected officials who serve them are at the heart of what is wrong with the American political system. Perot was most effective in attacking the nation's political elites and rallying his supporters around the populist banner of "United We Stand." As one commentator pointed out, "Far more than most leading Democrats and Republicans, Perot has a feel for how millions of ordinary people actually experience life in contemporary America, and he expresses that understanding keenly."[50] As a result, he was able to rally supporters who were concerned about undemocratic abuses of power at the same time that they wished to have more meaningful involvement in the political system. To his most avid supporters, many of whom had become angry and frustrated with American politics, it did not seem to matter that to critics Perot appeared to be "an egomaniac with a clever sales pitch and a fortune to spend."[51] In the end, both Democrats and Republicans recognized that the Perot phenomenon would not quickly disappear. In July 1993 the **Democratic Leadership Council (DLC)**, a group of elected officials who wanted to overhaul the party's liberal image and move the party to the center of the ideological spectrum, especially on social issues, published a document designed to provide Democrats with the building blocks for a leadership, policy, and electoral strategy to persuade Perot supporters to support the Democrats in future elections. It concluded, in part:

> The Perot bloc is for real and has considerable staying-power. Perot voters remain committed to the 1992 vote and, for the moment, want to stick with Perot in 1996—even if he were to run as a Republican. That is a measure of their independence and alienation which will remain important in our future national elections.[52]

Perot's ability to win 19 percent of the popular vote in the 1992 presidential election provides more empirical evidence for the claim that many Americans are increasingly disheartened with "politics as usual." However, his disappointing showing in the 1996 presidential election (8.5 percent of the popular vote) is a reminder of the barriers that third parties face at the national level.

Ralph Nader's third-party challenge as the Green Party candidate in the 2000 presidential campaign also tapped into citizen frustration with the two-party system. Nader's campaign, which was energized by the response of students to his many campus speaking engagements, especially appealed to progressives who were worried about growing economic inequalities and the dominance of corporate influence in the public arena. His candidacy provided an avenue for a broader critique of the failure of the Democratic and Republican parties to respond to that influence in meaningful ways. But in the end, Nader received no electoral votes and garnered only a paltry 2.7 percent of the popular vote. His poor electoral performance did not stop angry Democrats from pinning the results of the 2000 election on his having taken away crucial votes from Al Gore in the highly contested state of Florida.

Republican party candidate Ron Paul did well in recruiting a committed group of students nationwide to support his long-shot candidacy in the 2008 election. When Paul announced his presidential campaign in 2007, recent Texas A&M graduate Jeff Frazee founded the organization Students for Ron Paul, which became the unofficial youth wing of the campaign. The organization raised $30,000 for Paul's campaign, and Frazee's hard work was rewarded with his being hired as the National Youth Coordinator.[53] Paul and Frazee hope that their organizing efforts in the 2008 presidential campaign will help to recruit students to libertarian causes in future elections. With that in mind, a new organization, Young Americans for Liberty, was established on December 2, 2008. In support of that organization, Paul argued that "a youth-based movement for liberty is essential to our cause. It is these young men and women who will become tomorrow's champions of liberty. That's why I am giving my enthusiastic endorsement to Young Americans for Liberty (YAL); an organization that is built directly on the success of Students for Ron Paul."[54] Like Ross Perot and Ralph Nader before him, Ron Paul built on the citizenry's frustrations with politics as usual.

Citizen alienation and frustration has also manifested itself in the increased popularity of television and radio call-in talk shows, which are often devoted to discussions of politics. *Newsweek* devoted a February 1993 cover story to the popularity of the talk-show format and reported that call-in shows were growing so fast that they represented nearly 1,000 of the nation's 10,000 radio shows. At that time, *Larry King Live* was the highest-rated show broadcast on the Cable News Network (CNN).[55] Rush Limbaugh emerged as such an unrelenting critic of the Clinton presidency that President Clinton unleashed a barrage of public criticism against the conservative talk-show host in June 1994. The president recognized that he could not let Limbaugh's continuous attacks go unanswered.

What is the broader significance of all of this "noise" across the airwaves? At one level, it surely signifies that a portion of the American electorate continues to be frustrated by the normal operation of American politics and desires more meaningful opportunities to participate in decisions that affect the quality and direction of their lives. At the same time, politicians who wince because of what they hear on television or radio talk shows are surely overreacting. To be sure, only the most outraged, motivated, and devoted listeners call in. They constitute only about 2 or 3 percent of the total audience.[56] As a result, the angry voices often heard in the talk-show format are hardly representative of the larger public. What the talk shows do signify, however, is that attention is being paid to citizen disaffection at a time when both scholars and average citizens are discussing issues of democracy, citizenship, and accountability. This is certainly true of the amount of attention devoted to young people's beliefs and values regarding politics, which I discuss next.

American Youth and Civic Indifference

Many studies through the years have provided considerable evidence to support the conclusion that young people are largely apathetic, uninterested, indifferent, and disengaged when it comes to politics. One political scientist recently claimed that "today's young adults are less politically interested and informed than any cohort of young people on record."[57] Indeed, studies of the political lives of contemporary youth provide additional support for this claim. Yet these studies also "reflect two contradictory stereotypes: that of an apathetic Me Generation and that of a college population motivated by idealism."[58] The tension between these two stereotypes warrants further examination. In addition, we need to explore the reasons why many young people appear to be indifferent toward politics.

When eighteen- to twenty-year-olds were given the right to vote with the passage of the Twenty-sixth Amendment in 1971, it was thought that the extension of the franchise would do much to address youth alienation. Indeed, at the time 11 million new voters gained the right to vote.[59] Since that time, however, there has been a steady decline in young voters' interest and participation in the political process. This lack of interest in voting fell to a new low in the 1990 off-year elections, when just one in five eighteen- to twenty-year-olds bothered to vote.[60]

The Census Bureau reports that 50 percent of eighteen- to twenty-four-year-olds voted in 1972, but in 1996 only 32 percent of those in this age group voted. According to the Voter News Service, turnout was even lower in the 1998 midterm elections, when eighteen- to twenty-four-year-olds accounted for only 28 percent of voters.[61] In the 2002 midterm elections, the turnout among eighteen- to twenty-four-year-olds hit an embarrassing low of 17 percent.[62] Although there was an upturn in voter turnout among eighteen- to twenty-four-year-olds in the 1992 elections (42 percent[63]) and in 2000 (32 percent), those elections appear to have been an anomaly.[64]

One group particularly concerned about Generation X's voting behavior is the Third Millennium, an organization that sponsored the Neglection 2000 project, designed to target young people in ways that would inspire them to vote in the 2000 elections. The organizers worried that young people were increasingly becoming disengaged from the political process, and at an even greater rate than the rest of the population. A second organization, the New Voters Project, "a nonpartisan effort to register and get them to the polls on Election Day,"[65] was created in time for the 2004 election campaign. The organization's founders decided to "bring unprecedented resources to a professionally run field operation that will use peer-to-peer voter registration and voter contact as the central strategies."[66] Their goal was to target eighteen- to twenty-four-year-olds in six states—Colorado, Iowa, New Mexico, Nevada, Oregon, and Wisconsin—which together have a population of 2 million eligible voters in that age range. The New Voters Project, which is a project of the Student PIRGS (Public Interest Research Groups), continued its organizing efforts for the 2008 presidential campaign, recognizing that "young people haven't been full participants."[67] What is most impressive about this organization's grassroots efforts is the underlying belief "that young people are a viable constituency that can be mobilized using tried and true techniques."[68] The organizers recognized the importance of reaching out to young people in an effort to persuade them to participate in mainstream electoral politics, despite what appear to be serious barriers.

For example, a study by the Center for Information and Research on Civic Learning and Engagement (CIRCLE) found that "strong pluralities of young people [eighteen- to twenty-four-year-olds] surveyed said they were certain they would not participate in politics." In addition, the study "reported that nearly 75 percent of the young people surveyed believe they really don't count, that candidates would prefer to address older or wealthier voters." As if these findings weren't depressing enough, the CIRCLE study provides more evidence to support the claim that young people are turned off by mainstream politics: "Fifty-seven percent said they almost surely would never run for elective office, fifty-three percent said they will not join a political party," and "forty-six percent said they would not be likely to volunteer in a political campaign."[69] The study also "found that young Americans are also less likely than their (admittedly also pretty disengaged) elders to have participated in traditional forms of civic engagement—writing a letter to their congressman or newspaper, for example, or marching in a demonstration."[70] These findings raise serious questions about the future of American democracy unless current generations "of young people come to see both the value of and necessity for civic engagement and political participation."[71]

Indeed, studies of college students conducted by the University of California, Los Angeles (UCLA)/American Council on Education, "The American Freshman" and the annual "Roper College Track" report, found that college freshmen matriculating during the 1994–1995 academic year were "more disengaged from politics than any previous entering class; only 31.9 percent of the fall 1994 freshmen—lowest [up to that time] in the history of the survey—say that 'keeping up with political affairs' is an important goal in life, compared to 42.4 percent in 1990, and 57.8 percent in 1966." The authors of the report concluded that "considering that the figure from 1993—a nonelection year—was 37.6 percent, the sharp drop in the fall 1994 election year survey is all the more unexpected." The UCLA findings provide more evidence of disengagement from politics. The percentage of "freshmen who say they frequently 'discuss politics' reached its lowest point ever in the fall 1994 survey: 16.0 percent, compared to 18.8 percent the previous year and 24.6 percent in 1992 (the highest point of 29.9 percent was recorded during the 1968 election year)."[72]

The UCLA data for the 2001, 2002, and 2003 entering college classes provide evidence that first-year students are becoming slightly more interested in political concerns. For example, the percentage of students who are committed "to keeping up to date with political affairs as an important life goal" increased: 31.4 percent (2001), 32.9 percent (2002), and 33.9 percent (2003). And the percentage of students who discuss politics frequently also increased to the highest point since 1993 in 2003, though there was a downturn in 2002: 20.9 percent (2001), 19.4 percent (2002), and 22.5 percent (2003). Finally, the percentage of freshmen who "performed volunteer work" during their last year in high school also increased between 2001 and 2003: 82.6 percent (2001), 82.6 percent (2002), and 83.1 percent (2003).[73]

Perhaps the slight percentage increases in responses to these questions between 2001 and 2003 reflect student reactions to post–September 11, 2001, events. There are other possible explanations, however, including that many high school curricula now require a public service component as a condition for graduation and that most schools stress the importance of public service for college applicants. But when these survey results are placed within the broader context of other recent data (quantitative and qualitative) concerning student engagement with politics, it is clear that students continue to be disengaged from and indifferent to politics, but connected to community service.

These positive trends continue in the UCLA study of the entering 2008 freshman class. The percentage of freshmen who say that they frequently discuss politics rose significantly, to 35.6 percent, while 39.5 percent claim that they are interested in keeping up with political affairs. One obvious explanation for these increases is that the survey was administered in the midst of the 2008 presidential election, when the country at large was most likely to be interested in politics. What is also striking is that the percentage of freshmen who performed volunteer work during their last year in high school rose to 84.4 percent, thus providing more evidence that community service is becoming more ubiquitous as students enter college.[74]

The positive trends are also reflected by an increase in youth voter-turnout rates in the 2008 presidential election (see Table 3.4). Youth activist Michael Connery reminds us that the Millennial Generation (those born between 1985 and 2004) are unlike previous recent generations of young people because they are not "disinterested [sic] or apathetic, but if early evidence proves correct, they may be the most civic-minded generation since the much-celebrated GI 'Greatest' Generation of World War II."[75] The political influence of the Millennial Generation will only increase in future "as the share who are old enough to vote rises from about one-third in 2008 to more than half in 2016. But their greatest mark may come in reinvigorating civic life after years of concern that the U.S. had atomized into a nation of 'bowling alone'."[76] CIRCLE's 2008 study of the youth vote offered this hopeful conclusion: "The turnout rate among young people in 2008 was one of the highest recorded. The increase suggests that the confluence of extensive voter outreach efforts, a close election, and high levels of interest in the 2008 campaign all worked to drive voter turnout among young people to levels not seen since 1992. The increase is a continuation of the trend observed in the 2004 and 2006 elections."[77] Barack Obama's attempts to target the

TABLE 3.4　Selected Voter Turnout in Presidential Election Years, 1972–2008

	U.S. Total*			
Presidential Election Year	18–24 Citizens	25 and older Citizens	18–29 Citizens	30 and older Citizens
1972	52.1%	68.4%	55.4%	69.5%
1976	44.4%	65.4%	48.8%	67.0%
1980	43.4%	68.5%	48.2%	70.6%
1984	44.3%	68.9%	49.1%	71.2%
1988	39.9%	65.8%	43.8%	68.5%
1992	48.6%	70.5%	52.0%	72.4%
1996	35.6%	61.6%	39.6%	63.6%
2000	36.1%	62.9%	40.3%	64.6%
2004	46.7%	66.3%	49.0%	67.7%
2008	48.5%	65.8%	51.1%	67.0%

Source: www.civicyouth.org

young in his campaign was a point of departure from mainstream politicians in recent years and paid real dividends in both the primary and general elections. In his decisive general election victory, Obama defeated McCain by 34 percentage points among voters under thirty (Reagan in 1984 and Clinton in 1992 secured 19-point advantages among these voters; those numbers were viewed as impressive until Obama's achievement in securing the youth vote in 2008).[78] Obama's efforts suggest that "youth may be willing to participate if the effort is made to draw out that participation."[79]

One explanation for the poor youth voter-turnout rates in the 1990s (the 1992 presidential election was an exception) is that "political parties, social movements, and organized lobbies began to ignore youth altogether, producing a downward spiral that probably had negative effects on young people's group membership, interest in the news, and other matters beyond voting."[80] Perhaps this explanation helps to account for the survey figures on entering freshmen reporting that those engaged by politics remain embarrassingly low. One explanation for college students' disengagement from politics is that they did not have a chance to confront their potential roles as citizens prior to entering college. The UCLA studies measure the attitudes only of entering first-year college students; they do not address the attitudes of upper-division students, who might have developed an interest in politics and public life as a result of their college educational experiences. To be sure, a college education reinforces the notion that one has a duty to participate in civic affairs, if only through voting in periodic elections.

There is another explanation, however, for young people's apparent civic disengagement. One political scientist believes that many young Americans have virtually no sense of civic duty or societal obligation. They "regard themselves solely as the clientele of government"[81] and demand rights without responsibilities. It is this view that has led some to call this generation of youth the Me Generation.

Indeed, several studies provide support for this grim conclusion. For example, a 1989 study for People for the American Way conducted by Peter D. Hart Research Associates found the following:

1. Young people cherish America's freedoms without understanding what it takes to preserve them.
2. This generation is—by its own admission and in the eyes of teachers—markedly less involved and less interested in public life than previous generations.
3. Institutions with the best opportunity to teach young people citizenship—family, school, and government—have let them down.[82]

A 1990 *Times Mirror* study found that "today's young Americans, aged eighteen to thirty, know less and care less about news and public affairs than any other generation of Americans in the past fifty years." The authors of this study labeled this generation of youth "the age of indifference."[83] Although these studies are now dated, they offer conclusions that are still relevant as we try to understand why so many young people remain disengaged from politics in a country that purports to adhere to democratic values.

Previous generations of young people have surely been preoccupied with personal concerns such as individual happiness and career success. Indeed, these two goals are often linked by the importance of making enough money to provide for one's family and pursue a variety of materialistic pleasures. But there is a sense that the present generation of youth is more preoccupied with career goals and making money than were previous generations. It may well be that students perceive that they face numerous pressures stimulated by a changing and more unfriendly economy, changes that could mean that the young may not be able to achieve the kind of material well-being their parents and grandparents had. The headlines of the early 1990s reminded students of the difficult job market: "Economic Trend for the 90s: Fear"; "Middle-Class and Jobless, They Share Sorrows"; and "Graduates March Down Aisle into Job Nightmare,"[84] and the job market is still very tight for current college graduates, especially given the collapse of the economy in 2008. The *Wall Street Journal* captured these challenges well with this headline: "The Curse of the Class of 2009." And the lead to this article dramatized what awaited that graduating class: "The bad news for this spring's college graduates is that they're entering the toughest labor market in at least 25 years. The worse news: Even those who land jobs will likely suffer lower wages for a decade or more compared to those lucky enough to graduate in better times, studies show."[85] Current challenges include inadequate health-care coverage, worsening job prospects, and how to pay off increased levels of debt (much of which comes from student loans). As a result of these economic pressures, much of America's youth embraces the kind of radical individualism discussed in Chapter 2.

One of the most exhaustive studies of college students' views in the past twenty years was conducted in 1992–1993 by the Harwood Group for the Kettering Foundation. First-year and upper-division students from ten college campuses across the country were brought together in ten discussion focus groups and asked to explore the following questions:

1. What do college students believe it means to be a citizen?
2. How do college students view politics today?
3. How have college students come to learn what they know about politics and citizenship?
4. How would college students like to see politics practiced?
5. What opportunities do college students see for learning politics at the university?[86]

The strength of this study is that it goes far beyond merely reporting what students think about politics, instead exploring why they hold certain political views and how they think about politics.

In addressing these broader issues, the Kettering study offered three main findings. The first was that "many students have concluded that politics is irrelevant."[87] Students in this study held a narrow conception of politics and identified three basic ways that they might participate in the American political system—all rooted in individual action. Students perceived that they could participate by voting, signing petitions, joining interest groups, or protesting, though they saw little value in any of these four forms. In light of this evidence, the researchers concluded that "the politics of pessimism" best captured the mood of the students.

A second and more hopeful conclusion was that "students can imagine a different politics." For many of the students interviewed, this different politics would be rooted in bringing people together at the community level to "find ways to talk and act on problems." In this way, politics would be more engaging to the average citizen. But students also recognized that the way U.S. politics was practiced did not correspond to this alternative vision.

Finally, the study found that "students say that they are not learning to practice politics." They offered a specific indictment of political education at the college level, saying that campus conversations reinforced "everything that they believe to be wrong with politics." More specifically, campus discussions of politics tended to be far too polarized.[88] A Wake Forest student provided evidence to support this claim: "People are very opinionated in my classes. There is no moderation at all and [the discussion] gets totally out of bounds." A related problem is that when people take such strident positions both inside and outside the classroom, it is difficult to discuss possible solutions to the problems at hand. As a result, these heated arguments have little relevance for addressing major policy concerns. One Morgan State student concluded, "There are no solutions discussed; it is all rhetoric."[89]

In sum, this study revealed that many students were alienated from politics and not particularly hopeful about the future. It is little wonder, then, that despite the increase in voter turnout among college-age youth in the 1992 presidential election, voter turnout among the young fell far below the national average even in the riveting 2008 presidential election. The students' views echoed the attitudes of the citizens interviewed for *Citizens and Politics,* the study prepared by the Harwood Group (1991) for the Kettering Foundation discussed earlier in this chapter. At the same time, however, there are some key differences between the two studies.

The first is that whereas "citizens are frustrated, students feel resigned."[90] The 1991 study had found that Americans were angry about politics because they perceived that they had been "pushed out" of the political process. Students, in contrast, "seem resigned to the conclusion that politics is what it is, that politics always has been this way, and that it may always be something that has little relevance to their lives."[91]

A second key difference is that whereas "citizens are seeking to reengage in politics, students see little purpose in ever becoming engaged."[92] At least citizens in the 1991 study had claimed that they desperately wanted to be more involved in meaningful ways in the political process, but they could not find the appropriate place to participate. College students were so convinced that politics did not solve real problems that they saw no real reason to participate.

The respective studies also point out that whereas "citizens argue that politics should be different, students seem to be missing a context for thinking about politics."[93] It is interesting that citizens in the 1991 study had recognized that the current conditions that shaped the political process should be different, but students accepted them as the norm. "Only when they are given the opportunity to imagine a new set of political practices do they see possibilities for change."[94]

Finally, whereas "citizens have a strong sense of civic duty, students see primarily entitlement."[95] Citizens in the 1991 study believed that for the political process to work effectively, they had to participate. In this sense, they perceived that they were a key part of the political process. Students, however, conceptualized citizenship "almost exclusively in terms of individual rights."[96] They saw little connection, then, between citizenship and politics.

CIRCLE attempted to replicate this study in 2006 and 2007 when their researchers "spoke with undergraduates in focus groups on 12 four-year college and university campuses across the United States."[97] Most of those interviewed belonged to the Millennial Generation. Their goal was to study "whether and how college students' civic engagement had changed after almost 15 years of tumultuous political events and work by colleges and universities."[98] Their research led to these conclusions:

1) This generation of college students is much more experienced "with volunteering (mostly face-to-face and local) and . . . believe in their obligation to work together with others on social issues. They are neither cynical nor highly individualistic."

2) "The Millennials appear to be much more comfortable and experienced with direct service than with politics, yet their feelings toward government, politicians, and the media are complex. They do not want to write off politics, despite their many criticisms; instead, they seek ways to engage politically."

3) "Students perceive politics, as it currently exists, as a polarized debate with no options for compromise or nuance."

4) "Colleges and universities are providing very unequal levels of opportunity for civic participation and learning."[99]

It is indeed disturbing that young people appear to be so indifferent toward and alienated from politics. On the other hand, the recent CIRCLE study of college students provides evidence that young people are willing to be engaged politically provided that the electoral and policy processes afford them genuine opportunities to do so.

When a group of thirty-three juniors and seniors representing twenty-seven colleges and universities gathered at the Wingspread Summit on Student Civic Engagement in March 2001, the students offered a different perspective on indifference with their analysis of "a new democracy," a perspective that is also reinforced by the CIRCLE study. I was fortunate enough to attend that conference, and while there I heard the voices of an array of thoughtful, committed, energetic, and diverse students (the students ranged from twenty to forty-seven years of age and the group comprised twelve men and twenty-one women). The conception of democracy that emerged out of that summit was defined "less in terms of civic obligation than in terms of the social responsibility of the individual."[100] Their view of conventional politics is worth quoting at length:

> For the most part, we are frustrated with conventional politics, viewing it as inaccessible. We discovered at Wingspread, however, a common sense that while we are disillusioned with conventional politics (and therefore most forms of political activity), we are deeply involved in civic issues through non-traditional forms of engagement. We are neither apathetic nor disengaged. In fact, what many perceive as a disengagement may actually be conscious choice; for example, a few of us at Wingspread actively avoided voting, not wanting to participate in what some of us perceive to be a deeply flawed electoral process. Others chose to vote solely on local referendums and initiatives. We have chosen to become involved in unconventional political activities. While we still hope to be able to participate in our political system effectively through traditional means, service is a viable and preferable (if not superior) alternative at this time.[101]

The views expressed at the Wingspread Summit echo the earlier findings of the 1991 Kettering study of college students:

> College students will engage in politics, but only if it is a different kind of politics—one that challenges them to learn new political skills and provides

opportunities to put those skills to use. More "politics as usual" will only deepen their sense of the irrelevance of the political process.[102]

"liberal arts Colleges"

It is also worth emphasizing that college students perceived that the educational process failed to provide them with meaningful and alternative ways to conceive of politics and to become involved in decisions of import on their campuses and in the larger society. Chapter 6 devotes considerable attention to exploring alternative models for conceptualizing how colleges and universities might restructure their general curricula to address the concerns that college students identified in the Kettering study, the CIRCLE study, and at the Wingspread Summit on Student Civic Engagement. In the meantime, we need to examine the evidence for the rise in citizen activism.

Sources of Citizen Activism

The study *Main Street America*[103] found that the key to citizen participation, identified by those who actually participated, was the possibility of change, not the certainty of success. If this study is at all accurate, then Americans can overcome obstacles to civic engagement if they perceive that their participation may have a meaningful effect—"that there is some opportunity to create and witness change." One woman offered this realistic observation: "You just keep trying. That doesn't mean that you will win all the time." The possibility of change thus becomes an important force for reconnecting citizens and politics.[104]

Those who subscribe to the democratic theory of elitism believe that citizens have little interest in politics, have minimal knowledge of what is happening politically, and fail to participate because they perceive that the system is working well enough as it is. But those who embrace the more participatory democratic perspective challenge the notion of civic indifference by identifying various ways that citizens have become more meaningfully involved politically in their communities. Citizens do care, and they struggle in all sorts of ways to find opportunities to have their voices heard in decisions at all levels of government that affect their lives.

The *Main Street America* study revealed that citizens wanted more meaningful public dialogue on key public policy issues. Citizens identified three specific problems with politics as usual: "the way the political agenda is set, the way policy issues are framed, and the limited opportunities for public deliberation." Citizens were particularly vocal about the way that the public agenda was set in American politics. As a woman from Texas succinctly stated, "The issues that policymakers jump on the bandwagon and carry on about aren't really the issues that deal with mainstream people."[105] What citizens want to avoid is the kind of polarization of emotional issues in public discourse, such as abortion and school prayer, which E. J. Dionne contends is a major factor in why so many Americans hate politics.

The study found that many of the citizens who expressed helplessness about the political process participated in their communities "in many ways and with great intensity of purpose." Their involvement takes a number of different forms—membership in neighborhood organizations, crime-watch groups, school committees, and ad hoc bodies that have been formed to address specific problems in the community. At the same time that voter turnout has been in decline, we have witnessed an explosion of citizen activism. During the past three and a half decades, more Americans have become involved in an array of grassroots citizen groups such as ACORN (Association of Community Organizations for Reform Now), the various state PIRGs (Public Interest Research Groups), and Clean Water Action. These organizations are increasingly playing a more active role in local policy debates and decisions. *Main Street America* concluded that citizens were involved in these organizations because they believed that their participation could make a difference and that there was a direct connection between their actions and possible policy solutions.[106] As I discuss later in this book, participation in these citizen organizations is one element of the New Citizenship.

College students, too, have shown renewed attention to broader community concerns and issues of social justice. A wide variety of community service programs and student literacy programs have spread across college campuses as students yearn for the opportunity to make a connection between what goes on in the classroom and the larger communities in which they live. A number of colleges, including Bates College, Colby College, Colgate University, Connecticut College, LeMoyne College, the University of Minnesota, Providence College, Rutgers University, Stanford University, Syracuse University, and Hobart and William Smith Colleges, have offered specific courses that require some form of community service. I devote considerable attention to these course offerings and their connection to broader issues of democracy, citizenship, and difference in Chapter 6.

Like their counterparts in the 1960s, today's progressive students protest acts of social injustice involved with issues of racial, gender, and sexual discrimination. When President Bush built up American troops in the Middle East during the summer and fall of 1990 as a prelude to the Persian Gulf War, college students organized antiwar protests. Indeed, my own campus, Hobart and William Smith Colleges, had one of the first college antiwar rallies, in November 1990. In more recent years, students across college campuses have organized to protest the wars in Afghanistan and Iraq, as well as restrictions on individual freedoms and liberties associated with the Patriot Act, which was quickly passed by Congress and signed into law by President George W. Bush in the aftermath of the attacks of September 11, 2001.

To be sure, what separates this generation of college students from their 1960s peers is the presence of outspoken conservative voices on many campuses and in the classroom who attack their more progressive colleagues and college faculty supporters as kowtowing to "political correctness." This often contributes to the polarized climate and discourse in the classroom and in the broader college community that students lamented in the Harwood study. At the same time, the rise on college campuses of community service programs and discussions of highly charged political issues such as race, gender, class, and sexual orientation indicate that students are interested in linking their courses of study with public policy solutions to current societal problems. This, too, is a central element of the New Citizenship and a source of optimism as we consider the ways citizens can be more meaningfully connected to the American political system.

Conclusion

This chapter has emphasized the importance of conceptualizing political participation far more broadly than mere participation in periodic elections. The right to vote may well be the central element of any democracy, but if that is the case, American voter-turnout rates suggest that the nation is characterized by civic indifference. Indeed, those who do vote in elections are overwhelmingly from the upper and middle classes, thus reinforcing the class bias in American politics.

Several studies of the electorate point out that many citizens are apathetic and uninterested in "politics as usual," which they perceive as dominated by special interests and closed to meaningful participation by the average citizen. At the same time, these studies suggest that Americans wish to have more meaningful opportunities to participate in the political system.

America's youth mirror and reinforce the political indifference of the larger society. If anything, the young are less informed and less inclined to participate in mainstream electoral politics, even taking into consideration the extraordinary 2008 presidential primary and general election campaign that helped to galvanize voters under age thirty (the Millennial Generation) for the first time. College students, however, appear to be more likely to vote than American youth as a whole. These same students report that they are increasingly disgusted by the polarized discourse in the larger society and on college campuses as well.

There is reason for optimism, however. At all levels of society, citizens wish to expand their sense of civic responsibility. In other words, citizens wish to go beyond voting and participate meaningfully in decisions that affect the quality and direction of their lives in both their communities and their workplaces, a perspective that may be more pronounced since the September 11, 2001, terrorist attacks on American soil.

It is this desire for public participation that is at the core of the New Citizenship. To fully understand the elements of the New Citizenship, we need to examine the political movements and community organizations of the 1960s that were rooted in a broader vision of citizenship associated with the participatory democratic tradition. After examining the legacy of these movements, particularly the civil rights movement, one can more meaningfully evaluate contemporary proposals for increasing citizen involvement in public life. It is not enough, however, merely to discuss the political movements growing out of the 1960s. Indeed, if the central dilemma of this book is how can a polity strike a balance between the varieties of political participation engaged in by its citizens, then I must also address contemporary organizations of both the left and the right whose approach to politics potentially threatens overall system stability. These issues are explored in Chapter 4.

4

....

Civility, Stability, and Foundations for the New Citizenship

At 9:02 A.M. on April 19, 1995, when many parents had just dropped their children at the second-floor day care center of the Alfred P. Murrah Federal Building in Oklahoma City, a truck bomb went off, shredding the front of the building, collapsing its nine stories like playing cards, and leaving behind bloody rubble, body parts, a thirty-foot-wide crater, and at least 167 dead. It was the worst terrorist attack and the most egregious mass murder in American history. It was also a warning shot by those who would make civil war in America.

–Kenneth Stern, *A Force upon the Plain*

IN THE IMMEDIATE aftermath of the Oklahoma City bombing, many suspected that only foreign terrorists could be capable of such massive devastation and destruction. The country soon learned, however, that individuals associated with the American militia movement were charged in the crime. In many ways, the militia movement is the realization of the constitutional framers' worst fear—large numbers of individuals organized around a set of emotional issues working outside the normal confines of Madisonian democracy. Those who constitute the various militia groups in states throughout the United States are engaged in the kind of factious activity that the framers hoped to prevent. Indeed, in the face of the Oklahoma City bombing, *Newsweek* concluded that "the militia movement may have 10,000 adherents,"[1] In fact, the contemporary American scene is littered with groups on both the left and the right whose members embrace unconventional politics and factious activity as a response to those in power. At a bare minimum, these groups contribute to the growing incivility and breakdown of community increasingly associated with American politics. To the extent that they endorse and encourage violence, they threaten overall system stability.

Of course, not all movements and groups that support unconventional politics foment violence in an attempt to disrupt system stability. Indeed, the African American civil rights movement of the 1960s embraced **nonviolent civil disobedience**, the deliberate breaking of an "unjust" law, and voter education as central strategies to force those in power to confront its demands. In so doing, the civil rights movement helped lay the groundwork for the New Citizenship today. Some of that movement's tactics and strategies have also been embraced by organizations across the ideological spectrum in their attempt to attract media attention and to prompt meaningful policy responses from governing elites.

As we saw in Chapter 2, during the decade of the 1960s a host of political and social movements and community-based organizations rooted in participatory democratic principles flourished. I now turn to a discussion of the period in American politics in which there was considerable organizing and activism, especially on the part of college students. To understand the foundations of the New Citizenship, we must first understand why some people called for expanding democracy four and a half decades ago. To be sure, the efforts of those working in the civil rights movement of the 1950s and 1960s have had consequences for American politics more generally; for the women's, student, antiwar, and economic justice movements; and for those activists who participated in the respective movements. My focus is largely on the specific roles played by students. It is usually argued that social movements are a central vehicle through which meaningful social, political, and economic change can occur, as evidenced by policies embraced at the national level under the rubric of Lyndon Johnson's **Great Society** in the 1960s.

As one scholar put it, the decade of the 1960s is remarkable because "large numbers of people began, through their choices, to challenge all manner of long-standing social, political and cultural arrangements."[2] That is particularly true of the civil rights movement. It was in this movement, as well, that participants learned how to be both educators and organizers. As I make clear, students played central roles. The civil rights movement provides a concrete and useful example of how a renewal of democratic citizenship and the extension of basic civil rights at the national level might be achieved.

1960's = Social Mobilization / Civil Rights

The Civil Rights Movement and Foundations for the New Citizenship

The importance of the civil rights movement of the 1950s and 1960s cannot be overestimated. It helped to inspire widespread political action, particularly among college students, for political and social reform. One scholar has called it the "second reconstruction,"[3] and another contends that it "had a profound impact on American society" for two central reasons.[4] First, it dismantled those components of the American political system that severely restricted the right of African Americans to vote. Second, "the movement altered and expanded American politics by providing other oppressed groups with organizational and tactical models, allowing them to enter directly into the political arena through the politics of protest."[5]

How did the civil rights movement accomplish these goals? The goals were largely accomplished by pursuing unconventional politics, a politics that required participants to go outside the formal channels of the American political system and embrace the politics of protest and mass involvement. Civil rights organizers used the **boycott** (the refusal to buy products or services of a business or public utility), marches and demonstrations, and nonviolent civil disobedience as vehicles for attracting media coverage, helping to dramatize the grievances of African Americans, and highlighting racial injustices. These techniques became effective tools for mobilizing the African American population throughout the nation by providing collective power in ways that helped to create a base for further successful political and social struggle. In addition, these strategies served the purpose of disrupting "normal patterns of life" and thus the ability of business and government to conduct their daily activities. The disruption of daily business and governmental affairs through nonviolent means of protest foreshadowed the violent protest in the form of urban riots that erupted in America's cities in the middle to latter part of the 1960s. Much of the violence was directed against symbols of civic authority, such as the police, as well as white business establishments that had a reputation for exploiting ghetto residents.[6]

Here, however, I wish to focus attention on the portion of the civil rights movement that most closely connects to the New Citizenship. Therefore, I turn now to a discussion of the educative component of the civil rights movement and the specific role played by students. In so doing, we must address the role of citizenship schools as well as the **Mississippi Freedom Summer**, when a thousand college students came to Mississippi from around the country to make white violence against blacks impossible for federal officials to ignore. This educative component, rooted in participatory democratic principles, coupled with a commitment to unconventional politics as a vehicle for capturing the attention of public policy elites, provides a direct connection to the New Citizenship today.

· College Students/ Students = Civil disobedience in

Citizenship Schools   *Tnc New Citizenship*

African American disfranchisement was widespread in the South during the late 1950s. Indeed, the overwhelming majority of African Americans were not even registered to vote. To be sure, this disfranchisement resulted from a deliberate attempt by powerful southern whites to deny African Americans the right to vote because of the color of their skin. Whites used a number of tactics to prevent African Americans from voting, including literacy tests; the **grandfather clause**, which denied the vote to those whose grandfathers had been slaves; all-white primaries; the **poll tax**; state-imposed tax on voters; outright violence; and economic reprisals.[7]

· Congregations + Civil Rights movement

In response to these repressive tactics, the **Southern Christian Leadership Conference (SCLC)**, under the direction of Rev. Martin Luther King Jr., organized a new mass movement whose central goal was to gain the franchise. Black churches played a central role in the origins of the movement.[8] Conservative church-going elements of the African American community were particularly ripe for the kind of nonviolent direct action associated with SCLC. One scholar of social movements concludes, "Externally, they [nonviolent direct action] counterpoised the well-dressed peaceful marchers of the movement to the thuggery of the police, while turning the religiosity of the southern black middle class into a basis of solidarity."[9] Thus one of the major goals of the civil rights organizers of the early 1960s was to incorporate local ministers into the movement and persuade them to encourage their congregations to participate in civil rights organizing.[10] After a considerable amount of hard work, the organizers were successful in enlisting church support.

The central goal of the **Crusade for Citizenship** program, as the new movement was called, and the citizenship schools that developed throughout the South was to **empower citizens through education**. With the organizing and training support of the Highlander Folk School in Tennessee, the civil rights movement of the 1950s recognized the importance of literacy education so that African Americans could overcome the obstacles to voting. Another goal was to prepare the people for meaningful social and political change. In the words of Myles Horton, Highlander's founder and director, "The job of Highlander was to multiply leadership for radical social change."[11]

In the 1950s many southern states required all eligible voters to pass a literacy test before they could even register to vote. Literacy tests were largely used to "disfranchise blacks, as the white registrars enforced the requirement stringently for blacks and leniently or not at all for white registrants." Most African Americans could not pass the test and were thus disqualified from voting on the grounds that they were illiterate.[12] Such tests became an important means for denying African Americans the basic right of democracy, the right to vote.

White resistance and repression undermined the efforts of the civil rights movement organizers. Whites opposed to southern integration used a number of tactics to blunt the impact of civil rights organizers, including **gerrymandering,** that is, redrawing legislative districts in partisan ways; delaying tactics by white registrars; economic reprisals; and legal maneuvers designed to neutralize the monitoring power of the Civil Rights Commission. In Louisiana the SCLC came close to achieving its goal of a mass citizenship movement but faced still-insurmountable barriers such as those described by this movement organizer: "When blacks went to register they were cut off the welfare rolls. . . . We had people who actually had difficulty selling their crops and things because they did go register."[13]

The SCLC's efforts in the late 1950s provided a foundation for the political, educational, and social change that was to emerge more forcefully with the roles played by SCLC, the Congress on Racial Equality (CORE), and the Student Nonviolent Coordinating Committee (SNCC) in the civil rights movement of the 1960s. The partnership between the Highlander Folk School and SCLC around citizenship education had consequences for the role of students in the civil rights movement and for the development of SNCC. At one level, SNCC surely benefited from the resources and ideological direction of the two previously established organizations.[14] At another level, students in the civil rights movement soon recognized that united African American support for their efforts would better enable them to achieve their goals. These goals and the strategies for achieving them are discussed next.

SNCC, Sit-ins, and the Mississippi Freedom Summer

SNCC was born out of a realization that for idealistic young people, political and social struggle occurring outside the normal framework of American politics was the only viable means for expressing their resentment of racial prejudice. SNCC's founding conference, held in Raleigh, North Carolina, on April 16–18, 1960, was called by Ella Baker, then executive director of SCLC. Baker encouraged the students to assert their independence from the SCLC leadership, but the students also "affirmed their commitment to the nonviolent doctrines popularized by King." The young people quickly made it clear, however, that they were not drawn to these ideas merely because they were associated with Martin Luther King but "because they provided an appropriate rationale for student protest." Indeed, there was at least one important difference between SCLC and SNCC. SCLC had a formal, centralized decision-making group headed by King, whereas SNCC was founded as a loosely structured coordinating committee, one that had "little power of control over local groups."[15] According to historian Clayborne Carson, "SNCC's founding was an important step in the transformation of a limited student movement to desegregate lunch counters into a broad and sustained movement to achieve major social reforms."[16]

No one national organization or leader initiated the lunch counter sit-ins that spread throughout the South in 1960.[17] It is true, however, that the sit-ins and the birth of SNCC in 1960 brought a new kind of intensity to the civil rights movement. To a large extent the sit-ins were a spontaneous phenomenon organized by college students; they emerged from the grass roots.

The most celebrated of the lunch counter sit-ins occurred at a Woolworth's in Greensboro, North Carolina, on February 1, 1960. By their courageous act, four African American North Carolina college students, Franklin McCain, Ezell Blair Jr., David Richmond, and Joseph McNeil, helped to launch sit-ins throughout the South. In their college dormitory the previous fall, the four young men had discussed the question, "At what point does the moral man act against injustice?" Reflecting on the experience several years later, McCain said, "I think the thing that precipitated the sit-in, the idea of the sit-in, more than anything else, was that little bit of incentive and that little bit of courage that each of us instilled within each other."[18] On the day of the sit-in, the four students purchased several items at the downtown F. W. Woolworth store and then asked to be served at a "lunch counter long reserved for whites through custom and tradition."[19] Not surprisingly, they were refused service. When asked why they had chosen Woolworth's, McCain explained:

> They advertise in public media, newspapers, radios, television, that sort of thing. They tell you to come in: "Yes, buy the toothpaste; yes, come in and buy the notebook paper. . . . No, we don't separate your money in this cash register, but, no, please don't step down to the hot dog stand." . . . The whole system, of course, was unjust, but that just seemed like insult added to injury. That was just like pouring salt into an open wound. That's inviting you to do something.[20]

The initial Greensboro sit-in was both polite and peaceful, but subsequent sit-ins in the South became much more assertive and occasionally unruly. Over time, the demonstrations attracted increased crowds and thus were perceived as threats to the social order because they disrupted the normal activities associated with daily business life. The sit-ins by African American college students "were characterized by strict discipline among the protesters."[21] Violence broke out in sporadic cases, for example, when the demonstrations included high school protesters in Portsmouth, Virginia, and Chattanooga, Tennessee. But the protesters largely embraced the nonviolent tactics associated with Martin Luther King Jr. Former SNCC activist John Lewis describes how he adapted such tactics: "One method of practicing this approach [nonviolent civil disobedience] is to imagine that person—actually *visualize* him or her—as an infant, as a baby. If you can see this full-grown attacker who faces you as the pure, innocent child that he or she once was—that we *all* once were—it is not hard to find compassion in your heart. It is not hard to find forgiveness."[22] As Clayborne Carson points out, "Nonviolent tactics, particularly when accompanied by a rationale based on Christian principles, offered African American students an appealing combination of rewards: a sense of moral superiority, an emotional release through militancy, and a possibility of achieving desegregation." Indeed, nonviolent civil disobedience ushered in a new stage in the civil rights movement, one that would be a rallying point for African American students as well as a catalyst for "the emergence of a new political consciousness among oppressed people" throughout the country and the world.[23]

The sit-ins and the emergence of SNCC had a profound impact on activist-oriented students at predominantly white northern colleges and universities, which spread to colleges across the country. Students at these schools were inspired by the impact of the sit-ins rapidly spreading throughout the South, as well as by the fact that most of the participants were African American college students. In his study of the Students for a Democratic Society (SDS), Kirkpatrick Sale discusses the impact of the sit-ins on white college students:

> By the end of that spring students at perhaps a hundred northern colleges had been mobilized in support, and over the next year civil-rights activity touched almost every campus in the country: support groups formed, fund raising committees were established, local sit-ins and pickets took place, campus civil-rights clubs began, students from around the country traveled to the South.[24]

The impact of the 1960 southern sit-ins was so great on white student activists that SDS actually borrowed much of its organizational structure from SNCC. In this way, then, the sit-ins helped generate "the activist stage of the modern white student movement."[25]

Ultimately the 1960 sit-in campaigns had much to do with exposing and dramatizing the racist underside of life in the South. By the end of 1960, the demonstrations had moved from lunch counters to parks, theaters, swimming pools, restaurants, libraries, interstate transportation, beaches, laundromats, courtrooms, churches, museums, and art galleries. In addition, students demanded an end to all employment discrimination and embraced voter registration projects as a key element of their broader interest in grassroots political organizing. As 1960 came to a close, these were no longer isolated incidents but were a part of a broader movement for political and social change.[26] Such efforts helped pave the way for the student-organized **freedom rides** of 1961, in which interracial groups of civil rights movement activists traveled throughout the South in an effort to desegregate vehicles engaged in interstate transportation. Many were beaten and stoned by whites for attempting to sit in the "whites-only" sections of buses and terminals.

The significance of the freedom rides is that they both led to the desegregation of southern transportation facilities and contributed to the development of a radical student movement, which laid the foundation for the 1964 Mississippi Freedom Summer. Unlike the 1960 sit-ins, which were widespread throughout the South, the 1961 freedom rides directly involved only several hundred protesters. Yet they had a far greater impact on the nation as well as "on the political consciousness of the participants, who suddenly became aware of their collective ability to provoke a crisis that would attract international publicity and compel federal intervention."[27]

The central goal of the freedom rides was to attract publicity by testing "compliance with court orders to desegregate interstate transportation terminals." Public buses throughout the Deep South were targets of these interracial freedom rides, which the organizers anticipated would prompt racial violence in the heartland of Jim Crow laws and thus force the federal government to vigorously protect African American rights.[28] On May 4, 1961, two small integrated groups rode a Trailways bus and a Greyhound bus from Washington, D.C., to New Orleans in an effort to "test whether buses and terminal facilities were desegregated."[29] Organized by CORE, the freedom rides included young members of SNCC. They were met in some cases by the most brutal forms of violence.

The freedom rides placed considerable moral pressure on the Kennedy administration to address segregated interstate transportation terminals in the South, but the administration did not want to be too closely tied to what it perceived as radical civil rights demands. In late 1962, however, CORE announced that segregation in interstate travel had been virtually ended as a result of the freedom riders' courageous efforts.[30] Once again, nonviolent civil disobedience had been a powerful weapon for challenging the most racist elements of the Deep South.

The efforts of the early civil rights movement in the form of citizenship schools, sit-ins, and freedom rides reached a climax with the 1963 inter-racial March on Washington. The central purpose of this march was to demand strong protection of African American rights by the federal government. Organized by veteran civil rights activist A. Philip Randolph and coordinated by Bayard Rustin, the March on Washington was labeled an immediate success because of its size (roughly 250,000 people) and the fact that it helped galvanize attention (through media coverage) to the plight of African Americans nationwide, but particularly in the South. Ultimately, most scholars agree that the march and other civil rights protests in the 1950s and early 1960s prompted the federal government to pass the Civil Rights Act of 1964 and the Voting Rights Act of 1965 (see Box 4.1). It also prompted grassroots civil rights organizers to redouble their efforts in the South. These efforts culminated in the 1964 Mississippi Freedom Summer.

The Mississippi Freedom Summer, or "Summer Project" as it was then called, was organized by SNCC and lasted less than three months, from early June through late August 1964. Over the course of those three months, more than 1,000 people journeyed to Mississippi to work in one of the forty-four local projects that were the central elements of the campaign. The vast majority of the participants were northern college students. The volunteers lived in communal "Freedom Houses" or were housed by local African American families who refused to be intimidated by the threat of possible segregationist violence. The principal daily activities of the volunteers included teaching in freedom schools and registering African American voters.[31] The freedom schools had to compensate for the inadequacies of Mississippi's segregated, impoverished public school system. Summer Project volunteers attempted to do so by offering young African Americans a sense of their own past, while also teaching them to think and act for themselves. There were classes in adult literacy, African American history, journalism, and French.[32] A central goal of the project was simply to integrate Mississippi en masse by northern white student volunteers in summer 1964. This goal was clearly accomplished.

BOX 4.1 Civil Rights Movement Timeline, 1954–2010

1954   In its *Brown v. Board of Education* decision, the Supreme Court rules that in education, separate facilities are inherently unequal. In making this decision, the court overturned the precedent set in its 1896 *Plessy v. Ferguson* decision, thus rendering segregated schools unconstitutional.

1955   Martin Luther King Jr. leads a widespread bus boycott in Montgomery, Alabama.

1957   A Little Rock, Arkansas, high school is forced to desegregate by federal troops, which were dispatched by President Dwight Eisenhower, who had initially opposed the Supreme Court's *Brown v. Board of Education* ruling.

1963   More than two hundred thousand people of all races attend the historic March on Washington to protest racial segregation. As a part of this march, Dr. King gives his immortal "I Have a Dream" speech.

1964   The Twenty-fourth Amendment to the Constitution ends the poll tax in federal elections.
         Congress passes the Civil Rights Act of 1964, in response to vigorous lobbying by President Lyndon Johnson. The comprehensive legislation affords the federal government an array of powers to force states to end racial discrimination practices.

1965   After strong support and lobbying by President Lyndon Johnson, Congress passes the Voting Rights Act. The act awards registrars the power to impound ballots and sends federal registrars to southern counties and states to protect African Americans' right to vote. Riots occur in the Watts section of Los Angeles and other cities and recur every summer in various cities over the course of the next five years.

1966   The U.S. Supreme Court invalidates poll taxes in state elections in *Harper v. Virginia Board of Elections*. This decision forbids making a tax a condition of voting in any election.

1967   With the election of Carl Stokes, Cleveland becomes the first major city to be headed by an African American mayor. Lyndon Johnson appoints Appeals Court judge and U.S. solicitor general and director counsel of the NAACP legal defense fund Thurgood Marshall to the Supreme Court; he is the first nonwhite to sit on the court.

1968   Dr. Martin Luther King Jr. is assassinated in Memphis, Tennessee. Shirley Chisholm is elected to represent New York's Twelfth District in the U.S. House of Representatives; she is the first African American female representative.

(continues)

(continued)

1971   The Supreme Court's *Swann v. Charlotte-Mecklenberg County Schools* decision approves of busing as a means of combating state-enforced segregation.

1972   Congresswoman Shirley Chisholm runs for president; she is the first African American to launch a serious campaign for the American presidency.

1978   The Supreme Court's *California Board of Regents v. Bakke* decision forbids the use of racial quotas for medical school admissions but does not forbid the consideration of race as a factor in admissions decisions.

1979   The Supreme Court's *United Steelworkers of America v. Weber* decision permits an affirmative action program to favor African Americans if the program is designed to remedy past discrimination.

1984   Rev. Jesse Jackson becomes the first African American candidate to run for president within one of the two major political parties when he decides to enter the Democratic primary process.

1989   L. Douglas Wilder becomes the first African American to be elected governor of a state when he defeats Marshall Coleman in a close Virginia election. David Dinkins is the first African American elected mayor of New York City.

1995   The Supreme Court's *Adarand Constructors v. Pena* decision states that affirmative action programs must undergo strict scrutiny to determine that they are narrowly tailored to serve a compelling governmental interest.

2003   The Supreme Court's *Gratz v. Bollinger* decision struck down the University of Michigan's undergraduate admissions policy because it assigned points to applicants based on certain admissions criteria, including race and ethnicity. But in *Grutter v. Bollinger* the U.S. Supreme Court permitted the University of Michigan's consideration of race in its law school admission process as a means for diversifying the law school student body because the admission's plan did not violate the Constitution's 14th Amendment equal protection clause.

2007   The Supreme Court's *Parents Involved in Community Schools v. Seattle School District No. 1* decision limited race-based systems for primary and secondary assignments in schools, except for those districts that were ordered by courts to remedy the indignities of prior official segregation.

2008   Barack Obama is elected president of the United States.

2009   The Supreme Court's *Ricci v. DeStefano* decision ruled that New Haven, Connecticut's promotion exam policy had discriminated against a group of mostly white firefighters who were punished unfairly when the exam was thrown out because no African Americans had scored well enough to be promoted. In doing so, the Supreme Court established a new standard for employers' use of race as a criteria in hiring decisions.

Robert Moses, the chief architect of the Freedom Summer, concluded in early 1964 that federal government intervention was desperately needed to combat southern segregationist resistance. Like other SNCC workers, Moses recognized that "his earlier strategy of relying mainly on local black organizers could not succeed in registering large numbers of black voters."[33] As a result, Moses and other SNCC organizers planned a weeklong training session for student volunteers at Western College for Women in Oxford, Ohio, in June 1964. Moses targeted affluent white college students because, in his words: "These students bring the rest of the country with them. They're from good schools and their parents are influential. The interest of the country is awakened, and when that happens, the Government responds to that interest." Volunteers were expected to pay for their own transportation, give up summer jobs, and provide their own bond money if they were arrested. This helped to ensure that the students who participated in both the training sessions and in the Freedom Project belonged to the target socioeconomic group.[34]

Participants in the Freedom Project endured the murders of James Chaney, Michael Schwerner, and Andrew Goodman; thirty-five shooting incidents; the bombing of thirty homes and other buildings; the beating of eighty persons; the arrest of a thousand; the burning of thirty-five churches; and widespread lynchings.[35] Yet the volunteers persevered and, in the end, managed to teach literacy skills and conveyed the importance of registering to vote to many African American Mississippians. James Foreman, a leading SNCC activist, offered this analysis of the power of the organizing efforts: "It seemed important then just to do, to act, as a means of overcoming the lethargy and hopelessness of so many black people.... Working in the rural south, facing constant death, trying to heighten consciousness seemed in itself an ideology around which all could rally."[36] Yet that was only a part of their full contribution to the civil rights movement. On July 19, 1964, Robert Moses distributed an "Emergency Memorandum," urging that "everyone who is not working in freedom schools or community centers must devote all their time to organizing for the [Mississippi Freedom Democratic Party] convention challenge."[37] This effort ultimately led to the challenge of the Mississippi Freedom Democratic Party (MFDP) at the 1964 Democratic convention in Atlantic City, which featured the eloquent speech of Fannie Lou Hamer. Organized by the Council of Federated Organizations (COFO), which included SCLC, SNCC, and CORE, the MFDP was created to inform the nation that the regular Democratic Party routinely excluded African

Americans. Under COFO's direction, the MFDP elected its own delegates with the avowed purpose of challenging the seating of regular Democratic Party delegates at the 1964 convention.[38]

The events of the summer of 1964 had profound consequences for the civil rights movement and the participants, as well as for other major movements of the era, including the women's, student, and antiwar movements.[39] In his exhaustive study of the Mississippi Freedom Summer, Doug McAdam concludes that "perhaps the most important cultural contribution of Freedom Summer was the early behavioral expression it gave the link between personal liberation and social change."[40] McAdam devotes a considerable amount of attention to exploring the consequences of the summer for the participants' conception of their roles as democratic citizens. He concludes: "The volunteers came to believe that it was just as important to free themselves from the constraints of their racial or class backgrounds as it was to register black voters. They became as much the project as the freedom schools they taught in."[41] This sense of linking one's self-development to contributions to the larger community is a central element of the New Citizenship, which I examine in Chapter 6. But for now, it is important to recognize that the civil rights movement had profound consequences for the women's, student, and antiwar movements of the 1960s. All these movements embraced a strong belief in participatory democracy, equality of opportunity and equality of results, the notion that the personal is political, and the importance of changing the quality of human relationships.[42] In addition, the civil rights movement had a major impact on the kind of policy emanating from the federal government to address problems of racism and poverty.

Writing in 1986, historian William Chafe offered this analysis of the impact and importance of the civil rights movement:

> Without question, the movement for black freedom and equality constituted the most important domestic development of post-war America, arguably, the most important domestic event in the 20th century. The civil rights movement provided the energy, the inspiration, and the model for virtually every effort of social reform that emerged in the remarkable decade of the 1960s. The women's movement, the antiwar movement, the student movement, the movement to end poverty, the struggle for Indian rights, Chicano rights, and gay rights—none of these would have been conceivable were it not for the driving force of the civil rights movement. If the movement

achieved nothing more than to provide the leadership for other social activists in the 1960s and 70s, this alone would be sufficient.[43]

But as we now know, the civil rights movement achieved much more than those accomplishments suggest. Under Lyndon Johnson's leadership, the 1964 Civil Rights Act and the 1965 Voting Rights Act were passed by Congress. The Civil Rights Act helped end a decade of paralysis in school desegregation that had followed the Supreme Court's 1954 ***Brown v. Board of Education*** decision, when the Court declared that schools segregated by race were unconstitutional. In addition, it destroyed Jim Crow in public accommodations by prohibiting discrimination in businesses such as hotels, motels, cafeterias, restaurants, theaters, and service stations. Finally, the Civil Rights Act barred discrimination on the basis of race, religion, color, national origin, or sex. The Voting Rights Act eliminated all barriers to voting except for residency, age, and criminal record. In so doing, it got rid of the literacy test and rendered discriminatory voting regulations illegal. Its passage immediately led to the registration of many African Americans as well as southern white voters who could not pass literacy tests.[44]

In addition to these policy accomplishments, the civil rights movement offered African Americans who had been excluded from public life the opportunity to develop their public capacities and their voices. In this way, the movement provided the foundation for the New Citizenship in contemporary American politics.

Yet to the extent that the movement embraced unconventional politics, it also established a foundation for disruptive politics and potential threats to system stability, which the constitutional framers had feared. To be sure, contemporary groups across the political spectrum have embraced unconventional politics as a way to attract attention to their grievances and to prompt substantive policy responses. By those maneuvers, however, they have disrupted civility in public discourse. My focus shifts now to those groups.

Challenges to the New Citizenship

ACT UP

Like other grassroots organizations, ACT UP (the AIDS Coalition to Unleash Power) has been influenced by the civil rights movement to the extent that ACT UP has used the boycott, marches and demonstrations, and non-

ACT UP, supported by a coalition of AIDS activists, protests New York Governor George Pataki's and Mayor Rudolph Giuliani's proposed 1995 budget cuts to AIDS and other health-related services. *Credit:* Carolina Kroon/Impact Visuals.

violent civil disobedience to attract media coverage of its direct action. ACT UP, however, has eschewed violence.

ACT UP was founded in March 1987 by playwright and AIDS activist Larry Kramer. In a March 10, 1987, speech at the New York City Lesbian and Gay Community Services Center, Kramer challenged the gay and lesbian movement to organize, mobilize, and demand an effective AIDS policy response. He reminded the audience of gay men that two-thirds of them might be dead within five years. To Kramer, the mass media were the central vehicle for conveying the message that the government had hardly begun to address the AIDS crisis. As part of his speech, he asked, "Do we want to start a new organization devoted solely to political action?" By early 1988 strong chapters of ACT UP had appeared in various cities throughout the United States and the world. However, ACT UP New York routinely drew more than eight hundred people to its weekly meetings, thus becoming the largest and most influential of all the chapters.

The original goal of ACT UP, which identified itself as a diverse nonpartisan group united in anger and commitment to direct action to end the

AIDS crisis, was to demand the release of experimental AIDS drugs. This central goal is stated before every ACT UP meeting. ACT UP's commitment to direct activism emerged as a response to the more conservative elements of the gay and lesbian movement.

Over the years, ACT UP has broadened its original purpose to embrace a number of specific and practical goals. It has demanded that the Food and Drug Administration (FDA) release drugs that could help people with AIDS in a timely manner by shortening the drug-approval process and has asked that private health insurance as well as Medicaid be forced to pay for experimental drug therapies. Ten years into the AIDS crisis, ACT UP questioned why only one toxic drug had been approved for treatment. The organization demanded answers from policy elites. ACT UP has also demanded the creation and implementation of a federal needle-exchange program, called for condom distribution at the local level in a federally controlled and funded program, and asked for a serious sex education program in primary and secondary schools, a curriculum that would be created and monitored by the federal Department of Education. In addition, it has called for a national policy on AIDS.

Thousands of people joined ACT UP groups in response to what they felt to be an outrageous lack of governmental support for addressing AIDS. Many were motivated by anger, but they shared Larry Kramer's belief that direct political action on behalf of their lives should be a key element of any organizing strategy. The media were a central target for communicating ACT UP's grievances. ACT UP secured media attention from the start, by embracing slogans such as "Silence = Death." ACT UP also used political art as a way to convey its message to the larger society. ACT UP members with backgrounds in public relations and the news handled the media, and as a result, the organization communicated greater awareness of AIDS issues to both the gay and lesbian community and the larger society. ACT UP's creative approach to the media has been recognized by social movement scholars for its effective use of "aesthetically rich images, accompanied by witty, sound-bite-worthy slogans."[45] The media covered ACT UP's first demonstration, which was held on Wall Street on March 24, 1987. The goal of this demonstration was to heighten awareness of the FDA's inability to overcome its own bureaucracy and release experimental drugs in a timely fashion. This demonstration became a model for future ACT UP activities. It was carefully orchestrated and choreographed to attract media attention and to convey a practical political message.[46]

Over the years, other ACT UP demonstrations received considerable media coverage. A 1987 protest at New York's Memorial Sloan-Kettering Hospital called for an increase in the number of drugs used in the treatment of HIV. Also in 1987, a demonstration targeted Northwest Airlines for refusing to seat a man with AIDS, and in 1988 the editorial offices of *Cosmopolitan* were invaded as protesters challenged an article that claimed that hardly any women were likely to develop AIDS. In 1988 more than 1,000 protesters surrounded the FDA's Maryland building, in 1989 ACT UP activists demonstrated at the U.S. Civil Rights Commission's AIDS hearings to protest its ineptness in responding to AIDS, and in 1989 ACT UP New York's "Stop the Church" disrupted Cardinal John O'Connor's mass to protest his opposition to condom distribution. ACT UP members invaded the studio of the *MacNeil/Lehrer NewsHour* on January 22, 1991, chained themselves to Robert MacNeil's desk during a live broadcast, and flashed signs declaring, "The AIDS Crisis Is Not Over." That was the ultimate media event.[47]

In light of some of these actions, particularly the "Stop the Church" demonstration, ACT UP found itself responding to criticism from within and outside the organization that it had simply gone too far in its efforts to dramatize its grievances. One social movement scholar offers a deeper understanding of what motivated its creative response to political activism:

> ACT-UP's tacit strategy was to force on public officials, church, and business leaders their most horrific nightmare: exposure by means of actions that signify disrespect. By presenting itself as an "out-of-control" intransigent mélange of queers and misfits, it reveals a capacity to opt out of what is expected of a "responsible" civic organization: to play by the rules. From the perspective of the Establishment's code, to refuse these rules is to engage in the politics of *terror*.[48]

There had always been a tension within the gay and lesbian movement between those who favored more traditional lobbying activities and those who embraced the radical direct action associated with ACT UP. Many ACT UP activists became increasingly intolerant of those who worried that direct action alienated important policy elites.

By 1992 there were also divisions within ACT UP over what political strategy was appropriate. Since ACT UP's creation in 1987, AIDS activists had directed their anger toward perceived enemies—Congress, the president,

Protest politics at work: opposition to health care reform and big government in Reston, Virginia, August 2009. *Credit:* Tim Sloan/AFP/Getty Images.

federal agencies, drug companies, the media, the Catholic Church, and homophobic politicians in positions of power at all levels of society. The divisions within ACT UP undermined organizational and movement solidarity.

Today ACT UP is plagued with internal division over appropriate tactics and its relationship to the larger gay and lesbian movement, and its membership is depleted by the loss of life as it attempts to press ahead. Nevertheless, ACT UP chapters continue to play an important role in the fight against AIDS, especially at the global level, by demanding greater access to affordable generic drugs for African nations. The organization's use of direct action politics is an example of the effectiveness of unconventional politics in the face of the unresponsiveness of policy elites. Many worry that this kind of politics contributes to overall system instability and incivility in the larger public discourse. Ironically, ACT UP's radicalism has made the more mainstream gay and lesbian organizations seem much more moderate as they interact with the American policy process on AIDS-related issues. In this and other ways, ACT UP has made an invaluable contribution to saving people's lives in the face of governmental indifference.

Earth First!

Earth First! was founded in the early 1980s by former Wilderness Society members David Foreman and Bart Koehler, as well as by Howie Wolke of the Wyoming chapter of Friends of the Earth and two associates, Mike Roselle and Ron Kezar. On a spring 1980 camping trip, the five men decided that mainstream environmentalism simply was not working and that what was needed was a pro-wilderness organization, one that was militant and uncompromising in its defense of the earth.[49] Unlike the mainstream national environmental organizations, which work within established political and economic frameworks, Earth First! challenges those who embrace environmental compromise and pursue environmental objectives through traditional Madisonian interest group and lobbying processes. Instead, members of Earth First! believe that the natural world must be defended through direct action, civil disobedience, and ecosabotage of the kind advocated by writer Edward Abbey in the form of "monkey wrenching" (see Box 4.2). Earth First! identified itself as a warrior society from the very beginning.[50] In pursuing their objectives, some Earth First! members and their supporters have placed their bodies in front of logging trucks, chained themselves to the upper branches of trees that were to be cut down by the timber industry, destroyed survey stakes for an oil exploration project, and driven iron spikes into trees to prevent loggers from cutting into the wood.[51] One historian writes that "this romantic mix of direct action and the culture of enchantment made Earth First! extraordinarily appealing to people who had little or no previous involvement in environmental groups."[52]

In justifying the existence of the organization and its use of unconventional politics, Foreman said:

> We aren't an environmental group. Environmental groups worry about health hazards to human beings, they worry about clean air and water for the benefit of the people and ask us why we're so wrapped up in something as irrelevant and tangential and elitist as wilderness. Well, I can tell you a wolf or a redwood or a grizzly bear doesn't think that wilderness is elitist. Wilderness is the essence of everything. It's the real world.[53]

In the late 1980s, many Earth First! members were building upon Foreman's approach by arguing, as Christopher Manes did, that the Earth must come first in "all decisions, even ahead of human welfare if necessary."[54]

BOX 4.2   Why Earth First! Embraces Environmental Radicalism

- To state honestly the views held by many conservationists.
- To demonstrate that the Sierra Club and its allies were raging moderates, believers in the system, and to refute the Reagan/Watt contention that they were "environmental extremists."
- To balance such antienvironmental radicals as the Grand County commission and provide a broader spectrum of viewpoints.
- To return vigor, joy, and enthusiasm to the tired, unimaginative environmental movement.
- To keep the established groups honest. By stating a pure, no-compromise, pro-Earth position, we felt that Earth First! could help keep the other groups from straying too far from their original philosophical base.
- To give an outlet to many hard-line conservationists who were no longer active because of disenchantment with compromise politics and the co-option of environmental organizations.
- To provide a productive fringe, since ideas, creativity, and energy tend to spring up on the edge and later spread into the center.
- To inspire others to carry out activities straight from the pages of *The Monkey Wrench Gang* (a novel of environmental sabotage by Edward Abbey), even though Earth First!, we agreed, would itself be ostensibly law-abiding.
- To help develop a new worldview, a biocentric paradigm, an Earth philosophy.
- To fight, with uncompromising passion, for Earth.

Source: Dave Foreman, *Confessions of an Eco-Warrior* (New York: Harmony Books, 1991), p. 18.

By the early 1990s, splits had developed within Earth First! over tactics and strategy. Indeed, not all Earth First! members embraced ecosabotage as a response to human degradation of the planet. Foreman and two of his associates were arrested in 1989 by the Federal Bureau of Investigation on charges that they were planning to blow up power lines to the Central Arizona Project, a massive federal irrigation program.[55] Their arrests for potential monkey-wrenching activities forced organizational members to confront whether monkey wrenching was a wise strategy in the face of governmental indifference.

Governmental authorities treated Earth First! and its members as if they were threats to the overall stability of the American political system. In this sense, Earth First! is an excellent example of the kind of factious activity that the constitutional framers feared would disrupt system stability. To be sure, if many citizens embraced monkey-wrenching strategies in response to governmental decisions impinging on the environment, then stability and civility would surely be disrupted. But from the vantage point of many Earth First! members, radical responses were both needed and justified in the face of governmental indifference. In this way, then, Earth First! embraced the sort of unconventional politics popularized and used with great effectiveness by the civil rights movement. But the use of these actions always provokes the resistance of government authorities, who recognize the potential threat to system stability and civility.

Earth Liberation Front

Like Earth First!, the Earth Liberation Front (ELF) believes that direct action is the way to protect and promote the interests of the planet in the short and long term. Modeled after the Animal Liberation Front, the Earth Liberation Front was founded in England in 1992 as a splinter group from Earth First![56] According to its Web site, all ELF actions must conform to the following guidelines: (1) "to inflict economic damage on those profiting from the destruction and exploitation of the natural environment," (2) "to reveal and educate the public on the atrocities committed against the earth and all species that populate it," (3) "to take all necessary precautions against harming any animal, human and non-human."[57] Like ACT UP, the ELF structure is nonhierarchical; individuals involved in unconventional direct actions "control their own activities." In addition, the effectiveness and security of ELF activities are maximized by the creation of "cells, which are small groups that consist of one to several people." The cells are anonymous "not only to the public but also to one another. This decentralized structure helps keep activists out of jail and free to continue conducting actions."[58] Finally, there is no official "membership" in the organization per se. Instead, "individuals who choose to do actions under the banner of the ELF are driven only by their personal conscience or decisions taken by their cell while adhering to the stated guidelines."[59]

What kinds of activities have been undertaken by ELF? The *New York Times* reports that "since 1997, members in North America are believed to have caused more than $100 million in damage to real estate developers' offices, houses and construction and logging sites."[60] On August 1, 2003, a fire in San Diego, California, destroyed a partially completed five-story condominium complex. This action, which caused $50 million in damage, received considerable publicity because the complex was owned by Garden Communities, the second largest Southern California developer. ELF responded to what they perceived as a disastrous Clinton administration logging policy in the Pacific Northwest, one "that opened many national forests to the timber industry,"[61] by burning "a U.S. Forest station and a truck in Willamette National Forest"[62] near Eugene, Oregon, in October 1996. The ELF began carrying out unconventional political actions on a much larger scale when it burned an expansion of new buildings and chair lifts at Vail Ski Resort, Colorado.[63] The organization targeted global capitalism and consumerism after demonstrations against the World Trade Organization in Seattle in 1999. How did it do so? "Research labs working on genetically modified organisms, like special grasses for golf courses, were destroyed."[64] In recent years the organization has also targeted sport utility vehicles (SUVs) because of the damage that these gas-guzzling vehicles cause the environment. SUVs parked at car dealerships have been spray painted with graffiti (and in some cases set on fire) in at least five areas throughout the United States, mostly on the West Coast: Los Angeles, California; Santa Cruz, California; Eugene, Oregon; Seattle, Washington; and Erie, Pennsylvania. All of these actions have received considerable mainstream press attention, which is, of course, a central goal of those who want to dramatize their grievances by using unconventional politics.

Operation Rescue

Violence targeted at abortion clinics represents the kind of extreme factious activity that the constitutional framers believed would threaten overall system stability. Clinic violence began in the 1980s but erupted with greater frequency in the 1990s. As we have seen in recent years, physicians who perform abortions have been harassed, injured, and in some cases, killed. In this violent climate, many doctors who had formerly performed abortions have stopped offering such medical services, thus making it difficult for some women to have access to safe abortions.

The murder of Dr. David Gunn illustrates well the broader issues associated with antiabortion violence. On March 10, 1993, Gunn drove to the Pensacola, Florida, abortion clinic where he worked on a regular basis. As he got out of his car to enter the clinic's back door, he heard the cries of antiabortion protesters. His name was already well known to many antiabortion activists; it regularly appeared on posters that urged pro-life activists to make his life and his family's lives miserable. As he approached the clinic to begin his day's work, he was shot three times in the back at point-blank range by an antiabortion protester. The case received considerable national attention at a time when authorities feared that antiabortion violence was an increased threat to stability.

The May 2009 murder of Dr. George Tiller in Wichita, Kansas, brought violence once again to the forefront of the abortion debate in the United States. Tiller was one of a very few doctors nationwide who courageously performed abortions late in a woman's pregnancy. He and his family (and his supporters) knew that he was a potential target for antiabortion advocates who might embrace violence as a way to dramatize their cause. Indeed, in 1993 Rachelle Shannon shot Dr. Tiller in both of his arms. And "two years earlier, during Operation Rescue's 'Summer of Mercy' protests, thousands of anti-abortion protesters tried to block off the clinic, the site of a bombing in 1986."[65] Scott Roeder was arrested and charged with the crime; Roeder had posted messages to the Operation Rescue Web site in the past, but Troy Newman, president of the organization, said that Roeder is "not a friend, not a contributor, not a volunteer."[66]

Law enforcement officials monitoring radical antiabortion activity had reason for concern as early as December 1994, when John C. Salvi opened fire at two abortion clinics in Brookline, Massachusetts. He murdered two receptionists and wounded five others in his violent rampage.

To be sure, many in the antiabortion movement have distanced themselves from such violent responses to legalized abortion in the United States. Indeed, in the aftermath of the killing of Dr. Tiller, many antiabortion rights advocates distanced themselves forcefully from violence and Roeder's actions. Newman said: "Operation Rescue has worked tirelessly on peaceful, nonviolent measures to bring him [Dr. Tiller] to justice through the legal system, the legislative system. We are pro-life, and this act was antithetical to what we believe."[67] Operation Rescue, a leading national antiabortion organization, may reject violence per se, but it has embraced aggressive measures to stop abortion, including barring access to clinics where abortions are performed. The organization was created in the 1980s by those right-to-life supporters who were continually frustrated by the mainstream antiabortion movement's incremental national effort to end abortions. The mainstream movement has pursued traditional lobbying strategies and processes and has largely eschewed violence.

Operation Rescue garnered national attention in 1988 when it organized a series of demonstrations in New York City. More than fifteen hundred participants were arrested for physically blocking entrances to abortion clinics in an effort to shut them down. In an attempt to attract even more media attention, Randall Terry, the organization's director, orchestrated a "Siege on Atlanta," where hordes of news crews had gathered to cover the 1988 Democratic National Convention. About twelve hundred antiabortion demonstrators blockaded the entrances to Atlanta abortion clinics. As a result of Terry's efforts, Operation Rescue enjoyed a sharp increase in financial contributions. Before the Atlanta event, the group's income was about $5,000 per month; four months later it exceeded $60,000 per month. The overall success of the New York and Atlanta blockade efforts led the organization to expand its blockade strategy to numerous cities and hundreds of abortion clinics throughout the United States.[68] Taking a page from the organizing efforts of the civil rights movement, Operation Rescue quickly learned that nonviolent civil disobedience could attract the media attention necessary to communicate a political message. But for those who worry about deteriorating civility and stability, Operation Rescue poses a threat to the extent that it inflames emotions around a very controversial public policy issue—abortion. And to the extent that Operation Rescue and other antiabortion groups embrace unconventional politics, they may well encourage the kind of violent activity embraced by John Salvi, Scott Roeder, and their sympathizers.

The Militias

On April 19, 1995, right-wing extremists blew up the federal building in Oklahoma City, killing 168 people. At the time, it was the worst terrorist attack and mass murder in American history. In the immediate aftermath of the attack, the authorities, the press, and ordinary Americans were convinced that Islamic extremists were responsible. In the weeks that followed, the principal suspect turned out to be a fellow traveler of the "militias," and militia organizations throughout the United States underwent considerable scrutiny.

One precursor of militia organizations was the Posse Comitatus, an armed right-wing group formed in 1969 in Portland, Oregon. The Posse Comitatus was especially active in the early to mid-1980s. Members share a number of core beliefs, including the principle that all governments

August Kreis, the head of the "Messiah's Militia," displays two central icons of Patriot ideology—a handgun and a Bible. *Credit:* Buffalo News.

above the county level are illegitimate. "'Posse Comitatus' is [Medieval] Latin for 'Power of the County.'" To Posse Comitatus members, the county sheriff is seen as the highest level of legitimate government authority. They believe that federal and state governments are taking away their freedoms, especially in the form of excessive taxes and gun control. Some Posse Comitatus members refuse to pay state and local taxes and embrace a virulent form of anti-Semitism, one that contends that "our nation is now completely under the control of the International Invisible government of the World Jewry."[69] Their goal is to extend "the Christian Identity doctrine into a complex theory of constitutional government based on the notion that the United States is not a democracy but a Christian republic, lawfully governed by so-called Christian common law rather than legislative statutes and court decisions." To Posse Comitatus propagandists, the governing institutions of the United States "had been usurped by the 'anti-Christ Jewry.'"[70]

The militia organizations, which exist in a number of states, share some of the principles associated with the Posse Comitatus (see Box 4.3). In

---

BOX 4.3   The Beliefs of the Montana Militia

The security of a free state is not found in the citizens having guns in the closet. It is found in the citizenry being trained, prepared, organized, equipped and lead [sic] properly so that if the government uses its force against the citizens, the people can respond with a superior amount of arms, and appropriately defend their rights.... Remember Thomas Jefferson's words that the primary purpose of the second amendment was to ensure that Americans as a last resort would be able to defend themselves against a tyrannical government, ...

To balance the military power of the nation with the might of the militia will put at odds any scheme by government officials to use the force of the government against the people. Therefore, when the codes and statutes are unjust for the majority of the people, the people will rightly revolt and the government will have to acquiesce without a shot being fired, because the militia stands vigilant in carrying out the will of the people in defense of rights, liberty, and freedom.

The purpose of government is in the protection of the rights of the people, when it does not accomplish this, the militia is the crusader who steps forward, and upon it rests the mantle of the rights of the people.

Source: Kenneth S. Stern, *A Force upon the Plain* (New York: Simon & Schuster, 1996), pp. 71, 75–76.

---

many ways, the militia organizations are the constitutional framers' worst nightmare—factious groups of individuals with their own private armies, ready to make war with the American government. One student of right-wing extremism contends that there are 10,000 to 40,000 active members of militia organizations in the United States and that hundreds of thousands of Americans sympathize with them.

In fall 1994 the Michigan Militia claimed that it had 10,000 members and units in sixty-three of the state's eighty-three counties. The central goal of the Michigan Militia is to "stand against tyranny, globalism, relativism, humanism, and the New World Order threatening to undermine the United States of America." One Michigan Militia leader, Norman Olson, wrote that in order to promote these values, "many thousands are prepared to go to Washington in uniform, carry their guns, prepared to present the ultimatum to the President and to the Congress." In 1994 Olson declared, "If this country doesn't change, armed conflict is inevitable. Who is the enemy? Anyone who threatens us."[71] With such bellicose rhetoric, Olson directly challenged the authority, order, civility, and ultimately the stability of the political and economic system.

The militia movement was galvanized by the Bureau of Alcohol, Tobacco, and Firearms' decision to raid the Branch Davidian compound in Waco, Texas, on April 19, 1993. The tragic outcome of the government's action (more than seventy cult members died) reinforced the widespread view held by militia supporters that the federal government was capable only of abusing power. One member of a Florida militia said: "Waco awakened the whole [movement]. That put the fear of God into us."[72] To many militia members, the federal assault on the Branch Davidians represented the ideological equivalent of Pearl Harbor. In any event, the federal government's attack on the Branch Davidians and the response of militia supporters to that attack suggest that such incidents pose challenges to overall system stability and civility.

With the election of Barack Obama, militia groups have expanded their organizing activity. In doing so, they have built on their racism and "virulent anti-government, anti-taxation and anti-immigrant agenda." A law enforcement official claimed that "this is the most significant growth we've seen in 10 to 12 years . . . All it's lacking is a spark . . . and it is only a matter of time before you see threats and violence."[73] The key difference between radical right organizing now and in previous years is, according to a Southern Poverty Law Center (SPLC) study, that the federal government, which "almost the entire radical right views as its primary enemy—is headed by a black man."[74] The current radical right organizing has tapped "into the latent rage of white supremacist culture."[75] In February 2009 the SPLC reported that "there has been a 54-percent rise in race-based hate groups in the United States since 2000, from 602 then to 926 in 2008." The SPLC study drew "direct correlations between Barack Obama's presidency and numerous murders of law-enforcement officials this year."[76] And this radical right organizing is occurring at the very moment when many Americans (regardless of political affiliation) and people in countries throughout the world have acknowledged, and in some cases, celebrated, the first African American president of the United States.

Conclusion

This chapter has identified the difficulties associated with striking the proper balance among various forms of political participation. In recent years, the inability to do so has led to growing incivility and occasional threats to overall system stability.

The central contribution of the civil rights movement is that it opened up the political system to African Americans by embracing unconventional politics throughout the 1950s and 1960s. Much of what civil rights organizers accomplished was rooted in participatory democratic principles. As we have seen, the events and strategies associated with the civil rights movement have had profound consequences for movements that developed during and since that time, as well as for individual participants. It provided new movements of the left and the right with a strategy for promoting political, social, and economic change. The use of unconventional politics by groups across the political and economic spectrum also suggests that participatory democratic politics is often messy and can lead to undesirable outcomes, especially if civility is an important societal goal. In important ways, unconventional politics often promotes incivility and challenges existing societal institutions. Such challenges are often deemed necessary by groups that are located at the margins of American society.

At a time when meaningful opportunities for political participation are lacking in America and civic indifference is widespread, we would do well as a nation to reexamine the courage and commitment of those associated with the struggle for basic civil rights. The expansive conception of citizenship embraced by many in the 1960s redefined citizenship and provides the foundation for the New Citizenship today. Chapter 5 examines contemporary perspectives of the New Citizenship and discusses how these forms of participation promote overall civility and stability.

5

··

Contemporary Reflections on the New Citizenship

In the sit-ins, the marches, the jailhouse songs, I saw the African-American community becoming more than just the place where you'd been born or the house where you'd been raised. Through organizing, through shared sacrifice, membership had been earned. And because membership had been earned—because this community I imagined was still in the making, built on the promise that the larger American community, black, white, and brown could somehow redefine itself—I believed that it might, over time, admit the uniqueness of my own life.

That was my idea of organizing. It was a promise of redemption.

—Barack Obama, *Dreams from My Father*

Organizing to stop dioxin exposure is fundamentally organizing to rebuild democracy. We can't change the corporate decisions that result in dioxin exposure without challenging the dominance corporations now have over public life. Our campaigns must not be only about the danger of dioxin, but also about the dangers of a society where money buys power. To create the equality and justice of a true democracy, our organizing must restore the people's inalienable right to govern and protect themselves.

—Lois Marie Gibbs, *Dying from Dioxin*

SOCIAL COMMENTATORS ARE fond of referring to the decade of the 1970s as the Me Decade and to the young people who came of age during the 1970s and 1980s as the Me Generation. This chapter will provide an alternative explanation for the developments of the 1970s and 1980s by focusing on the grassroots organizing activity that developed in the 1960s and that has continued in many communities throughout the United States. This grassroots activity and the new sources of citizen participation, which go far beyond merely voting, are the central elements of the New Citizenship. Grassroots mobilization and community participation, service learning, and the Internet are components of the New Citizenship, a concept that extends the participatory democratic vision articulated in the 1960s as it attempts to bridge the gap between the public and the private. My goal here is to link all these various forms of participation to the central dilemma of this book—how to enhance the quality of democracy, bringing people of all backgrounds and interests together in a spirit of toleration, respect, trust, and social and political engagement. The New Citizenship attempts to foster an environment that promotes both an honest exchange of ideas and civility in contemporary American politics.

As we have seen throughout this book, two different conceptions of the role of the citizenry in American development have coexisted in a tense relationship. The first is electoral-representative democracy, which emphasizes the importance of elections and the lobbying of interest groups at the national, state, and local levels. Bargaining and compromise typify the decision-making process. Citizen participation is assumed to be the same as voter participation. It is this conception of citizenship that grows out of the democratic theory of elitism, discussed in Chapter 2. A second conception, steeped in participatory democratic principles, emphasizes grassroots organizing and mobilization rooted in community building, cooperation, alliance formation, and self-help. As we saw in Chapter 4, the civil rights movement demanded voting rights for all Americans and contributed a foundation for the kind of grassroots democracy that has flourished at the local level over the past forty-five years.

Taking voter-turnout figures as an indicator of the health of American democracy, one can see that America is a nation characterized by civic indifference. But merely using voter-turnout figures to assess the vitality of democracy ignores the explosion of grassroots, community-based activity that is a central element of the New Citizenship. This chapter examines contemporary perspectives on the New Citizenship and devotes particular attention to grassroots neighborhood and environmental organizations as well as student organizations that have developed in the 1980s, the 1990s, and the early part of the twenty-first century. But before we can evaluate the New Citizenship in its appropriate contemporary context, we must first examine the sources of the Me Generation. The goal is to ascertain whether such a label is an accurate and useful description of young people who have come of age since the 1960s.

The Me Generation

Social commentators have found it useful to stereotype decades in much the same way as people are often stereotyped. We tend to refer to the 1950s as the decade of affluence, the era of good feeling, the **end of ideology**, the perception that there is widespread consensus regarding basic values in the United States—individualism, equality of opportunity, representative democracy, and freedom. We think of the 1950s as largely conformist, despite the fact that it was in this decade that we saw the rise of the civil rights movement and rock and roll. In contrast, the 1960s have been labeled the decade of raucous rebellion, as a result of student protests on college campuses against the Vietnam War as well as the urban riots. Yet it is indeed the case that the overwhelming majority of people (including students) remained largely uninvolved and apathetic in the 1960s. The 1970s have been identified as the Me Decade, because personal concerns supposedly replaced social activism as the central quality of the era.[1]

But there are a number of problems with the Me Decade characterization as well. For example, most commentators failed to explore the sources of these values, ignoring the broader political and economic framework and the political socialization process, discussed at length in Chapter 2. In addition, the values of radical individualism and careerism were surely part of the American experience long before the 1970s. There was also little doubt that young people's preoccupation with success and pursuing the American dream was a rational response to a more difficult economy, one

Participants in the AFL-CIO's Union Summer program join striking Detroit newspaper workers in June 1996 in picketing a scab's house. *Credit:* Jim West/Impact Visuals.

in which the young would have a challenge in maintaining the quality of life of their parents and grandparents. From this vantage point, then, who could blame America's youth for being concerned about their economic well-being?

Of course, many people who have come of age over the past thirty-five years have rejected the values that are typically associated with the Me Generation, despite their prominence in the larger society. Some who reject these values have been involved in grassroots political organizing activity in communities throughout the United States. It is to a discussion of these neighborhood, grassroots political organizing activities that we now turn to outline the central components of the New Citizenship.

New Citizenship Components

Neighborhood Organizations

Largely in response to the events of the 1960s and the economic instability that followed, neighborhood organizations proliferated in the United States during the decade of the 1970s. In 1977 the *Christian Science Monitor* devoted a series of articles to examining the "groundswell movement of citizens calling for the return of political and economic power to the local level." One scholar estimates that by the end of the decade, more than 20 million Americans were actively involved in a variety of neighborhood groups throughout the United States.[2] Others have concluded that these voluntary neighborhood structures are the building blocks for a revitalized ethos of citizenship, which will spawn a new political and social movement rooted in participatory democratic principles.

The rise of these neighborhood organizations has been deemed the **new populism**. Unlike socialist movements that identify capitalism as the major target for transformation, the new populism views unaccountable power wielded by policy elites as the fundamental problem. In addition, whereas many neighborhood organizers cut their teeth in participation in the civil rights, women's, and antiwar movements, advocates of the new populism reject single-minded attention to a particular constituency—whether African Americans, women, or students—and instead embrace a "majoritarian strategy," one "rooted primarily in the communities and traditions of white and black, low and moderate income people." A central goal of the new populism is to win power and build organizations that are controlled by working-class people. Like the civil rights movement, these neighborhood-based organizations often ally with traditional community institutions, such as churches and unions.[3]

Yet it is indeed the case that much of the citizen activism that has developed over the past thirty years has addressed a fairly narrow range of issues. As Harry Boyte points out, "Activists have not often asked what their work 'means' in a larger sense, where they are going in the long run, or how their particular efforts might add up to more than the particular or localized campaigns they engage in."[4] In this way, such community-based efforts reinforce narrow interests and are largely divorced from a broader political and social vision. At the same time, however, Boyte and other scholars of community-based organizing recognize that citizen activism has afforded relatively powerless communities, such as the poor, an opportunity to develop their political voices on issues of meaning in their communities.

In theory, urban populist movements, which are at the heart of the new populism, attempt to strengthen all city neighborhoods by promoting an active and highly participatory community life. Ideally, residents have a meaningful participatory role to play in decisions about how public funds are spent for community development projects. In addition, neighborhood groups and organizations participate in the planning, development, and implementation of projects and service delivery. Neighborhood block-watch programs grow out of community-based efforts to prevent and control crime. The emphasis here is on collective preventive efforts, which instill a sense of responsibility for others and enhance community.

There has been a tendency to assume that all the 1970s-style neighborhood organizations enjoy considerable unity and common ground on a wide variety of issues. However, students of neighborhood organizing have identified significant differences in origins, goals, structure, and strategies among the groups that have come to represent the new populism and neighborhood organizing throughout the United States.[5] To show how these neighborhood populist groups have worked in practice, I offer some concrete examples.

ACORN. The Association of Community Organizations for Reform Now is representative of the more politically active and "consciously left-oriented wing of the new populism."[6] Based on the philosophy of Saul Alinsky, a veteran community organizer, and founded in 1970, ACORN embraced the neighborhood as the central "training ground" for mounting larger challenges for equity, justice, and democracy.[7] Alinsky's strategy was to develop mass political organizations that were rooted in neighborhoods and embraced local concerns. Ultimately, such organizations attempt to advance social and economic democracy, "empower people, and challenge power relations within and beyond the neighborhood."[8] All Alinsky organizations embrace central elements of the new populism—participatory democracy, self-reliance, decentralization, empowerment of low- and moderate-income people, and mistrust of corporate and government institutions.[9] ACORN also shares these characteristics and pursues these goals. Steve McDonald, president of ACORN's Executive Board, described his organization this way:

> Some people say what does ACORN want? The answer is simple: We want sufficient power in our cities and states to speak—and be heard—and heeded—for the interests of the majority of citizens. We want to participate in community and civil affairs, not as second-class citizens because we don't drive Rolls Royces, but as men and women committed to a better future where our concerns are met with justice and dignity; where wealth, race and religion are insufficient excuses to prevent equal participation and impact in government; where any person can protect his or her family and join with others in community strength; and where, as ACORN's slogan goes, "The People Shall Rule." That is what America is. That is what ACORN wants. Nothing more and nothing less.[10]

Since 1970 ACORN has mobilized thousands of college students (mostly nonminority) to engage in community organizing, often as summer jobs or jobs upon graduation. In 1982 ACORN job advertisements offered this promise: "A job you can believe in. ACORN needs organizers to work with low and moderate income families in 26 states for political and economic justice. . . . Tangible results. Long hours and low pay. Training provided." The organizing method used by ACORN is similar to the early efforts of SNCC in the Deep South.[11] In recent years ACORN has continued its organizing against banks that routinely practice predatory lending, while also fighting to restore funding for federal, state, and local programs that assist poor people, including funding for fuel assistance. In addition, ACORN has done important organizing work on behalf of a living wage, welfare reform, public education, and voting rights. "ACORN and its affiliates have an annual budget of over $100 million, over 1,000 employees, and nearly 500,000 dues-paying families." It has chapters in 103 cities in 38 different states.[12] Ultimately, ACORN attempts to empower ordinary people to decide what

ACORN meeting in Washington, D.C., held to rally citizens to protest lead poisoning from paint. *Credit:* Rick Reinhardt/Impact Visuals.

services should be provided and how they should be delivered in neighborhoods, recognizing broader structural inequalities that are rooted in the American political and economic system.

ACORN endured an embezzlement scandal in 2008, which John McCain attempted to make an issue in the 2008 presidential campaign. The scandal "involved the brother of the organization's founder, Wade Rathke,"[13] who at the time was the organization's chief financial officer, and who was later charged with embezzling nearly $1 million from the organization in 2000. Wade Rathke covered up his brother's embezzlement of funds and kept him on the payroll after the embezzlement was discovered by a whistleblower. All of the funds were eventually returned to ACORN, but Wade Rathke resigned, and his brother, Dale, was fired.[14] How did the McCain campaign attempt to link Barack Obama to the ACORN scandal? Obama had worked with ACORN, among other community-based organizations, in his Chicago community organizing efforts during the 1980s. In addition, he was director of Project Vote in 1992, which led voter registration efforts that included ACORN. He also "served as a lawyer for ACORN in 1995 in a case against Illinois to increase access to the polls."[15] McCain's efforts to link Obama to ACORN's financial troubles, however, did not become a serious issue in the 2008 campaign. Perhaps citizens recognized that compared to the corporate scandals of recent years, the ACORN incident did not warrant much attention.

In September 2009 ACORN was again the focus of considerable negative publicity when both houses of Congress voted, in a decisive bipartisan vote, to cut off federal funding to the organization. What prompted such a decision? The votes were taken "just a few days after the release of a series of (now infamous) videos in which young right-wing activists James O'Keefe and Hannah Giles pose as a pimp and as a prostitute."[16] The conservative activists arrived in a number of ACORN tax preparation offices with a hidden camera, ostensibly to seek business and tax advice. What they captured on tape so alarmed both Democrats and Republicans that federal funds were cut off and politicians of both parties distanced themselves from the organization. What is clear, however, is that the organization's grassroots organizing mission made it a target for conservative scrutiny. It is also likely that the young conservative activists targeted ACORN to once again connect President Obama to the organization and to raise anew questions about his organizing past. As one thoughtful analyst suggested in the wake of this entire affair, "For all its organizational problems, ACORN does vital, indispensable, unglamorous work: it trains legions of organizers, builds grassroots leadership, and wages disciplined and effective local and statewide campaigns, such as its minimum-wage effort in Florida in 2004."[17] Despite the setbacks of 2008 and 2009, ACORN continues to organize on behalf of low-income voters at the grass roots in communities throughout the United States.

SECO. Whereas Alinsky-style groups, such as ACORN, are politically active and represent a left-oriented wing of the new populism, there also exists a community development trend that is more conservative and more localist. Like the Alinskyite groups, development-oriented organizations share a "let the people decide" ideology; an acceptance of conflict tactics; and a frustration with the policies of corporate executives, bureaucrats, and elected officials. Development-oriented groups are often found in blue-collar, white ethnic neighborhoods, communities where there was little civil rights or left-oriented political activity in the 1960s. Such organizations also appear, however, in Hispanic, black, and white working-class neighborhoods that have had long histories of struggle.[18] The Southeast Baltimore Community Organization (SECO) is an excellent example of this community development approach. Since its creation, SECO has been "run as a democratically controlled organization that would enable community residents to participate in decisions that affected their lives. One of SECO's primary goals was to build the capacity of grassroots leaders to identify needs and take advantage of opportunities in their community."[19] The organization has inspired citizens to "democratically and effectively improve their community in the areas of health, education, recreation, transportation, safety, culture, taxation, economics, and other areas affecting the general well being of the neighborhood. In fulfilling these purposes, SECO aims to reflect the geographical, sociological, economic, and cultural diversity of the community."[20]

The origins of SECO go back to 1966, when the Baltimore City Council unveiled plans to build a six-lane highway (later, Interstate 83) through several southeast Baltimore neighborhoods. This project would have meant the demolition of hundreds of homes and the displacement of many residents. A number of people in the affected communities were so upset that they tried to prevent the road's destruction of their neighborhoods, and the Southeast Council Against the Road (SCAR) was formed to oppose the building of the highway in that part of Baltimore. The group succeeded by lobbying for the naming of the Fell's Point neighborhood to the National Register of Historic Places, which meant that it was off-limits to bulldozers. Baltimore residents point with pride today to the fact that Interstate 83 stops in downtown Baltimore without disrupting nearby neighborhoods.[21]

Residents soon learned, however, that the highway project was just one of several projects planned by city leaders under the rubric of urban renewal. SCAR activists revealed plans, labeled "development projects," that proposed the rezoning of one community area for industry. Another section of Baltimore was targeted for demolition and "renewal." The city government had neglected the neighborhood for decades, thus contributing to the economic deterioration of the community. As a result, Baltimore banks had engaged in **redlining**, which meant that this neighborhood would not receive the mortgage or home improvement loans that were needed. In this way, the banks encouraged what has come to be known as a "neighborhood cycle" of "slow deterioration, demolition, and renewal."[22]

In April 1971 more than 1,000 people representing about ninety organizations attended what came to be the founding meeting of SECO. A coalition of neighborhood groups, including church groups, local unions, block clubs, and ethnic fraternal organizations had been formed. Local groups were determined that the newly formed community organization would be rooted in the already existing structures of the people who resided there. Like Alinsky organizations, SECO used direct action and confrontation tactics at the outset.

What did SECO actually accomplish? How effective was its overall strategy for neighborhood revitalization and community development? SECO organized a neighborhood-based health cooperative, housing inspection teams, a public school reform program, and a Youth Diversion Project, which is credited with having contributed to reducing neighborhood juvenile delinquency recidivism rates. In addition, SECO worked closely with city officials to persuade the Department of Housing and Community Development to investigate redlining. The banks worked out a compromise with SECO and agreed "to stop redlining Baltimore's poorer neighborhoods if southeast neighborhood people supported lifting the 8 percent usury ceiling imposed by the state legislature." One student of neighborhood organizations believes that this compromise signaled the end of SECO's "confrontational" phase and the beginning of an approach rooted in neighborhood development.[23]

How was this more conciliatory approach reflected in SECO's approach to advancing neighborhood interests? At virtually every stage of the organization's existence, SECO was willing to work with and occasionally depend on an array of city officials, especially the commissioner of housing and community development. In addition, unlike ACORN, SECO never really agitated for more fundamental political, economic, and social change in Baltimore and throughout the United States. The immediate results of SECO's efforts provided evidence to reinforce a less confrontational and more conciliatory revitalization strategy,[24] a strategy that has been embraced by a number of neighborhood groups over the years.

BUILD. Baltimore United in Leadership Development was founded in 1977 because of concern about Baltimore's quality of life as measured by jobs, education, and the cultural infrastructure. Today BUILD "is a faith-based, non-partisan, multi-denominational, ecumenical, city-wide citizen organization of 50 religious congregations and other associations with a 25 year history of acting to transform neighborhoods by training and developing neighborhood leaders to address community issues, public institutions, public life and building power for families in Baltimore City."[25] The organization has focused its attention on the repeal of federal welfare reform (the

Personal Responsibility Act of 1996), car insurance rates, predatory lending by banks, crime and safety concerns, voter education, and fighting for a living wage. In the mid-1980s it created the Baltimore Commonwealth, an ambitious plan to revitalize Baltimore's public schools. Harry Boyte describes the central elements of BUILD's public school revitalization plan:

> It combines a remarkable incentive plan for high school graduates with a strategy for wide-ranging devolution of power and responsibility to teachers and the community. Moreover, it represents a potent redefinition of the very function of schools, reviving the old tradition which saw education as the instrument of democracy itself, teaching young people to be full, active participants in the life and decision-making processes of their communities.[26]

Through their success with BUILD, African Americans have played and continue to play an important prophetic role in reminding us of the democratic possibilities within the existing American political system. On November 8, 1987, when BUILD held its tenth anniversary convention, the membership was still largely African American, but it was increasingly becoming more diverse. In 1987 forty-two churches, including several white congregations, three labor unions, the Murphy Homes Improvement Association, a public housing tenants' group, and the Baltimore association of school principals also belonged to BUILD.[27] The central element of the 1987 meeting was "Empowering the BUILD Agenda," which included an exchange between BUILD leaders and Baltimore's public leaders in four key program areas: education, employment, neighborhood development, and public housing. The presence of city leaders, including mayor-elect Kurt Schmoke, Michael Middleton, executive vice president of the Maryland National Bank, Leo Molinaro, a representative from the Rouse Company, one of the country's largest builders, and Mary Pat Clarke, the president-elect of the City Council, helped to give BUILD even greater visibility and power. Schmoke and Clarke both agreed to meet with BUILD on a regular basis. Soon Schmoke endorsed the Baltimore Commonwealth plan for public schools and ultimately made it a central element of his administration.

In recent years BUILD has focused its attention largely on youth issues, highlighting youth homicide, gang violence, and the failure of Baltimore (and the nation writ large) to respond by financing community-based recreation centers and creating jobs. BUILD has embraced a "Save Our Youth, Save Our City" agenda, one that "targets the lack of opportunity and lack of safe spaces for our young people."[28] The organization has offered specific policy recommendations:

> 1) Create 30 fully funded, fully staffed recreation centers . . . that are open nights and weekends; 2) Work with corporate leaders to double the number of summer jobs for youth; 3) Create a $100 million fund to rebuild neighborhoods so families can raise their children in safe, affordable homes; 4) Provide an additional 2,000 young people with after-school opportunities and make after-school programs part of the city's annual budget.[29]

BUILD leaders use every opportunity to develop new organizing strategies not only related to specific issues but also to policy questions and broader concerns of public life and politics. The Baltimore Commonwealth, dealing with America's educational future, is an important initiative. Gerald Taylor, BUILD's lead organizer, offered the following analysis of BUILD's grassroots organizing efforts:

> The first struggle for the black community, coming out of a segregated history, is the fight to be recognized. When you've been out of power so long, there's a tendency to not want to be responsible or to be held accountable. But to participate in creating history, one must move into power. Moving into power [is] to negotiate, compromise, understand others have power and ways of viewing the world other than your own.[30]

The key here is that BUILD has moved from beyond a mere strategy of confrontation and alienation to one that embraces working with people in positions of power to achieve policy goals. These goals reflect the concerns of people whose voices are rarely heard in the local policy process. The policy goals are part of a larger struggle for extending participatory democratic principles at all levels of society. Public life is viewed as a "contested, turbulent arena that mixes values, interests, and differences with common purposes."[31] BUILD is a showcase of what happens when people mobilize at the grass roots for meaningful social, political, and economic change, rooted in a participatory democratic vision.

The Institute for the Study of Civic Values. Founded in Philadelphia in 1973, the Institute for Civic Values rejects the Alinsky notion that people get involved politically merely to advance particular interests and that out of this particularistic organizing, people will develop a sense of citizenship, "if not at once, at least after oppressive conditions have been eliminated."[32] The institute is organized on the assumption that this old view of political organizing needs to be challenged in ways that affirm a more positive understanding of what motivates community organizing at the outset. At its core, the institute bases its local organizing and political education efforts on a substantive notion of justice that draws leadership and support from churches, labor unions, and other traditional community groups. Its mission statement claims that "at a time when political leaders and commentators are struggling to identify the values that we share, civic idealists believe that the principles set forth in the Declaration of Independence, the Constitution, and the Bill of Rights—life, liberty, and the pursuit of happiness; equality and justice—are the civic values that should guide us in meeting the challenges facing America today."[33] Edward Schwartz, a longtime leader of the institute, argues that genuine citizenship education at all levels of society must be developed, especially in our "antipolitical system," which he defines as

> the network of large corporations that controls most of the wealth of the country, that employs a large percentage of our people, but disparages politics and tries to insulate itself against governmental control. This antipolitical system elevates individual achievement in the quest for wealth and power above the collective effort of communities to determine common destinies.[34]

Working out of Philadelphia, a city with severe racial tensions and divisions, the institute has faced the challenge of organizing participation around "civic values," in the broader context of intense rivalries among neighborhood and racial groups for private and/or governmental resources in a time of increased resource scarcity. It has attempted to offer research and civic understanding for those groups and individuals interested in grassroots political action. How has the institute attempted to pursue this goal? It has built ties with church groups, labor educational programs, and college and university faculty who have an interest in stemming the decline of Philadelphia's neighborhoods. When industries departed from Philadelphia in the 1970s and 1980s as a part of the broader change from basic manufacturing to service industries, the **deindustrialization of America**, "the institute supported the creation of a citywide umbrella council of neighborhood organizations to act as advocate for city services and federal aid."[35]

In addition, the institute created a program of locally run and controlled credit unions, which were designed to stimulate housing programs and local economic activity throughout Philadelphia. One group of scholars concludes that the institute has done well in "empowering citizens across racial lines in large enough numbers to create an effective 'neighborhood presence' in Philadelphia's political and economic life."[36] In recent years it has developed an urban voters' campaign in Philadelphia that is designed to mobilize voters in important elections, has worked "with the Alliance for Better Campaigns to expand free air time for candidates discussing issues in primary and general elections," and has established NeighborhoodsOnline, a "pioneering Web site serving neighborhood and community activists throughout the country."[37] In addition, the institute launched its "Communities Matter" initiative in 2009, "a campaign to strengthen federal support for America's communities. The 'Communities Matter.org' web site is focusing on the economic recovery strategies of the Obama campaign, to restore economic growth and put America back to work."[38] In so doing, the institute has been successful in consistently raising questions about the purpose of community action and cooperation, with an emphasis on justice and power as the ultimate end of politics.

The Labor/Community Strategy Center. Headquartered in Los Angeles, the Labor/Community Strategy Center also embraces justice and power as the ultimate goal of politics. A multiracial center for policy, strategy, and organizing, it is representative of the progressive grassroots organizations discussed earlier in this chapter and emphasizes the needs of the labor movement, workers, and communities of color. With the help of its Watchdog Environmental Organization, the center has organized on behalf of environmental justice in Los Angeles, with particular attention to the smog problem (see Figure 5.1).

In addressing environmental concerns, the center embraces "a model of community action that forces companies to stop producing toxins right on the spot, even if that means temporarily shutting down production."[39] At the core of the center's organizing strategy is a call for a new social movement, "one that demands democratic control over basic corporate production decisions to stop . . . pollution . . . and demands the production of non-polluting alternatives."[40] The center has focused on the auto, oil, and rubber-tire industries; the petrochemical industry; and all factories that use and emit dangerous chemicals as worthy targets for democratic control over

BOYCOTT TEXACO!

COMMUNITIES AND WORKERS DEMAND
PUBLIC HEALTH BEFORE CORPORATE PROFITS!

✪ Texaco annually emits 248,000 lbs. of carcinogens, reproductive toxins, and neurotoxins into homes, schools and neighborhoods in the L.A. Harbor Area whose residents are predominantly workers and people of color.

✪ Texaco, through the Western States Petroleum Association (WSPA), spends millions of dollars to undermine air pollution regulations passed by the Air Quality Management District (AQMD). Many AQMD rules, virtually written by Texaco and WSPA, legalize continued and even increased air pollution and toxins.

✪ Texaco ignored a warning letter about corroded pipes causing an explosion and four-day fire at their Wilmington Refinery in October 1992. The result: hundreds evacuated and 2000 health related claims for symptoms of severe headaches, vomiting, broken bones, loss of hearing, skin rashes and psychological trauma.

✪ Texaco dumped over 17 million gallons of crude oil and 20 billion gallons of toxic waste water into the Ecuadoran rain forest and rivers, destroying the homeland and water supplies for more than 300,000 people, as well as causing and exacerbating cancers, respiratory illnesses and other diseases.

The Texaco Boycott Campaign Demands:

1) **Reduce emissions of toxics and criteria pollutants at the Wilmington plant by 50 percent over a period of 5 years (10 percent per year).** By its own admission, Texaco's Wilmington plant pours out 248,000 pounds of toxic chemicals per year—chemicals such as the carcinogen benzene, and xylene, which causes birth defects. Furthermore, its reformulated gas project will allow Texaco to increase its "routine" emissions by 41 percent!

2) **Fund an independent, community-based, community-run free health clinic** that specializes in the diagnosis and treatment of diseases associated with chemical exposure. Texaco, as the first of other oil companies, must begin to take responsibility for exposing residents to toxins.

3) **Provide full access to the plant for a community chosen inspector** who will have the power to slow down production schedules, modify production processes, implement safety measures and, if necessary, shut down the plant until severe problems are resolved, if the inspector concludes that continued operation constitutes a threat to community and worker health and safety. This inspector must also have the power to ensure that effective evacuation plans are prepared and publicized by the company for area residents.

4) **Meet the Demands of the Ecuadoran Texaco Boycott organized by Acción Ecológica:** Submit to a comprehensive, independent, public investigation • Perform a thorough cleanup of damage caused by drilling operations • Where the damage is irreversible—provide health care, drinking water, and funds for community development • Repair corroded pipelines and modernize the obsolete oil infrastructure.

JOIN THE BOYCOTT!

➥ Don't buy Texaco Gasoline or Star Mart products
➥ Don't buy Havoline Motor Oil
➥ Don't use Star Lube Oil Change stations
➥ Cut up and mail your Texaco Card, with a letter stating why, to:
(Alfred De Crane, CEO; Texaco, Inc.; 2000 Westchester Ave; White Plains NY 10650. Please send copies of all correspondance to us (including xeroxes of cut cards) so that Texaco cannot deny receiving them.)

JOIN THE WATCHDOG !

➥ Join us at our weekly pickets in front of Texaco gas stations throughout L.A. County
➥ Help build a long-term multiracial anti-corporate movement for social change—become a member of the Labor/Community WATCHDOG
➥ Send a donation to the WATCHDOG BOYCOTT CAMPAIGN

The Labor/Community WATCHDOG

3780 Wilshire Blvd, Suite 1200
Los Angeles, CA 90010
(213) 387-2600

1142 N. Avalon, Suite #1
Wilmington, CA 90744
(310) 834-9795

The WATCHDOG's Texaco Boycott is supported by the Sierra Club, Greenpeace, Acción Ecológica, and Rainforest Action Network

FIGURE 5.1 Poster Urging Texaco Boycott

their basic corporate production decisions. Is such a goal even possible in a system of capitalism in which private decisions on the part of corporate officials are protected in the name of individual freedom and the right to maximize profits? From the vantage point of the center, private decisions by various Los Angeles industries have had harmful public consequences for the environment. As a result, community organizers must mobilize those who are adversely affected by these corporate decisions—workers in factories and offices, high school and college students, women, African Americans, Latinos, Native Americans, Asian Americans, white working people, farmworkers working with pesticides on a daily basis, and inner-city residents who face groundwater contamination, air pollution, and waste incineration.[41] Their goal is to "build consciousness, leadership, and organization among those who face discrimination and societal attack—people of color, women, immigrants, workers, LGBT people, youth, all of whom comprise our membership."[42] In doing so, they attempt to link "mass struggles to the need for radical, structural change" by developing "campaigns and demands that help build a revitalized world united front that can stop the rising tides of war, racism and imperialism, the ecological crisis and the growing police state."[43]

The center embraces a global perspective as it works with its Watchdog Environmental Organization to mobilize across class, racial, ethnic, and gender lines in response to the Los Angeles air pollution problem. In *L.A.'s Lethal Air,* the Labor/Community Strategy Center presents these policy demands:[44]

1. Create a superfund for workers that would guarantee income maintenance, high school and college education funds, and long-term retraining for any workers temporarily or permanently laid-off because of the cessation of production due to company-caused environmental hazards. . . .
2. Restrict capital flight and stop companies from running away from Los Angeles to evade environmental regulation and union organization. . . .
3. Oppose U.S. firms dumping toxics in the Third World. . . .
4. Develop less-polluting auto transportation. . . .
5. Organize for low-fare, convenient, safe public transportation. . . .
6. Reduce the total number of cars on the road: make the employers pay. . . .

7. Initiate community development programs. . . .
8. Institute progressive and corporate taxation. . . .
9. Take consumer action to demand environmentally safe consumer products. . . .

Driven by a vision of participatory democracy, the center hopes to extend the civil rights movement of the 1950s and 1960s in an effort to pursue environmental justice and challenge both the short- and the long-term corporate decision making that lacks accountability. The center is attempting to build a movement that is rooted in economic and political democracy and that integrates the environment, union organizing, racial equality, community empowerment, women's rights, world peace, and international solidarity.[45] As it attempts to reach this goal, the organization has played an active role in the movement against the U.S. invasion and occupation of Iraq, led a movement to end the MTA-imposed transit strike in Los Angeles, and created the People's Bus emergency service for those dependent on transportation. The center has also helped to organize a campaign for improved access for students to the reduced-cost bus pass, won a proposed order from the federal courts for 117 buses powered by clean-burning natural gas in the greater Los Angeles area, and developed a new Global Warming/Public Health Campaign (www.thestrategycenter.org/body-projects.html). In addition, the center hosts a national school for community organizing. The center's organizing strategy is far more comprehensive and ambitious than that of most neighborhood organizations that have developed over the past forty years.

Center for Health, Environment, and Justice. The Center for Health, Environment, and Justice (originally named the Citizens Clearinghouse for Hazardous Waste) is a national organization that supports, encourages, and organizes thousands of grassroots groups throughout the United States. Founded in 1981 by Lois Marie Gibbs, who is also executive director, the organization continually raises questions about the primacy of corporate power and the nature of "democracy" in the United States.

As a young housewife and mother, in 1978 Gibbs organized neighborhood families who were living in the midst of a chemical swamp located in the suburbs of Buffalo, New York. In the early 1950s, Hooker Chemical, a subsidiary of Occidental Petroleum, had dumped more than 20,000 tons of chemical poisons on a twenty-four-acre site that became known as Love

Canal. Hooker Chemical later sold this land to the city of Niagara Falls, which used it to develop residential properties and a school.[46]

The Love Canal organizers used a strategy that became a model for thousands of other communities that tried to protect community and neighborhood interests in the face of urban development and land-use decisions that had negative consequences for local environments (see Box 5.1). These activists learned how to embrace politics "very rude and very crude," in the words of Lois Gibbs. For example, when New York's governor came to address their concerns in the late 1970s, the mothers and their young children filled the stage after his speech and insisted that he do everything possible to protect their children from the deadly chemicals associated with Love Canal. Surrounded by young children, the governor immediately capitulated. Reflecting on these early organizing experiences, Gibbs said, "When I started, I believed democracy worked. I believed everything I had learned in civics class. What I saw is that decisions are made on the basis of politics and costs. Money."[47]

Today the Center for Health, Environment, and Justice embraces many of the strategies used by Gibbs at Love Canal in the late 1970s. The organization challenges the right of corporations to make decisions that lead to environmental degradation. Its statement of purpose endorses environmental justice: "CHEJ believes in environmental justice, the principle that people have the right to a clean and healthy environment regardless of their race or economic standing. Our experience has shown that the most effective way to win environmental justice is from the bottom up through community organizing and empowerment."[48] How is CHEJ different from other environmental organizations? "It was created out of a commitment and passion to work with communities at risk, to empower local families to take steps to protect their neighborhoods and families from unnecessary chemical threats."[49] What have been the organization's major public policy accomplishments? "CHEJ was instrumental in establishing some of the first national policies critical to protecting community health like the Superfund Program, Right-to-know and others. By pioneering the effort nationwide to protect communities from exposures to dangerous environmental chemicals, in the air, water, and soil, CHEJ has become the preeminent national leader among grassroots groups reducing the burden of toxic substances on our environment."[50]

Like other environmental organizations that are concerned with the local consequences of elite decision making, the organization is criticized for fos-

• •

BOX 5.1   The Basics of Organizing

- Talk and listen
- Figure out who you should talk and listen to first
- Create and distribute fact sheets
- Recruit new members
- Conduct meetings
- Create an organizational structure
- Set goals
- Identify targets
- Conduct research
- Take direct action
- Target the media
- Use laws and science to support organizing

Source: Adapted from Lois Marie Gibbs, *Dying from Dioxin: A Citizen's Guide to Reclaiming Our Health and Rebuilding Democracy* (Boston: South End Press, 1995), pp. 159–160.

• •

tering a **NIMBY** ("not in my backyard") mentality, one that puts the interests of individual neighborhoods ahead of the larger society. Of course, this charge is unfair to the extent that the organization and many other environmental organizations embrace "a public-spirited goal that is more positive and ambitious than the government's—to stop the corporations from dumping their stuff in anyone's backyard."[51]

Connections can be made between the civil rights movement of the 1950s and 1960s, on the one hand, and the Labor/Community Watchdog Environmental Organization and the Center for Health, Environment, and Justice on the other. Like the members of SNCC, the citizens who constitute these organizations are distant from power. They are also scattered voices who advocate on behalf of their families and communities but work far below the formal structure of American politics. In addition, they organize at the grass roots in the hope that their efforts will contribute to a broader political movement, one based on environmental justice.

Citizen organizations of the type discussed in this chapter have undoubtedly expanded and increased participation, particularly at the local level. The paradox is, of course, that this increase has occurred at a time when

most empirical evidence suggests that political participation has deterio-
rated and civic indifference has increased, at least as measured by traditional
participation indicators. For example, as we saw in Chapter 3, U.S. voting-
turnout rates remain quite low, especially when compared to those of other
Western democracies. The public continues to distrust political institutions
in general and politicians more specifically.[52]

The New Citizenship enables us to conceptualize what it means to be a
citizen much more broadly than merely voting in periodic elections. Indeed,
citizen organizations are a central element of the New Citizenship. Organizations that appeal to college students and recent college graduates are also
an integral part of the New Citizenship.

Student Organizations

Public Allies. One organization that targets college students and recent
college graduates is Public Allies, an organization founded by two young
women, Vanessa Kirsch and Katrina Browne, who were frustrated by the
ways that their generation had been portrayed in the popular press. Public
Allies was created in 1991 when Kirsch questioned the results of a poll
that she had helped to compile while working with Peter Hart, a noted
pollster based in Washington, D.C. Kirsch claims that she "was just so disappointed by the results of the poll that showed how apathetic our generation was. It did not reflect the potential of my generation."[53] With those
concerns in mind, Kirsch and Browne were determined to create an organization that would enable college students and recent graduates (as
well as others) to demonstrate their commitment to active citizenship and
working in communities to foster political, social, and economic change.
The organization's vision and mission statement captures its goals well:
"Public Allies envisions communities where people of different backgrounds, beliefs and experiences work together and share responsibility
for improving their own lives and the lives of those around them. Public
Allies advances diverse young leaders to strengthen communities, non-
profits and civic participation."[54]

How has Public Allies attempted to achieve these goals over the years?
The organization has been most successful in recruiting "leadership minded
young adults, ages 18–30, who want a career in nonprofit work [and plac-
ing] them in locally based community organizations that apply for their
services."[55] Public Allies has been a proud partner of the AmeriCorps pro-

gram since 1994; indeed, it worked with the White House and other organizations to help create the Corporation for National Service and the AmeriCorps program, which I discuss more fully in Chapter 6. Moreover, the organization is recognized as a model for national service excellence in light of the quality of the work that it has achieved in placing more than 1,350 "Allies" in eleven communities throughout the United States.[56] A strategic plan, adopted in June 2001, envisioned expanding to twenty cities and "more than 450 Allies will serve at over 300 Partner Organizations annually by 2006." In addition, the organization hoped to take advantage of its growing alumni network (a network that would "grow to more than 2,500 with 80 percent continuing careers in public service") by creating Ally Lifetime Leadership Programs, which would provide a "series of leadership, learning, and networking opportunities."[57]

Public Allies is an excellent example of the New Citizenship because it stresses the importance of mobilizing and training young people as they interact with diverse individuals in communities throughout the United States. It celebrates grassroots organizing and connects these organizing efforts to the important work of community-based nonprofit organizations. Indeed, it "partners with local universities and nonprofit organizations to operate our local programs in communities across the country."[58] Finally, it affords young people the opportunity to develop the leadership, communication, organizing, and public policy skills necessary to effect political, social, and economic change. The many accomplishments of Public Allies stand as a direct challenge to those who believe that young people today have little interest in community service or civic engagement.

Campus Green Vote. The central purpose of Campus Green Vote, an organization founded in 1991 by Harvard undergraduate student Brian Trelstad, is to educate and train college students to engage in public problem solving of national, state, and local environmental crises. The organization provides college students "with the necessary tools for active and sustainable participation in the public dialogue about our planet's future."[59] Representatives visit college campuses around the country to teach students how to mobilize their peers to political action in response to environmental concerns. Campus Green Vote also sponsors summer training academies in several major cities throughout the United States. Specifically, the organization focuses its training sessions on how to run a voter registration campaign, how to lobby members of Congress, and how to interact with the local media. In recent years, it has also tried to mobilize potential young leaders in communities of color, as they deal on a daily basis with environmental justice issues.

Campus Green Vote has also developed the Shadow Congress Information Network, which has an Internet mailing list that has distributed more than 20,000 action alerts to students in all fifty states since its creation in 1993.[60] The network's purpose is to "combine a series of grassroots trainings (discussing issues of power, diversity, the legislative process, the media and basic campaign skills) with a computer communications system that will provide up to the minute legislative information for campus environmentalists who want to stay on top of cutting edge state and national environmental politics." That empowers students to "jointly frame environmental problems and create a partnership that will work towards generating effective grassroots political power."[61] The legislative alerts provide students with the necessary background on controversial bills or actions on the floor of Congress. The hope is that students will then contact influential or swing congressional members by phone, fax, or e-mail. In this way, Campus Green Vote hopes to guarantee that the youth environmental movement is heard. Members of Congress will thus be held more accountable to informed and politically active citizens as they vote on environmental matters. Raney Corey, former field director of Campus Green Vote, put it this way: "Once you turn people out at the polls, politicians will listen."[62]

What have been the accomplishments of Campus Green Vote thus far? In fall 1992 the organization trained more than 280 student environmental leaders in twenty-seven states to organize issue education campaigns and voter registration drives. Before the 1992 election, Campus Green Vote joined forces with the United States Student Association, Rock the Vote, the Center for Policy Alternatives, Americans for Democratic Action, and the National Abortion Rights League in a get-out-the-vote coalition that helped increase youth voter participation by 7 percent. Campus Green Vote claims that it registered more than 107,000 students nationwide. The organization mobilized even more college students for the 2000 and 2004 election campaigns.

In February 2006 Campus Green Vote's organizing activities, in addition to all activities associated with the Center for Environmental Citizenship, were subsumed under the League of Conservation Voters' Education Fund. Why did this incorporation occur? The League of Conservation Voters claimed it "enhances LCVEF's ability to educate college students across

America on key environmental issues."[63] At the time, Brian Trelstad concluded that "after thirteen years of independent organizing on college campuses, it is gratifying that the Center for Environmental Citizenship's programs will now be integrated into LCVEF—one of the nation's premiere environmental organizations."[64] It is also true that this incorporation allowed Campus Green Vote to survive into the future while relying on the League of Conservation Voters' financial, computer network, and organizing efforts. This case is also a reminder of the challenges that grassroots student organizations face if they wish to survive for the long term.

Campus Green Vote continues to challenge the notion of civic indifference among America's youth by educating and mobilizing college-age students to participate in politics around environmental concerns. In so doing, it has provided a model for other national organizations. Although their focus is largely on voting, Campus Green Vote organizers (working through the League of Conservation Voters) hope that their education campaigns will inspire young Americans to consider an array of grassroots participatory forms as they mobilize on behalf of the environment. In this way, Campus Green Vote is a good example of the New Citizenship in practice.

COOL. The Campus Outreach Opportunity League was organized in 1984 by recent college graduates to provide assistance and encouragement for student-initiated service programs.[65] It is "a national nonprofit organization dedicated to the education and empowerment of college students to strengthen our nation through community service."[66] In late 2003 COOL merged with Action Without Borders, which had created Idealist.org, "the largest online resource for those interested in non-profit careers and social justice work." COOL organizers believe that "this will be a powerful partnership that can deliver the networks, content, and resources that engage students and youth in volunteerism and social change and prepare them for a lifelong commitment to public service."[67] Indeed, a major advantage of this merger is that "Idealist on Campus offers resources, events, educational tools, networking opportunities, and other programs that support students and campuses in strengthening communities through service, activism, and civic engagement."[68]

For many involved in COOL, the strength of the organization rests in its "ability to transcend partisan politics and reach out to all students, regardless of perspective."[69] Paul Loeb provides an overview of how the organization grew out of an idea of a Harvard student Wayne Meisel:

In 1978, this son of a liberal Presbyterian minister was cut from the Harvard soccer team. He responded by convincing 150 fellow students, including other frustrated former high school jocks, to help set up a local youth soccer league. As one of his friends described it, "Wayne's encounters with kids who were not middle class, white, or well taken care of, 'brought Wayne into the twentieth century.'" Wayne himself credited his involvement with curing the "anxious paralysis" he felt when he read newspaper headlines or heard political arguments, then hung back, too overwhelmed to act. Having been one of the silent, he felt angry at media stereotypes that branded his generation as apathetic and callous. Although Harvard had long had a community service center, Phillips Brooks House, Wayne wanted to draw in a new group of participants. He soon set to work pairing the school's residential houses with projects in specific Cambridge neighborhoods. He encouraged their students to work in local day-care centers, music and dance programs, boys clubs, and wherever their passions and talents would fit in. After Wayne graduated, he spent the next year extending this approach throughout the Harvard campus. In 1984, he joined with several friends to found COOL as a vehicle to promote comparable efforts nationwide.[70]

Wayne launched COOL with a "Walk for Action," which was designed to challenge "structural apathy" without engaging in direct political involvement. Meisel and several other students walked 1,500 miles, visiting about sixty-five colleges from Maine to Washington, D.C., in an effort to prove that students would respond to a message rooted in personal commitment. The publicity from this effort, as well as the conservative policies of the Reagan administration, led to a jump in attendance at COOL's annual conference, from 60 students in 1984, to 120 in 1985, to 1,700 in 1989. The organization in 2000 included more than 1,000 schools in its national network, and attendance at its national conference has averaged 1,500–2,000 students per year.

COOL's growth matches the growth of student service organizations on college campuses across the country. Countless students now volunteer their time in an array of community service projects. Some campuses have developed courses that allow students to link their community service experiences with course readings and classroom discussions that tackle issues of democracy, citizenship, and service. These courses are discussed in further detail in Chapter 6. The Clinton administration's national service initiatives, proposed in 1993 and adopted in a pared-down manner by Congress later that year, provided a national impetus for campus service activities and have helped galvanize COOL as the leading national service organization representing college students. To be sure, so many high school and college students engage in some form of service activity that service must be considered a central element of the New Citizenship.

United Students Against Sweatshops. Founded in 1997, United Students Against Sweatshops (USAS) "is an international student movement of campuses and individual students fighting for sweatshop free labor conditions and workers' rights."[71] It unabashedly embraces and celebrates forms of unconventional politics growing out of the African American civil rights movement. USAS has chapters at more than 200 colleges and universities throughout the United States. In late 1998 and 1999, students on a number of campuses—Duke University, Georgetown University, Harvard University, Macalester College, University of Michigan, University of North Carolina at Chapel Hill, University of Oregon, Tulane University, and the University of Wisconsin at Madison—held rallies, protests, and/or sit-ins of college presidents' offices to force administrators "to require manufacturers of products licensed by the university to enforce stricter labor standards."[72] Students at Purdue University even held an eleven-day hunger strike to protest the working conditions of those who make clothing with the Purdue logo. The University of North Carolina's antisweatshop group, Students for Economic Justice, embraced yet another form of unconventional politics. They hosted a "nude-optional party" called "I'd Rather Go Naked Than Wear Sweatshop Clothes." Not to be outdone, Syracuse students biked across their campus in the nude to protest exploitative sweatshop activity in the making of their campus logo products. These products include T-shirts, sweatshirts, and baseball caps. USAS supported and helped to organize these protest efforts in several cases. The organization insists that university standards need to support clothing that is made in "decent working conditions." More recently, students at the University of North Carolina "occupied chancellor James Moesser's office, demanding that the university purchase 75 percent of its light-blue logo gear from factories where workers are paid a living wage and can form unions."[73] Students enrolled at Appalachian State, Penn State, and the University of Montana also occupied administration offices in April 2009; all of these efforts were a part of the broader USAS campaign "to force universities to adopt the Designated Supplier Program, which requires garment producers like Champs, JanSport,

Nike and Adidas and their overseas suppliers to guarantee living wages and labor rights."[74]

How has USAS articulated and fought for its beliefs? It has demanded that colleges and universities "adopt ethically and legally strong codes of conduct, full public disclosure of company information and truly independent verification systems to ensure that sweatshop conditions are not happening." In addition, in November 2009 the organization achieved its biggest victory when "its pressure tactics persuaded one of the nation's leading sportswear companies, Russell Athletic, to agree to rehire 1,200 workers in Honduras who lost their jobs when Russell closed their factory soon after the workers had unionized."[75] The company also agreed not to challenge unionization in its seven companies in Honduras. How did USAS accomplish this goal? The organization galvanized a campaign against the company that extended across the United States. In doing so, it "persuaded the administrations of Boston College, Columbia, Harvard, New York University, Stanford, Michigan, North Carolina and 89 other colleges and universities to sever or suspend their licensing agreements with Russell," agreements that amounted to more than a million dollars in sales and permitted Russell to emblazon university logos on fleeces, sweatshirts and T-shirts.[76] Other colleges and universities are likely to do the same. What made this organizing effort most interesting is that the student activists did so well in organizing beyond their campuses. They picketed the 2009 NBA finals in Orlando and Los Angeles because the NBA has a licensing agreement with Russell. In addition, they targeted consumers by sending "Twitter messages to customers of Dick's Sporting Goods to urge them to boycott Russell products," and they gave fliers to customers inside Sports Authority sporting goods stores.[77] Mel Tenen, who is responsible for monitoring licensing agreements at the University of Miami, underscored the importance of USAS's accomplishments: "It's a very important breakthrough. It's not often that a major licensee will take such a necessary and drastic step to correct the injustices that affected its workers. This paves the way for us to seriously consider reopening our agreement with Russell."[78]

Their efforts have received considerable media coverage. "Activism Surges at Campuses Nationwide, and Labor Is at Issue," trumpeted a March 29, 1999, *New York Times* headline. The article placed this student organizing activity within the broader context of student activism around an array of issues: labor, affirmative action, and lesbian and gay rights. Although these identity-based campus organizing efforts have been prevalent on college campuses over the past decade, the emphasis on labor organizing is relatively new. One explanation for this development is that labor unions themselves have worked hard to attract committed students to their causes and to train them in serious organizing activity.[79] Summer internships in labor union organizing have been awarded, and many of these student interns, upon their return to campus, are ready to exercise leadership in political organizing on their respective campuses.

All of these campus organizing efforts are celebrated by the USAS; indeed, the organization has attempted to coordinate such activities across campuses. Their efforts have been so successful that the Nike corporation has begun to take notice. When Nike corporate boss Phil Knight learned that University of Oregon students were protesting his corporation's treatment of workers, he withdrew a $30 million donation to the university.[80] And USAS targets national politicians as well. The California Students Against Sweatshops and supporters marched at the 2000 Democratic National Convention to demand that the Democratic Party endorse policies that would "hold retailers accountable for sweatshop conditions at suppliers' factories."[81] USAS supporters protested the April 2000 World Trade Organization meetings in Seattle and the International World Bank/International Monetary Fund meeting held in Washington, D.C., several weeks later.

One analyst sees important parallels between USAS and the student antiapartheid movement of an earlier era. Joel Lefkowitz argues that "these student movements worked to redefine university investment and production decisions as public matters for democratic decision rather than private enterprise. . . . Both movements reverberated beyond the campus, not only increasing the visibility of the issues they raised but sparking decisions in other institutions, parallel to the student demands."[82] Moreover, Eric Schlosser, the author of the enlightening book *Fast Food Nation,* believes that the successful strategies used by USAS "can be used to help workers much closer to home—workers in the slaughterhouses and processing plants of the High Plains."[83] The political organizing efforts of USAS have clearly transcended the organization itself, which is another important connection to the New Citizenship in the twenty-first century.

The student movement for greater economic justice represents a significant shift in student organizing efforts, away from the fragmented and nationalistic identity politics prevalent on campuses in the early 1990s.

Although these latter efforts have resulted in greater understanding of the importance of campus diversity among administrators, faculty, and fellow students, they have also contributed to increased balkanization on college campuses. Identity-based organizing efforts have often appealed only to a narrow slice of college students. The efforts of USAS and its supporters transcend such identity-based organizing to the extent that economic equality, humane working conditions, and labor rights are much more universal issues. As a result, organizing around these issues has the potential to link student campus-organizing concerns with political and economic organizing well beyond the privileged confines of ivy-covered campuses. Indeed, the organization's strategy is "to raise public awareness of the exploitation of garment workers in the global economy and mobilize pressure on sweatshop producers by targeting the college apparel industry."[84] In this way, USAS embraces a form of outsider, unconventional politics that has historical connections to the African American civil rights movement, which is also a key element of the New Citizenship.

United States Student Association. One organization that practices both insider and outsider politics is the United States Student Association (USSA). Founded in 1947 as the National Student Association (NSA), the organization has been an important student activism channel, "fighting against, among other things, segregation, McCarthyism, and apartheid, and for access to higher education, which remains its primary focus today."[85] It represents over 4.5 million students on more than 400 campuses in the United States. The organization promotes and organizes "student voices at the local, state, and national levels by mobilizing grassroots power to win concrete victories on student issues."[86] In recent years USSA has moved away from broad statements "of belief on all matters foreign and domestic, and instead defined itself as a ground-level, political-savvy organization bent on advocating one goal: increased access to higher education."[87] Its vital advocacy work on behalf of students' access to higher education has been especially relevant at a time when the challenges of a troubled economy highlight larger structural inequalities. The organization's Web site highlights the importance of educational access: "USSA believes that education is a right and should be accessible for any student regardless of their socio-economic background and identity. We believe people who are affected directly by issues of access to higher education should be the ones identifying the solutions that make education accessible to them."[88] USAS hopes to develop student leaders who can advance a broader social justice agenda using both insider and outsider politics.

USSA's organizing efforts have ensured that the organization is an integral lobbying voice for students in the Washington, D.C., policymaking process concerning educational policy access issues. The group's representatives have frequently testified in the halls of Congress and worked "with the Department of Education on issues such as Pell Grants and increased Student Aid, the renewal of the Higher Education Act, the growing financial burdens placed upon students in exchange for an education, affirmative action for students from traditionally underserved communities, and access to education for immigrant children."[89] Early indications are that President Barack Obama intends to restructure the student loan program and ensure a much more active federal government role. As one reporter suggests, "When it comes to student loans, the president has shaken off his tendency to compromise—and is on the verge of reining in the loan sharks who prey on college students."[90] USSA has indicated that it would "like to see the elimination of predatory private lenders altogether,"[91] so Obama's efforts reflect one of the organization's chief goals over the years. But the issue of student debt reduction in a time of greater inequality and economic challenge must still be addressed. As Gregory Cendana, USSA president, said in late 2009, "Right now, our challenge is to persuade other millennials that we no longer have to fight for crumbs."[92] In pursuing its goals, the organization is an excellent example of the New Citizenship.

The Internet

A final element of the New Citizenship is the Internet, which has become a central tool in political organizing. The Internet has tremendous repercussions for the public sphere, by facilitating communication with other citizens and by allowing access to information that would otherwise be difficult to acquire. Through access to the Internet, citizens become better informed on public policy. In this way, citizen-based democracy can be revitalized by challenging corporate control of vital communications media.[93] As citizens become better informed, they can more effectively debate the issues of the day: "This kind of citizen-to-citizen discussion, backed up by facts available to all, could grow into the real basis for a possible electronic democracy in the future."[94]

Many nonprofit organizations now use the Internet to rally support for their research and lobbying efforts, raise donations, and gather relevant information. As noted above, Campus Green Vote has used the Internet to keep students informed on controversial congressional actions through its Shadow Congress Information Network.

The Internet was used, as well, to organize a day of demonstrations against the Contract with America in March 1995. This protest activity took place at more than one hundred colleges and universities throughout the United States and "is thought to be the first instance in which campus organizers have taken to the Internet to map a nationwide campaign." The ease and speed with which the protests were planned and the broad coalition of student groups involved via the Internet dramatically changed the way students communicated with one another. One University of Virginia student said, "Electronic mail is a means to really have a participatory democracy."[95] As a communication medium, the Internet is unique "because of its speed, low cost, easy capacity for forwarding messages, freedom from gatekeepers, and unlimited capacity."[96] It has become a crucial vehicle for dissemination of information regarding political organizing and campaigns. What was once communicated by mail or personal contacts is now replaced by e-mail, listservs, and Web sites.[97]

The Internet has been an essential tool in national organizing efforts. For example, many of the activities associated with the spring 2000 protest at the World Trade Organization meetings in Seattle and the World Bank/International Monetary Fund meetings in Washington relied on Internet communication and organizing through the use of e-mail distribution lists. A Web site coordinated the April 16 Seattle protests (www.a16.org), providing fact sheets, pamphlets, and poster art. Terra Lawson-Remer, a Yale undergraduate and a national organizer for the Student Alliance to Reform Corporations (STARC), testified to the crucial importance of Internet organizing to nationwide organizing efforts: "We don't have any money, but it's not a problem at all. We post all of our information and training packets on the web so campus groups can just download them. Almost every student has access to a computer."[98] Indeed, the Millennial Generation "is the first American generation to be raised with access to the Internet and the incredibly greater communication opportunities the web offers."[99]

Moveon.org, founded in late 1998 and with thirteen full-time employees as of November 2009, has become the model for the online organization of citizens for progressive causes. According to the organization's Web site, by

2009 it claimed more than five million members throughout the United States. Created at the time of the congressional hearings on the impeachment of President Clinton, Moveon.org organized citizens to contact members of Congress and urge them to "move on."[100] The organization's founders, Joan Blades and Wes Boyd, "sent an e-mail to 100 of their friends saying Congress should censure the President and move on." By creating an online petition submission form, they were able to generate roughly 500,000 sign-ons, thus providing a template for their future organizational efforts.[101] Those subsequent efforts have included raising money for the late Senator Paul Wellstone's (D-Minnesota) 2002 senatorial campaign and organizing opposition to the war in Iraq. How has it organized against the war in Iraq? By raising millions of dollars online to sponsor print ads and televised spots against the war, delivering "a petition of 1 million signatures to the UN Security Council, and persuading 200,000 people to call their Washington, D.C. representatives in Congress and President Bush in a single day."[102] In 2004 Moveon.org raised millions of dollars to create and run television ads in support of John Kerry in key battleground states during the general election campaign. More recently, it organized extensively on behalf of Barack Obama in 2008. Two students of Internet organizing have highlighted the integral role that organizations like Moveon.org can play in building a netroots movement:

> [The netroots] means citizen activists—real people—using the Internet to gather information to organize with other like-minded folks across the country, to plan events, to raise money, and to make the case for their candidate. Much of the activity takes place in person, not online.[103]

These impressive organizing efforts have brought Moveon.org considerable and well-deserved attention. Other organizations of various ideologies have also embraced Internet organizing, as we have seen over the past ten years. We can expect that conservatives will develop their online organizing strategies more fully as the Obama presidency unfolds. Indeed, they did so in August 2009 in opposition to the Democrats' efforts to address health-care reform. Americans for Prosperity, a conservative organization, "embraced Internet activism to energize its 700,000 members and to point them to dozens of town-hall meetings with lawmakers over the past few weeks."[104] The organization held a conference, Right Online, at which organizers trained participants in the "use of Facebook, Twitter, and other online megaphones to rally conservative opposition to what they consider ultra-liberal policies—strategies popularized by organizations such as Moveon.org and President Barack Obama's 2008 campaign."[105]

Indeed, as we have already seen, there is precedent for Obama's and the Right's Internet organizing efforts. Howard Dean's bid for the 2004 Democratic presidential nomination was fueled by a sophisticated Internet organizing campaign. "Internet Helps Make Dean a Contender" was the headline of a summer 2003 *New York Times* article, whose lead read, "Howard Dean's prominence among the nine Democrats running for president is largely attributable to his campaign's early embrace of the Internet for organizing supporters and raising money."[106] Dean's use of the Meetup.com Web site, which encourages people with similar interests to meet and connect, was the foundation of his fund-raising efforts. Internet technology enabled people to type in a zip code on the Meetup.com Web site and connect immediately to other Dean supporters in their area. The genius of the Web site, created in 2002, is that it encourages people to leave the privacy of their homes to interact with others face to face, thus fostering the personal connections that are associated with participatory democracy and the New Citizenship. Dean's Internet organizing efforts were so successful (even though he did not get the Democratic nomination) that other candidates (including John Kerry) followed his lead and began more sophisticated Internet fund-raising and organizing efforts. When it came time for John Kerry to announce John Edwards as his vice-presidential running mate in the 2004 election, he e-mailed his choice about an hour before his formal announcement to more than 1 million people who subscribed to his Web site. Dean's success in using the Internet provided a template that presidential candidate Barack Obama used with considerable success as a vehicle for raising money and building a grassroots organizing base during the 2008 campaign. To the extent that the Internet enables citizens to communicate with one another about politics and bring people physically together in the larger public sphere, it is a crucial element of the New Citizenship.

The Obama 2008 Presidential Campaign

The journalist Tim Dickinson has captured the essence of the Obama campaign's Internet organizing accomplishments: "By marrying online technology to grass-roots activism, Obama's brain trust mobilized 1.5 million donors, raised more than $250 million, derailed the Clinton juggernaut and built something new in Democratic politics."[107] Most striking about the Obama campaign strategy was its determination to register as many first-time voters as possible; in doing so, the campaign "united web and field recruitment."[108] For example, the campaign used Facebook, YouTube views, and MySpace friends, recognizing that these relatively new forms of Internet technology were excellent vehicles for targeting younger, first-time voters in particular. And how did the Obama campaign use these new forms of Internet technologies as organizing vehicles? In Virginia, one hundred of the 3,600 Obama Organizing Fellows, "a group of full-time volunteers fanning out across the country to oversee local registration efforts"[109] descended upon the state to register first-time voters who indicated support for the Democratic nominee. This mobilization effort in Virginia and other states was galvanized by "Obama's Internet operation specializing in reaching out to the younger voters who use social networking sites like Facebook."[110] The Obama campaign also expertly used YouTube as a way to garner free advertising. Joe Trippi, the mastermind behind Howard Dean's 2004 Internet campaign, claimed that YouTube videos "were more effective than television ads because viewers chose to watch them from a friend instead of having their television shows interrupted."[111] In evaluating the Obama campaign's successful use of YouTube, Trippi pointed out that "'the campaign's official stuff they created for YouTube was watched for 14.5 million hours. To buy 14.5 million hours on broadcast TV is $47 million'."[112]

The Internet organizing campaign continued after Obama assumed the presidency. For example, the Obama administration used its campaign grassroots organization as a vehicle for "enlisting its millions of foot soldiers to help push the economic-stimulus package through Congress."[113] The organization, now called Organizing for America, is located under the Democratic National Committee. Mitch Stewart, the organization's new director, wrote the following in an e-mail to some of the Obama campaign's most active volunteers, exhorting them to organize on behalf of the 2009 stimulus package: "'The economic crisis can seem overwhelming and complex. But you can help the people you know connect the recovery plan to their lives and learn more about why it's so important'."[114] The same organizing approach has been used in the fight over health-care reform. In this and in other ways, Barack Obama's Internet campaign helped to change American politics in fundamental ways.

The Critique of the Internet

Coalitions among like-minded citizens and organizations can be built much more broadly and quickly through the Internet. Nonetheless, the Internet as a means for promoting democracy is not without its critics. One argument is that some citizens still cannot afford to buy the hardware and services needed to connect to the Internet. The Internet access problem has been identified as the "digital divide," which encompasses "the patterns of unequal access to information technology based on income, race, ethnicity, gender, age, and geography that surfaced during the mid-1990s."[115] Indeed, one political scientist has gone so far as to argue that "the internet's image of openness and equality belies its inequities of race, geography, and age."[116] Acknowledging this problem, former House Speaker Newt Gingrich argued that "maybe we need a tax credit for the poorest Americans to buy a laptop." But even he recognized that many would regard this suggestion as "a nutty idea."[117] Others have pointed out that the Internet encourages people to zip off unreflective sound bites in response to the issues of the day, rather than making the thoughtful, reflective contributions that are associated with the ideal participatory democratic vision. And yet another critic has astutely pointed out that organizing on the Internet cannot possibly take the place of political action:

> Of course, it is marvelously useful, allows us to exchange information, find the facts we need, alert each other to the coming dangers and all the rest of it. But it also creates a false impression of action. It allows us to believe that we can change the world without leaving our chairs. We are heard! Our voices resonate around the world, provoking commentary and debate, inspiring some, enraging others. Something is happening! A movement is building! But by itself, as I know to my cost, writing, reading, debate and dissent changes nothing. They are of value only if they inspire action. Action means moving your legs.[118]

There are increased worries, too, that "the nation's obsession with the Internet is causing many Americans to spend less time with friends and family, less time shopping in stores and more time working at home." This was the conclusion of the first large-scale surveys of the Internet's impact on society. The principal investigator for the study, Stanford political scientist Norman Nie, reported in February 2000 that "the more hours people use the Internet, the less time they spend with real human beings."[119] In addition, the face-to-face vision of direct democracy cannot begin to be approximated on the Internet. Citizens do not have the opportunity to talk to and to listen to one another directly. As a result, they are not held accountable for their positions and do not have the benefit of learning from others through the give and take of the discussion process. Technological innovation cannot substitute for the kind of community building and participatory experiences associated with face-to-face democracy and the participatory democratic vision. A further worry is that people (especially the young) who are constantly using instant messaging, texting, e-mail, and cell phones (we must all be connected all of the time!) find it increasingly difficult to concentrate on the moment at hand. In this way, these new forms of technological "progress" serve as distractions and undermine the ability of people to concentrate and focus for sustained periods.

Despite these weaknesses, the Internet does potentially provide citizens with access to greater information, which can help them become better informed about public policy decisions that affect their lives. And through the use of e-mail, the Internet enables the kind of political organizing on a large scale that would be much more difficult, costly, and time-consuming without this important new technology. Some have argued that the Internet is the "dominant political medium" in the first decade of the twenty-first century.[120] More important, it is here to stay, and students of democracy will have to grapple with its broader consequences for citizenship and politics now and in the future. Perhaps Peter Levine has best summarized the current state of research on the impact of the Internet, especially as it affects the young: "It is impossible at this stage to predict whether the civic affects of these new forms of interaction will be positive."[121]

Conclusion

In this chapter I have argued that the study of politics and citizenship in America must move beyond the analysis of voting to capture the multiple ways citizens are involved in the American political system. To be sure, if we use voter-turnout figures as an indicator of the health of American democracy, we will see that America is a nation characterized by civic indifference. However, if we broaden our conception of citizenship to encompass what I call the New Citizenship, then it becomes clear that Americans have been actively involved in numerous grassroots and community-based organizations over the past thirty years. These citizen organizations have expanded and increased participation in American politics at the same time that many Americans eschew voting. Such organizations have proliferated on college campuses as well. To fully explain the meaning of the New Citizenship, I examine various conceptions of citizenship education in the final chapter. I outline the ways that teachers at all levels can engage their students in analyzing what it means to be a citizen on a college campus, in a neighborhood, and as a member of a global, interconnected community.

6

··

Service Learning and
the New Citizenship

... the ingenuity and idealism of the younger generations represent
a potent resource for civic renewal.

   —Robert D. Putnam, *Bowling Alone: The Collapse and Revival of
   American Community*

My heart is moved by all I cannot save. So much has been destroyed
I have cast my lot with those who, age after age, perversely, with no
extraordinary power, reconstitute the world.

   —Adrienne Rich, "Natural Resources"

I have harbored this dream for years. It was stoked in me by so many
thousands of experiences I cannot even recall. When the vice president and I went across the country last year, I was deeply moved by
the forces that were both good and bad that kept pushing me to believe that this was more important than so many of the other things
that all of us do in public life. . . . I watched people's dreams come to
life, I watched the old and the young relate in ways they hadn't. I
watched mean streets turn into safer and better and more humane
places. [National service] will help us to strengthen the cords that
bind us together as a people.

   —Bill Clinton, White House Ceremony

CLINTON'S SPEECH WAS delivered on the day that he signed the National and Community Service Trust Act of 1993 into law. The president and his advisers watched uneasily throughout the summer as Congress significantly scaled back his comprehensive national service plans, largely because of their perceived cost and the fact that many conservative critics were concerned about creating yet another Washington bureaucracy. Nonetheless, Clinton's idea ultimately carried the day, although his original proposal had largely been gutted by congressional policymakers. For Bill Clinton and his administration, passage of the National Service Act was a triumph of sorts. The president had embraced the popular idea of national service on the campaign trail and now was delivering on his promise.

This chapter discusses service as a central component of the New Citizenship. It offers an overview of service on college campuses as well as a discussion of the president's plan. It attempts to explain why service is so popular on college campuses and assesses its relationship to the New Citizenship. Finally, it connects service to civility and system stability, the central theme of this book.

Before I present the broader case for and against service, service itself must be placed within its appropriate theoretical context. To do that, I outline what is meant by the New Citizenship and examine various models of teaching citizenship education at the college level.

Critical Education for Citizenship and Educational Approaches

Those of us in higher education are uniquely situated to evaluate civic indifference and to devise strategies rooted in a curriculum that enables our students to grapple with the meaning of citizenship, democracy, and public participation in compelling ways. Students often arrive at college just out of high school with little interest in or understanding of politics and how their active engagement is crucial for a viable democracy. A rigorous liberal arts education should connect the many ways in which knowledge can inform our daily lives. Indeed, as some social scientists have written, "We believe that higher education has a critical role to play in shaping character and a sense of social responsibility in the U.S. citizenry because such a larger share of the population attends college for at least some period of time."[1] Political scientists like me tackle these issues in teaching, research, and community work. We can best achieve our educational goals by pursuing a model of education that we might call critical education for citizenship.[2]

A course on critical education for citizenship should have the following characteristics: (1) it should present the full critique of American democracy to the student; (2) it should allow students to see the importance of participating in public decisions; (3) it should ask educators and students to conceive of democracy broadly to include community discussions, community action, public service, and protest politics; (4) it should ask students to conceptualize participation very broadly to include workplace and community opportunities for participation; (5) it should encourage students to take into account the important relationships among gender, race, sexual orientation, and class concerns in the participatory process and to develop a respect for and understanding of difference; (6) it should place a discussion of democracy within its appropriate historical context, by focusing on democratic movements, such as the African American civil rights movement, the antiwar movement, and the women's movement; (7) it should ask students to confront their assumptions regarding power and leadership as well as the sources of such assumptions; and (8) it should prepare students for their place in the world by affording them a chance to make an informed choice about what it is that they want to do with their lives and how they connect what they do with the communities where they live and work.

Ultimately, college curricula should enable students to define what they mean by democracy and then provide opportunities for students to develop necessary skills for participation on their campuses, in their communities, and in the larger society. Students must see the connection between their college educational experiences and their participation in society upon graduation. Indeed, education is an important predictor of civic engagement. The Kettering Foundation has addressed these issues in a number of meaningful ways, including sponsorship of a national town meeting program called the National Issue Forums and an associated publishing program. A pamphlet published by the foundation, *Politics for the Twenty-First Century: What Should Be Done on Campus?*[3] offers several approaches to citizenship education that are particularly relevant as we explore the full meaning of critical education for citizenship and its connection to challenging civic indifference.

A first approach, rooted in community service, is "learning by doing—the public service component." The argument here is that students must look to the larger community if they are to be properly prepared for their roles as citizens in a democracy. From this vantage point, students should participate in their communities through involvement in service opportunities, political campaigns, or organizing for social change. Regardless of the form that involvement actually takes, students learn that hands-on experience outside their college campuses is a crucial component of their college education.[4] I explore this approach in more detail when I discuss the role played by community service in the New Citizenship later in this chapter.

A second option, "learning by talking—acquiring deliberative skills," rejects the notion that service should be at the core of an undergraduate education. Instead, this approach argues that service cannot begin to train people for politics, "because politics is actually about what we mean by 'the **public good**'." The latter is the good that we seek in common. The key here is that all students and citizens must be afforded the opportunity to develop their public deliberation skills so that they will be better equipped to participate meaningfully in politics at the community level. Proponents of this second approach think that "all citizens need to engage in reasoned political discussion about the sort of world they want to live in, and that a college should itself provide opportunities to practice deliberation and to hone the skills that public talk requires."[5]

A third perspective might be called "learning by practicing—democratizing the campus." Those who support this approach to citizenship education point out that direct participation by students in the creation of their own education and the structuring of their lives within their college or university affords them the best possible training in politics. The goal here is for students to transform the campus itself into an egalitarian, participatory community. As they do that, they will learn that "deliberation is meaningless without power and responsibility." In addition, they will come to reject hierarchy in all forms and recognize that "citizenship has to be practiced in order to be learned."[6]

Those who believe that "the key to a strong democracy lies in individuals who are well prepared intellectually" support a fourth approach. This approach might be called "learning by learning—a classical academic model."

Proponents of this perspective believe that the college or university should remain neutral in political affairs and students should not become too politicized. Instead, they should devote their attention to their studies and become trained in various intellectual disciplines, with the hope that they will develop the rigorous training needed to successfully analyze complex issues. In this way, they will actually strengthen democracy.[7]

As the Kettering pamphlet makes clear, these four approaches to citizenship education are not mutually exclusive. In fact, they all contribute in valuable ways to the elements of critical education for citizenship identified earlier. In addition, each of the four educational approaches either implicitly or explicitly challenges students to overcome the civic indifference often associated with their age group.

Of the four, the first—learning by doing—has received the most recent attention. This approach is the foundation of President Clinton's national service proposal as well as President George W. Bush's and President Barack Obama's policies on service. I turn now to an in-depth discussion of the Clinton, Bush, and Obama proposals and an overview of the strengths and limitations of service education.

The Clinton National Service Proposal and the Case for Service Learning

As a presidential candidate, Bill Clinton proposed creating the National Service Trust Fund as one of his top five priorities. The program would, in his words, "make it possible for every person in this country who wants to, to go to college." Clinton and his advisers proposed combining a major restructuring of the college loan program with national service. The initial proposal was that any young person, regardless of parental income, could borrow money for education from the federal government. How would these loans be repaid? According to the original Clinton plan, "They would repay their loans either through federal withholding from future wages or by serving their communities for one or two years doing work their country needs."[8]

The original Clinton plan identified Clinton as a **New Democrat**, more conservative than old-style Democrats. As a founding member of the Democratic Leadership Council, presidential candidate Clinton "wanted to show that Democrats could do more than throw money at the poor; that they could once again advocate mainstream middle-class values such as work,

Habitat for Humanity volunteers bringing a dishwasher into a house they are renovating on Detroit's east side. *Credit:* Jim West/Impact Visuals.

sacrifice, and mutual obligation." Clinton's proposal to offer aid to those young people who were willing to do service was a classic Clintonesque idea. From his vantage point, the great strength of the plan was that it was voluntary, it embraced tough conservative rhetoric, and at the same time it endorsed the generosity of liberalism.[9]

As an undergraduate at Georgetown University in the 1960s, Bill Clinton had tutored disadvantaged Washington kids in the Georgetown Community Action Program. His experience, however, was not completely positive, for he came away convinced that occasional volunteerism actually did much more for the volunteer than for the individuals being served. Clinton said,

"It made all the participants feel good and we learned a lot but I became convinced you had to have ongoing grassroots efforts."[10] Yet this concern did not prevent him from emphasizing the importance of service on the 1992 campaign trail.

Soon after assuming office, however, Clinton was informed by his top aides that his original national service proposal would be far too costly. Deficit concerns and the overall cost of the program prompted the administration to retreat from its original grandiose campaign promise. Then the president was attacked by the press for having abandoned yet another campaign promise. In retrospect, it is clear that Clinton promised far too much on the campaign trail and that economic and political realities made it difficult for him to translate his proposal for integrating educational assistance with community service into concrete public policy.

As a result, the administration settled for a much-scaled-down version of Clinton's original proposal. The resulting proposal was eventually split into two pieces of legislation: The first would establish a system whereby "young people could serve their communities in exchange for a college scholarship"; the second would discard the existing student loan program and enable college graduates to repay their loans "as a small percentage of their earnings over time."[11]

The legislation was signed into law at a time when many colleges across the country were expanding their own opportunities for service learning. The growing community service movement on college campuses is an attempt to overcome student frustration with American politics by giving students the opportunity to perform immediate and useful tasks, such as working in soup kitchens, teaching literacy skills, or volunteering with a local Big Brother/Big Sister program. The hope on the part of many organizers is that students who participate in service activities will begin to ask why tragedies such as illiteracy, hunger, and homelessness exist in our affluent society. Thus, such students, many of whom are apolitical, will begin to develop a social consciousness.

The AmeriCorps program is rooted in these broader principles regarding the importance of community service. Since its creation in 1994, it has justifiably received considerable attention for its many accomplishments. For example, in the first five years of the program's existence, more than 150,000 people joined AmeriCorps. As a comparison, it took the Peace Corps thirty-eight years to reach that level of participation. A recent evaluation of the Corporation for National Service found that AmeriCorps members are having a significant impact in classrooms, low-income communities, after-school programs, disaster response, and other diverse assignments. The same study reported that increasing "numbers of AmeriCorps members take advantage of the education award they receive for completing service—more than 23,000 former AmeriCorps members used their AmeriCorps education awards in 1999 alone."[12]

What are some of the most popular and interesting AmeriCorps programs? The AmeriCorps VISTA (Volunteers in Service to America) program comprised approximately 6,000 volunteers when VISTA celebrated its thirty-fifth anniversary in 2000. PowerUP, a major AmeriCorps VISTA initiative, was created in November 1999. This partnership program delivers "technological resources and expertise to disadvantaged communities." AmeriCorps VISTA participants are at the core of the program's implementation: "400 trained AmeriCorps VISTA members will serve full-time as mentors to young participants and train them in computer technologies they'll need to succeed in the digital age."[13]

AmeriCorps National Civilian Community Corps (NCCC) is an important component of the federal government's efforts to support and encourage community participation among the young. The importance and popularity of this program is reflected in its application pool. The NCCC received in excess of 3,000 applications for only 800 positions in 1999. Those fortunate enough to be selected engage in one of hundreds of successful service projects that are located in forty-nine states and Puerto Rico. Examples of service projects include disaster response in North Carolina after Hurricane Floyd; the Great River Sweep project, which "engaged 8,000 volunteers on a massive clean-up of the Hudson River to work with more than 30 Boys and Girls Clubs; the Habitat Collegiate Challenge Project that enabled over 2,000 high school and college students to devote their spring breaks to building homes for low-income families; and participation in the Special Olympics World Summer Games."[14] Although the AmeriCorps program is still relatively young, it has already enabled participating young people to build on their high school and/or college commitment to community service.

President George W. Bush created the USA Freedom Corps in the aftermath of the September 11, 2001, terrorist attacks. In March 2004 President Bush offered this justification for the USA Freedom Corps Program: "I created the USA Freedom Corps at the White House to encourage more Americans to serve and to foster a culture of service, citizenship, and responsibility for decades to come."[15] The AmeriCorps program was placed under this broader service initiative. Bush's endorsement of the AmeriCorps program and government-supported community and global service is a striking departure from the Republican Party's initial opposition to the Clinton plan. At the same time, however, George W. Bush was criticized for proposing significant cuts in funding for the AmeriCorps program as a part of his 2004 budgetary proposals. One observer estimated that if Congress did not restore the cuts, funding for AmeriCorps would be reduced by 58 percent and would prevent thousands of potential volunteers from participating.[16] Congress did restore a portion of Bush's proposed cutbacks, but they fell far short of sustaining all of AmeriCorps's potential participants. The continued popularity of the program indicates that some fifteen years after its inception, it remains an important element of America's national service commitment. To the extent that AmeriCorps encourages young people to link their service participation to political participation, then it plays an invaluable role in enhancing the New Citizenship.

Like Bill Clinton, presidential candidate Barack Obama embraced national service as an integral component of his campaign. And he followed through on his campaign promises, soon after his historic election, by securing a $200 million increase in AmeriCorps in the stimulus bill. This additional funding allowed for an increase in the number of staff from 75,000 to 250,000. High unemployment rates at the height of a serious economic recession contributed to a "surge in applications to America's most prominent service organizations, including an increase of 300 percent at AmeriCorps and 40 percent at Teach for America."[17] The legislation that allowed for this increase in funding renamed the program the "Edward M. Kennedy Serve America Act," in honor of the late Democratic senator "who was a main architect of the measure," and who championed "establishing new cadres of volunteers focused on health care, education, renewable energy and veterans."[18]

Many academic proponents contend that for community service programs and service learning to be successful in a college setting, they must be grounded in democracy and reflect various approaches to democratic citizenship. Some colleges and universities now offer courses that require service. Students are then given reading and writing assignments that require them to reflect critically on broader issues of race, class, gender, democracy, and citizenship concerns growing out of their service experiences. Colleges that offer such courses are redefining education to ensure that students become directly involved with citizenship concerns by working with others in the larger community.[19] The goal of such courses is to recognize that community service "is an indispensable prerequisite of citizenship and thus a condition for democracy's survival."[20] Service learning cannot play this role if it ultimately disconnects issues of social justice from those of social transformation and political empowerment.[21]

Others have argued persuasively that service learning ensures that students will be placed in direct contact with civic associations and civic spaces, both of which Tocqueville and Robert Putnam identified as vital if we are to have a "vibrant democratic life." If we assume that "such associational life is weakening" within our society, then these community-based connections are a crucial part of students' overall educational experiences.[22] And in the words of one recent college graduate, "College students are, for the most part, uniquely suited to have time for and to benefit from getting involved and addressing the needs of those around them."[23] Proponents of service learning also often argue that service should be viewed as a transformative activity—the "idea is to transform public service from a few hours of tutoring poor children or working in a homeless shelter to a lifelong commitment to civic engagement."[24] It is this important connection to long-term civic engagement that connects service learning to the New Citizenship.

Finally, service learning raises important questions about the connection between colleges and universities on the one hand and public life on the other. Service learning proponents understandably argue that colleges and universities make useful contributions to their surrounding communities to the extent that students interact with those communities in meaningful and important ways. For example, the Alternative Spring Break program, established several years ago, is an increasingly popular program with college students who wish to link their programs of study with community service. The goal is to place students in communities where they can "engage in positive social action and education, while participating in meaningful service. Students perform short-term projects for community agencies and also have an opportunity to live in a culture and geographical area different than their own."[25] As students participate in these alternative spring break experiences, it is hoped that they will connect them to a lifelong commitment to participatory service in their communities. Proponents of service learning extol the benefits of such innovative programs.

It is interesting that despite the popularity of community service, Republicans in Congress gave serious thought to eliminating Clinton's national service program, cutting almost all of its $500 million budget. One *New York Times* editorial regarding the Clinton program examined the work of more than twenty AmeriCorps volunteers who were rebuilding New Hampshire trails and winterizing cabins. When not working in the New Hampshire mountains, they served hot meals at a senior center and taught environmental classes at local schools. For their year of service, these volunteers would receive a modest living allowance and a $4,725 voucher for higher education. One volunteer, who hoped to attend graduate school in soil sciences, told political scientist Robert Putnam, "I simply cannot imagine leaving this project and not staying involved with community service."[26]

Despite the enthusiastic praise for Clinton's program and the increasing popularity of service learning opportunities on college campuses, there are some who offer a number of important criticisms of service.

The Critique of Service

Many of those opposed to courses that require students to participate in community or public service believe that such service simply cannot possibly achieve all that it purports to achieve. For example, Harry Boyte writes that "community service is not a cure for young people's political apathy," because "it teaches little about the arts of participation in public life."[27] In addition, it falls far short of providing the everyday connections to the political process that students must have. Furthermore, most courses that require community service fail to afford students the opportunity that they need "to work effectively toward solving society's problems."[28]

Other critics of service-based experiences lament the fact that most student participants avoid tackling larger policy questions and issues. In this sense, the participants often conceive of service as an alternative to politics. Indeed, service is often a way for participants to avoid talking about politics.[29] Boyte points out, for example, that the language of community service is infused with the jargon of "helping" rather than "a vocabulary that draws attention to the public world that extends beyond personal lives and local communities." Service volunteers rarely have the ability to grapple with the complex intersection of class, race, and power that is created when middle-class youths engage in projects in low-income areas. In the absence of "a conceptual framework that distinguishes between personal life and the public world, community service adopts the 'therapeutic language' that now pervades society."[30] It is this therapeutic approach that cannot begin to deal with the inequalities that structure the relationship between the so-called servers and the served. Boyte explains further that "the current emphasis of volunteerism 'dumbs down' citizenship by highlighting personal traits like caring and individual acts of kindness and eclipsing questions of power, collective action, the cultures and functioning of institutions, and larger systemic problems."[31] In the end, service activity is devoid of politics and therefore is a relatively empty way of tackling the complex structural issues that arise out of the conditions that prompt service activity in the first place. Some contend that it ultimately contributes to "the narrowing political role of American citizens."[32]

Yet another set of criticisms raises questions about the relationship of the individual to the State. According to Eric Gorham, "Community service is an institutional means by which the State uses political discourse and ideology to reproduce a postindustrial capitalist economy in the name of good citizenship."[33] For Gorham and other critics, community service reinforces the worst form of clientelism and tacitly accepts the structural inequalities growing out of the limited American welfare state. It does so by largely working within the confines of the current system without always affording students the opportunity to critique that system in a fundamental way. It thus promotes an invidious form of authoritarianism.[34] In addition, service assumes that all participants can afford to volunteer for little or no pay. Unfortunately, many students need one or two jobs merely to make ends meet while they pursue their undergraduate education. As a result, many are prevented from participating in service opportunities because of economic barriers.

Gorham raises serious practical considerations that need to be addressed by proponents of any community service. To Gorham, these are the most important questions:[35]

1. How well can the practice of national service fulfill its theoretical goals?
2. What does "inculcating civic education" mean in concrete terms? In what sense will national service offer opportunities for democracy, equality, and participation to those who serve?
3. Is the goal of citizenship appropriate to all people, regardless of their race or gender?
4. Does national service contribute to citizenship in any material way?
5. Furthermore, how should citizenship be nurtured?

BOX 6.1 Ten Crucial Choices in Developing Community
Service Courses

---

1. Should service be education based or extracurricular?
2. Should service be mandatory or voluntary?
3. Should service be civic or philanthropic?
4. Should service be for credit or not?
5. Should service be offered as a single course or as a multicourse program?
6. Should the community be a "client" or a "partner in education"?
7. Should students serve in group teams or as individuals?
8. Should the faculty also do community service?
9. Should the pedagogy of service emphasize patriotism and citizenship or critical thinking?
10. Should students participate in the planning process?

Source: Benjamin R. Barber and Richard Battistoni, "A Season of Service: Introducing Service Learning into the Liberal Arts Curriculum," *PS: Political Science and Politics* 26, no. 2 (June 1993), p. 236.

---

6. Do the ideas of the planners of national service coincide with those of the philosophers who might view it as appropriate to their ends?

Critics such as Eric Gorham point out that most proponents of service fail to ask these questions and, as a result, avoid discussing the kind of theoretical underpinnings that should be at the core of any courses that require students to participate in service activities (see Boxes 6.1 and 6.2).

The libertarian perspective offers a final critique of national service programs. Libertarians, for example Doug Bandow, point out that President Clinton's national service proposal will ultimately lead to government coercion because all government service programs assume at their core that citizens are not responsible to one another, but are responsible to the State. In this way, the "volunteers" are actually coerced by the government to participate in service programs, thus losing their liberty and freedom.[36] Bandow's critique is particularly relevant to the present analysis because it raises interesting questions about whether students should be required to participate in any service experience as a part of a college course or courses.

· ·

BOX 6.2   Criteria for Evaluating Service Learning Courses

1. Are the service learning placements challenging (providing growth in important moral and civic skills)?
2. Are students well prepared for the placements?
3. Do the field experiences contribute directly to the academic goals of the course?
4. Does the course have a structured reflection component that examines the issues addressed by the service in terms of systematic causes and policy responses as well as in interpersonal terms?
5. Do students use the reflection opportunities to think through their assumptions, values, and identities when appropriate as well as to focus on the substantive issues raised in the service experience?
6. Was the student participation effective from the point of view of the community partners?

Source: Anne Colby, Thomas Ehrlich, Elizabeth Beaumont and Jason Stephens, *Educating Citizens: Preparing Undergraduates for Lives of Moral and Civil Responsibility*. San Francisco: Jossey Bass, 2003, pp. 263–264.

· ·

In addressing this critique, I present an upper-level political science course at Hobart and William Smith Colleges in Geneva, New York: Social Policy and Community Activism, which requires students to be fully engaged in a semester-long community service/community action project. The course is about democracy, community, and difference, and it attempts to link the readings, assignments, and a service requirement to the model of critical education for citizenship discussed earlier. Students are to be fully engaged in the lives of people within the community and to be involved in thinking autobiographically about the effect of the service on their own lives, their perspectives on democracy, and their understanding of democratic citizenship.[37] The goal is for students to connect their service learning and community action problems with public policy debates and normative and ethical concerns regarding what constitutes a just society.[38]

The course encourages and rewards independent thought. It focuses on critical evaluation of both the readings and the field experience and how each serves to illuminate the other. Students are asked to reaffirm one central precept, namely, that learning requires a serious commitment to both the subject at hand and the voices and experiences of those engaged in the course and the community.[39]

Students are involved in community service/community action from two different perspectives. First, work in service involves students in the everyday lives of community members who face limited economic opportunities. Geneva, New York, and its surroundings is a community in need of serious economic and social assistance, as it deals with the consequences of the deindustrialization of America.[40]

Some of the students experienced empowerment and social transformation through their service experience. Several students revitalized the efforts of the local literacy program, working with individuals and families. Some of this involved work with migrant workers in the local wineries and vineyards. Literacy improvements were achieved in both Spanish and English. Literacy efforts, addressing the needs of both adults and children in a migrant population that is marginalized politically, socially, and economically, had profound consequences for personal self-esteem, individual competency, and collective initiative.[41]

Second, students approach service as a project in citizenship. The course asks students to explore the nature and current limits of democratic citizenship. This component of service learning is an essential issue in its own right.

In addressing this element of the course, I ask students to reflect on a number of questions: What is the role of the citizenry in the American political system? What should the role of the citizenry be? How does citizenship relate to various theories of justice, democracy, community, and difference? As students read an array of texts that address these issues, and as they work in the community, they have to tackle these important questions rooted in democratic theory, practice, and critical education for citizenship. The goal of this course is to join readings and experience with intellectual development and ethical growth. In its most successful moments, the course encourages students to develop the democratic imagination and personal commitments required to be an active citizen.[42]

One compelling example of student growth involved a student working with a local food group that is responsible for distributing groceries to low-income individuals and families. She wrote in her journal and her citizen autobiography about her intense feelings of guilt and her privileged position in society when compared to the plight of the people she worked with as a part of her service experience. She came from a middle-income family in

. . . .

> **BOX 6.3**   Community Service Projects of Students in "Community, Politics, and Service" Course
>
> ――
>
> 1. Two students worked with children at a Geneva, New York, recreation center.
> 2. A student worked with the Ontario Day Care Center.
> 3. Several students worked with Project Rise, tutoring underprivileged youth in reading and literacy skills.
> 4. A student met weekly with a migrant worker's son, in an attempt to provide him with a role model for success in school.
> 5. A student volunteered with the Rochester, New York, Jewish old-age home.
> 6. A student volunteer worked with children at the agricultural business child development center.
> 7. A student volunteered weekly at "neighbors' night" for St. Stevens Church and worked with children.
> 8. A student volunteered as an AIDS buddy in Geneva, New York.
> 9. A student volunteered with the local Red Cross.
> 10. A student volunteered with AIDS Rochester/Geneva.
> 11. A student volunteered with Planned Parenthood.
> 12. A student volunteered to work with children in Operation Head Start.

. . . .

New England, a family that embraced fairly progressive political positions and had keen sensitivities to the needs of others. Nevertheless, she experienced deep anxiety about her own feelings of social distance and privilege. Ultimately, however, she worked through these emotions to grapple coherently with issues of class, race, and difference within the context of her service experience. She thereby discovered crucial elements of what it means to be a citizen.

Another student worked at the local food pantry and had a transforming interaction there one morning. He reported in class discussion that a young man who shared his birthday (and who was also the same age) came in to get food for his girlfriend and their two children. The student, who came from a privileged background, stared in the face of poverty as if he had never seen it before. What he described in class to all of us made for a spellbinding listening experience, one that helped to set a context for issues regarding inequality and poverty that helped to frame the entire course. The student later wrote about this experience in his course journal by connecting it to larger analytical issues of poverty policy. What was particularly interesting about this journal entry was how he was able to situate his interaction in the community within the context of broader public policy course themes.[43]

Other students engaged in a wide variety of community projects (see Box 6.3), ranging from work as AIDS buddies, to visiting a Rochester, New York, Jewish old-age home, to active work with the rape crisis center and the "neighborhood watch" associations. On average, they worked from two to four hours a week over the course of a fifteen-week semester.

Individual student experience varied among the service opportunities. Some students truly challenged their own value systems, whereas others had rather routine involvement with agencies. One young woman working with a women's organization confronted issues of sexual abuse that resonated with her own personal experience. Her journal indicated deep reflection about the assigned readings, particularly those discussing issues of gender and difference as well as those analyzing conditions of empowerment. Although her field experience was deeply personal, it was not so qualitatively different from the experiences of many of the other students. Most of them were able to relate their service experiences to issues of equity, justice, and care. For almost all of them, it was their first opportunity to frame their community work in a larger context of rigorous intellectual work and group reflection.

Other students encountered firsthand some of the fundamental social barriers to ethnic and racial harmony within the Geneva community. Working with neighborhood improvement groups, they witnessed the underlying racial antagonism that surrounds such issues as including low-income tenants, usually Latino or African American, in neighborhood attempts to increase safety and in cleanup campaigns. Over time, the depth of racial and class divisions became very real to them, and most students increased their determination to reduce these divisions. The ability of some of these students to grapple with race, class, and social justice concerns within the context of their service experiences is a positive reason for requiring service in appropriate college courses.[44]

At the same time, however, the course has suffered from some of the weaknesses identified by critics of service learning. For example, some students were reluctant to relate the course reading and discussion materials to politics and the broader issues of democracy and citizenship. There are several possible explanations for their unwillingness to do so. First, it is possible that the faculty facilitator was not tough enough in encouraging the students to make the appropriate connections. Yet it is difficult to be forceful in a course that is rooted in participatory democratic principles. Second, there can be little doubt that most students have been socialized to accept the basic elements of American "democracy" without the questioning or critical self-reflection that the course and the notion of critical education for citizenship requires. As a result, we should not be surprised that students are reluctant to engage in this important critical process. Third, as some critics have pointed out, it may well be that there is a flaw in the structure and nature of courses that require service to the extent that they fail to connect service appropriately to issues of democracy, politics, and citizenship, as Harry Boyte has suggested.[45] Some students probably resisted discussing issues of democracy, politics, and citizenship because in their minds, their service activities had little relevance or connection to these broader issues. In addition, some students may hold antidemocratic or elitist attitudes, views that make them fundamentally hostile to the participatory democratic vision. Finally, a few students were uncomfortable with the service learning model and offered a radical critique, one that allowed them to think of politics much more broadly in terms of community organizing, advocacy, and creating progressive social movements.

I am also convinced that one course cannot possibly tackle issues of democracy, citizenship, diversity, and difference with the kind of depth and attention to detail that such important concerns deserve. A central question underlying the course is, How are democracy, citizenship, diversity, difference, and multiculturalism connected to or disconnected from one another? One cannot just assume that these connections will be readily apparent to all students. Participation in service learning gives some students an opportunity to confront some of these concerns, but it is in the classroom that the task of making important connections must take place. One semester-long course cannot possibly do justice to the magnitude of the issues raised by service learning and the literature on democracy, citizenship, and service.

As we have seen throughout this book, there are other models of inspiring students to think about their roles as citizens that go well beyond service per se. For example, Campus Compact has created its "Raise Your Voice Campaign" for college campuses, growing out of the Wingspread Summit on Student Civic Engagement discussed in Chapter 3. The campaign has three important overarching objectives: "(1) increase college student involvement in public life and connect these actions with a larger national student movement around civic engagement; (2) document student civic engagement activities and issues that are important to college students; (3) mobilize higher education in a way that gives more voice to students and makes civic engagement central to service learning."[46] This important campaign affords students the opportunity to develop their own thoughtful, critical voices within the broader context of their campus and surrounding communities and to potentially make connections to their programs of study. In addition, the American Democracy Project for Civic Engagement provides college campuses with another useful approach to connecting students' undergraduate education with civic engagement. It is a "national, multi-campus initiative," focused on public colleges and universities that "has created a collaborative network of 199 public colleges and universities, representing more than 1.7 million students."[47]

Of course, what all this means is that students need to have opportunities to tackle important citizenship issues within the broader context of several different courses. To be sure, courses on citizenship are limited to the extent that they do not connect students directly with politics and the policymaking process. But that does not mean that such courses should be abolished. Indeed, we need more courses that allow students to think as public citizens, that link their classroom discussions with concerns in the larger society. At a time when students are socialized to think in highly private ways, they need opportunities to connect to the larger public sphere, where they will spend much of their lives. Faculty should build on the obvious commitment to public service that many students bring with them when they arrive on their campuses. Robert Putnam has pointed out:

> Young Americans in the 1990s displayed a commitment to volunteerism without parallel among their immediate predecessors. This development is the most promising sign of any that I have discovered that America might be on the cusp of a new period of civic renewal, especially if this youthful volunteerism persists into adulthood and begins to expand beyond individual caregiving to broader engagement with social and political issues.[48]

This commitment on the part of young people is clearly a source for optimism about the future. Courses in community politics, organizing, and service-based learning can build on this commitment, by addressing the goals associated with the New Citizenship and by engaging students who are alienated from the political system at large.

Civic Indifference and the New Citizenship

In this book I have provided an analysis of the sources of civic indifference and how that civic indifference is being challenged within the broader context of the New Citizenship. Low voter-turnout figures are an indicator of the citizenry's indifference to mainstream electoral politics. But as noted in Chapter 3, many citizens are angry with "American politics as usual," and this anger is reflected in two ways. The increased popularity of television and radio call-in talk shows, which are often devoted to discussions of politics, enables frustrated citizens to voice their discontent with politics and politicians. Second, the number of congressional incumbents who have chosen to leave office voluntarily in response to their perception that they will be ousted by an angry electorate, and the popularity of **term limits**, prohibiting elected officials from holding office for more than a specified number of terms, at all levels of government, indicates that the citizenry is increasingly frustrated with professional politicians. These trends do not suggest that the citizenry is indifferent to politics, but that a significant proportion of people think that they have little control over elected and non-elected government officials. Moreover, they desire more meaningful opportunities to participate in decisions that affect the quality and direction of their lives.

This last point is an important one. Despite the fact that the framers of the Constitution attempted to limit the participation by the citizenry in an effort to control the passions of the mob and promote overall system stability, they did not prevent the rise of various political and social movements that have demanded a more participatory role in public decision making at all levels of government. As we saw in Chapter 4, that demand contributed to the rise of the African American civil rights movement, which has influenced other nascent political and social movements since the 1960s. Indeed, the language of democratic ideals has been part of the American political tradition since its inception, and it is this language that serves as the basis for the New Citizenship. In his study of political and social movements, Stewart Burns offers the following analysis: "Although half the American public does not even vote, and most of the rest have experienced only a semblance of democracy, the language of democratic ideals can still inspire people because it taps into core principles of the American creed—the only real commonality that citizens of this land share."[49] Burns's discussion is important because it reminds us of the possibilities for developing new ways of conceptualizing citizenship, even within the broader context of a political and economic system that has constrained opportunities for expanding citizen democracy through the years.

The New Citizenship is steeped in participatory democratic principles, emphasizing grassroots organizing and mobilization based on community building, cooperation, alliance formation, and self-help. The New Citizenship is reflected in unconventional protest politics that mobilize the citizenry against the forces of corporate capitalism and that attempt to fight gender, racial, and sexuality discrimination. It is reflected as well in the rise of citizen organizations at the grass roots and in the proliferation of college student organizations committed to economic, social, and environmental justice. The New Citizenship encompasses, too, the commitment on college campuses to service-based learning and to giving students the opportunities to link their own interests with serving the communities in which they live. Finally, communications technology through the Internet encourages citizens who have access to computers to communicate with other citizens and to use the information available online. In this way, citizens may become better informed regarding public policies. The Internet, then, is a powerful tool of the New Citizenship.

Underlying the development of a participatory conception of citizenship is a belief that education at all levels of society should prepare students for active participation in their communities and workplaces and in public policy decision making at the grass roots. Students should think of their roles as citizens in ways that will enable them to rise above merely voting in periodic elections and venting their frustrations on call-in talk shows. A curriculum rooted in critical education for citizenship enables students to explore these possibilities and the barriers and how the barriers might be overcome. The goal should be to challenge the traditional political socialization process to the extent that it prevents discussion of alternative conceptions of citizenship. Students might be asked to consider the desirability of constructing a society that enables all citizens to have "the right and ability to play active roles in shaping the public decisions that affect their lives," and to bring "more fully under democratic control an increasing percentage of the institutions in which we function."[50] Students should have an opportunity to consider whether these goals can be accomplished without overall system civility and stability being damaged. Ultimately, the goal is to challenge civic indifference and to encourage the young to understand the development of the American democratic tradition in its appropriate historical and contemporary context. All of this is vitally important as we celebrate young people for their energy, commitment, and dedication while they work with others to address the challenges in this post–9/11 world.

Conclusion

This chapter has argued that service learning and community service are important components of the New Citizenship. Many academic proponents of service contend that if community service programs and service learning are to be successful on college campuses, they must reflect varied approaches to democratic citizenship and be grounded in democratic theory. Some of those opposed to community or public service believe that such service cannot possibly achieve all that it purports to achieve. Other critics of service point out that most service programs fail to encourage participants to deal with larger policy questions and issues. To overcome these weaknesses, any successful service-based learning program must be placed within the broader context of critical education for citizenship. In this way, service programs can challenge limited notions of citizenship reinforced by the political socialization process and, ultimately, civic indifference. Students will then have an opportunity to experience the New Citizenship in ways that enable critical reflection and engagement rooted in democratic theory and practice.

Appendix 1

The Federalist No. 10

James Madison, 1787

To the People of the State of New York

Among the numerous advantages promised by a well-constructed union, none deserves to be more accurately developed than its tendency to break and control the violence of faction. The friend of popular governments, never finds himself so much alarmed for their character and fate, as when he contemplates their propensity to this dangerous vice. He will not fail, therefore, to set a due value on any plan which, without violating the principles to which he is attached, provides a proper cure for it. The instability, injustice, and confusion introduced into the public councils, have, in truth, been the moral diseases under which popular governments have everywhere perished; as they continue to be the favourite and fruitful topics from which the adversaries to liberty derive their most specious declamations. The valuable improvements made by the American constitutions on the popular models, both ancient and modern, cannot certainly be too much admired; but it would be an unwarrantable partiality, to contend that they have as effectually obviated the danger on this side, as was wished and expected. Complaints are everywhere heard from our most considerate and virtuous citizens, equally the friends of public and private faith, and of public and personal liberty, that our governments are too unstable; that the public good is disregarded in the conflicts of rival parties; and that measures are too often decided, not according to the rules of justice, and the rights of the minor party, but by the superior force of an interested and overbearing majority. However anxiously we may wish that these complaints had no foundation, the evidence of known facts will not permit us to deny that they are in some degree true. It will be found, indeed, on a candid review of our situation, that some of the distresses under which we labour have been erroneously charged on the operation of our governments; but it will be found, at the same time, that other causes will not alone account for many of our heaviest misfortunes; and, particularly, for that prevailing and increasing distrust of public engagements, and alarm for private rights, which are echoed from one end of the continent to the other. These must be chiefly, if not wholly, effects of the unsteadiness and injustice, with which a factious spirit has tainted our public administrations.

By a faction, I understand a number of citizens, whether amounting to a majority or minority of the whole, who are united and actuated by some common impulse of passion, or of interest, adverse to the rights of other citizens, or to the permanent and aggregate interests of the community.

There are two methods of curing the mischiefs of faction: The one, by removing its causes; the other, by controlling its effects.

There are again two methods of removing the causes of faction: The one, by destroying the liberty which is essential to its existence; the other, by giving to every citizen the same opinions, the same passions and the same interests.

It could never be more truly said, than of the first remedy, that it was worse than the disease. Liberty is to faction what air is to fire, an ailment without which it instantly expires. But it could not be less folly to abolish liberty, which is essential to political life, because it nourishes faction, than it would be to wish the annihilation of air, which is essential to animal life, because it imparts to fire its destructive agency.

The second expedient is as impracticable, as the first would be unwise. As long as the reason of man continues fallible, and he is at liberty to exercise it, different opinions will be formed. As long as the connection subsists between his reason and his self-love, his opinions and his passions will have a reciprocal influence on each other; and the former will be objects to which the latter will attach themselves. The diversity in the faculties of men, from which the rights of property originate, is not less an insuperable obstacle to an uniformity of interests. The protection of these faculties is the first object of government. From the protection of different and unequal faculties of acquiring property, the possession of different degrees of kinds of property immediately results; and from the influence of these on the sentiments and views of the respective proprietors, ensues a division of the society into different interests and parties.

The latent causes of action are thus sown in the nature of man; and we see them everywhere brought into different degrees of activity, according to the different circumstances of civil society. A zeal for different opinions concerning religion, concerning government, and many other points, as well of speculation as of practice; an attachment to different leaders ambitiously contending for preeminence and power; or to persons of other descriptions whose fortunes have been interesting to the human passions, have, in turn, divided mankind into parties, inflamed them with mutual animosity, and rendered them much more disposed to vex and oppress each other, than to cooperate for their common good. So strong is this propensity of mankind, to fall into mutual animosities, that where no substantial occasion presents itself, the most frivolous and fanciful distinctions have been sufficient to kindle their unfriendly passions and excite their most violent conflicts. But the most common and durable source of factions, has been the various and unequal distribution of property. Those who hold, and those who are without property, have ever formed distinct interests in society. Those who are creditors, and those who are debtors, fall under a like discrimination. A landed interest, a manufacturing interest, a mercantile interest, a moneyed interest, with many lesser interests, grow up of necessity in civilized nations, and divide them into different classes, actuated by different sentiments and views. The regulation of these various and interfering interests forms the principal task of modern legislation, and involves the spirit of the party and faction in the necessary and ordinary operations of the government.

No man is allowed to be a judge in his own cause; because his interest will certainly bias his judgment, and, not improbably, corrupt his integrity. With equal, nay, with greater reason, a body of men are unfit to be both judges and parties at the same time; yet what are many of the most important acts of legislation, but so many judicial determinations, not indeed concerning the right of single persons, but concerning the rights of large bodies of citizens? And what are the different classes of legislators, but advocates and parties to the causes which they determine? Is a law proposed concerning private debts? It is a question to which the creditors are parties on one side, and the debtors on the other. Justice ought to hold the balance between them. Yet the parties are, and must be, themselves the judges; and the most numerous party, or in other words, the most powerful faction, must be expected to prevail. Shall domestic manufactures be encouraged, and in what degree, by restrictions on foreign manufactures? are questions which would be differently decided by the landed and the manufacturing classes; and probably by neither with a sole regard to justice and the public good. The apportionment of taxes, on the various descriptions of property, is an act which seems to require the most exact impartiality; yet there is, perhaps, no legislative act, in which greater opportunity and temptation are given to a predominant party to trample on the rules of justice. Every shilling, with which they overburden the inferior number, is a shilling saved to their own pockets.

It is in vain to say, that enlightened statesmen will be able to adjust these clashing interests, and render them all subservient to the public good. Enlightened statesmen will not always be at the helm: nor, in many cases, can such an adjustment be made at all, without taking into view indirect and remote considerations, which will rarely prevail over the immediate interest which one party may find in disregarding the rights of another, or the good of the whole.

The inference to which we are brought is, that the causes of faction cannot be removed; and that relief is only to be sought in the means of controlling its effects.

If a faction consists of less than a majority, relief is supplied by the republican principle, which enables the majority to defeat its sinister views, by regular vote. It may clog the administration, it may convulse the society; but it will be unable to execute and mask its violence under the forms of the constitution. When a majority is included in a faction, the form of popular government, on the other hand, enables it to sacrifice to its ruling passion or interest, both the public good and the rights of other citizens. To secure the public good, and private rights, against the danger of such a faction, and at the same time to preserve the spirit and the form of popular government, is then the great object to which our inquiries are directed. Let me add, that it is the great desideratum, by which alone this form of government can be rescued from the opprobrium under which it has so long laboured, and be recommended to the esteem and adoption of mankind.

By what means is this object attainable? Evidently by one of two only. Either the existence of the same passion or interest in a majority, at the same time, must be prevented; or the majority, having such coexistent passion or interest, must be rendered, by their number and local situation, unable to concert and carry into effect schemes of oppression. If the impulse and the opportunity be suffered to coincide, we well know that neither moral nor religious motives can be relied on as an adequate control. They are not found to be such on the injustice and violence of individuals, and lose their efficacy in proportion to the number combined together; that is, in proportion as their efficacy becomes needful.

From this view of the subject, it may be concluded, that a pure democracy, by which I mean a society consisting of a small number of citizens, who assemble and administer the government in person, can admit of no cure for the mischiefs of faction. A common passion or interest will, in almost every case, be felt by a majority of the whole; a communication and concert, results from the form of government itself; and there is nothing to check the inducements to sacrifice the weaker party, or an obnoxious individual. Hence, it is, that such democracies have ever been spectacles of turbulence and contention; have ever been found incompatible with personal security, or the rights of property; and have in general been as short in their lives, as they have been violent in their deaths. Theoretic politicians, who have patronized this species of government, have erroneously supposed that by reducing mankind to be a perfect equality in their political rights, they would, at the same time, be perfectly equalized and assimilated in their possessions, their opinions, and their passions.

A republic, by which I mean a government in which the scheme of representation takes place, opens a different prospect, and promises the cure for which we are seeking. Let us examine the points in which it varies from pure democracy, and we shall comprehend both the nature of the cure and the efficacy which it must derive from the union.

The two great points of difference, between a democracy and a republic, are, first, the delegation of the government, in the latter, to a small number of citizens, elected by the rest; secondly, the greater number of citizens, and greater sphere of country, over which the latter may be extended.

The effect of the first difference is, on the one hand, to refine and enlarge the public views, by passing them through the medium of a chosen body of citizens, whose wisdom may best discern the true interest of their country, and whose patriotism and love of justice, will be least likely to sacrifice it to temporary or partial considerations. Under such a regulation, it may well happen, that the public voice, pronounced by the representatives of the people, will be more consonant to the public good, than if pronounced by the people themselves, convened for the purpose. On the other hand, the effect may be inverted. Men of factious tempers, of local prejudices, or of sinister designs, may by intrigue, by corruption, or by other means, first obtain the suffrages, and then betray the interest of the people. The question resulting is, whether small or extensive republics are most favourable to the election of proper guardians of the public weal; and it is clearly decided in favour of the latter by two obvious considerations.

In the first place, it is to be remarked that, however small the republic may be, the representatives must be raised to a certain number, in order to guard against the cabals of a few; and that however large it may be, they must be limited to a certain number, in order to guard against the confusion of a multitude. Hence, the greater number of representatives in the two cases not being in proportion to that of the constituents, and being proportionally greatest in the small republic, it follows, that if the proportion of fit characters be not less in the large than in the small republic, the former will present a greater option, and consequently a greater probability of a fit choice.

In the next place, as each representative will be chosen by a greater number of citizens in the large than in the small republic, it will be more difficult for unworthy candidates to practise with success the vicious arts, by which elections are too often carried; and the suffrages of the people being more free, will be more likely to centre in men who possess the most attractive merit, and the most diffusive and established characters.

It must be confessed, that in this, as in most other cases, there is a mean, on both sides of which inconveniences will be found to lie. By enlarging too much the number of electors, you render the representatives too little acquainted with all their local circumstances and lesser interests; as by reducing it too much, you render him unduly attached to these, and too little fit to comprehend and pursue great and national objects. The federal Constitution forms a happy combination in this respect; the great and aggregate interests being referred to the national, the local and particular to the state legislatures.

The other point of difference is, the greater number of citizens, and extent of territory, which may be brought within the compass of republican, than of democratic government; and it is this circumstance principally which renders factious combinations less to be dreaded in the former, than in the latter. The smaller the society, the fewer probably will be the distinct parties and interests composing it; the fewer the distinct parties and interests, the more frequently will a majority be found of the same party; and the smaller the number of individuals composing a majority, and the smaller the compass within which they are placed, the more easily will they concert and execute their plans of oppression. Extend the sphere, and you take in a greater variety of parties and interests; you make it less probable that a majority of the whole will have a common motive to invade the rights of others citizens; or if such a common motive exists, it will be more difficult for all who feel it to discover their own strength, and to act in unison with each other. Besides other impediments, it may be remarked, that where there is a consciousness of unjust or dishonourable purposes, communication is always checked by distrust, in proportion to the number whose concurrence is necessary.

Hence, it clearly appears, that the same advantage, which a republic has over a democracy, in controlling the effects of faction, is enjoyed by a large over a small republic, is enjoyed by the union over the states composing it. Does this advantage consist in the substitution of representatives, whose enlightened views and virtuous sentiments render them superior to local prejudices, and to schemes of injustice? It will not be denied that the representation of the union will be most likely to possess these requisite endowments. Does it consist in the greater security afforded by a greater variety of parties, against the event of any one party being able to outnumber and oppress the rest? In an equal degree does the increased variety of parties, comprised within the union, increase the security? Does it, in fine, consist in the greater obstacles opposed to the concert and accomplishment of the secret wishes of an unjust and interested majority? Here, again, the extent of the union gives it the most palpable advantage.

The influence of factious leaders may kindle a flame within their particular states, but will be unable to spread a general conflagration through the other states; a religious sect may degenerate into a political faction in a part of the confederacy; but the variety of sects dispersed over the entire face of it, must secure the national councils against any danger from that source: a rage for paper money, for an abolition of debts, for an equal division of property, or for any other improper or wicked project, will be less apt to pervade the whole body of the union than a particular member of it; in the same proportion as such a malady is more likely to taint a particular county or district, than an entire state.

In the extent and proper structure of the union, therefore, we behold a republican remedy for the diseases most incident to republican government. And according to the degree of pleasure and pride we feel in being republicans, ought to be our zeal in cherishing the spirit, and supporting character of federalists.

Publius

Appendix 2

Organizations for Political, Social, and Economic Change

AIDS Organizations

AIDS Action Council
223 M Street NW, Suite 802
Washington, DC 20030
202-293-2886
www.aidsaction.org

The Gay and Lesbian Community Services Center/AIDS Action Programs
1213 North Highland
Los Angeles, CA 90038
213-464-7400
laglc.convio.net/site/PageServer

Gay Men's Health Crisis
P.O. Box 274
132 West 24th Street
New York, NY 10011
212-807-6655
www.gmhc.org

Hispanic AIDS Forum
121 Avenue of the Americas, Room 505
New York, NY 10012
212-966-6336
www.hafnyc.org

National Association of People with AIDS
P.O. Box 34056
Washington, DC 20043
202-898-0414
www.napwa.org

National Minority AIDS Council
1931 13th Street NW
Washington, DC 20009
202-483-6622
www.nmac.org

Pediatric AIDS Foundation
2407 Wilshire Boulevard, #613
Santa Monica, CA 90403
213-395-9051
1-888-499-HOPE
www.pedaids.org

Animal Rights Organizations

American Fund for Alternatives to Animal Research (AFAAR)
175 West 12th Street, Suite 16-G
New York, NY 10011
212-989-8073
www.alternativestoanimalresearch.org

American Society for the Prevention of Cruelty to Animals (ASPCA)
441 East 92nd Street
New York, NY 10128
212-876-7700
www.aspca.org

Animal Political Action Committee
P.O. Box 2706
Washington, DC 20013
703-527-1539

Animal Welfare Institute
P.O. Box 3650
Washington, DC 20007
202-337-2332
www.awionline.org

Earth Island Institute
300 Broadway, Suite 28
San Francisco, CA 94133
415-788-3666
www.earthisland.org

The Humane Society of the United
States (HSUS)
2100 L Street NW
Washington, DC 20037
www.humanesociety.org

Humane USA
www.humaneusa.org

Society for Animal Protective
Legislation
P.O. Box 3719
Washington, DC 20007
www.saplonline.org

Environmental Organizations

Alliance for Sustainable Jobs and the
Environment
P.O. Box 1361
Eureka, CA 95502
707-498-4481
asje.org

The American Conservation
Association
1350 New York Avenue NW, Suite 300
Washington, DC 20005
202-624-9365
www.undueinfluence.com/aca.htm

American Council for an Energy-
Efficient Economy (ACEEE)
1001 Connecticut Avenue NW, Suite
535
Washington, DC 20036
202-429-8873
www.aceee.org

American Forestry Association (AFA)
1516 P Street NW
Washington, DC 20005
202-667-3300
www.amfor.org

American Oceans Campaign
1427 7th Street, Suite 3
Santa Monica, CA 90401
213-576-6162
www.americanoceans.org

American Rivers, Inc.
1025 Vermont Avenue NW, Suite 720
Washington, DC 20005
202-347-7550
www.amrivers.org

Americans for the Environment
1400 16th Street NW, 2nd Floor
Washington, DC 20036
202-707-6665
www.afore.org

American Solar Energy Society
2400 Central Avenue, #B1
Boulder, CO 80301
303-443-3130
www.ases.org

Apollo Alliance for Good Jobs and
Clean Energy
1025 Connecticut Avenue, Suite 205
Washington, DC 20036
202-955-5665
apolloalliance.org

The Better World Society
1100 17th Street NW, Suite 502
Washington, DC 20036
202-331-3770
www.globalideasbank.org

Campus Climate Challenge
1616 P Street NW, Suite 340
Washington, DC 20036
202-536-2845
climatechallenge.org

Campus Ecology
122 Maryland Avenue NE
Washington, DC 20002
202-544-1681
www.nwf.org/campus

Campus Green Vote/Center for
Environmental Citizenship
c/o League of Conservation Voters
1920 L Street NW, Suite 800
Washington, DC 20036
202-454-4557

Center for Energy Efficiency and
Renewable Technology
1100 Eleventh Street, Suite 311
Sacramento, CA 95814
916-442-7785
www.ceert.org

Center for Environmental Education
(CEE)
1725 DeSales Street NW, #500
Washington, DC 20036
202-429-5609

Center for Health, Environment,
and Justice
P.O. Box 6806
Falls Church, VA 22040
703-237-2249
www.chej.org

Center for Marine Conservation
1725 DeSales Street NW, Suite 600
Washington, DC 20036
202-429-5609
www.cmc-ocean.org

Center for Science and the
Public Interest
1875 Connecticut Avenue NW, Suite
300
Washington, DC 20009
202-332-9110
www.cspinet.orgwww.cspinet.org

Ceres Investors and Environmentalists
for Sustainable Prosperity
99 Chauncy Street, 6th Floor
Boston, MA 02111
617-247-0700
ceres.org

Cities for Climate Protection
ICLEI—Local Governments for
Sustainability, USA
436 14th Street, Suite 1520
Oakland, CA 94612
510-844-0699
iclei.org

Citizens for a Better Environment
942 Market Street, #505
San Francisco, CA 94102
415-788-0690

Clean Water Action
1010 Vermont Avenue NW, Suite 1100
Washington, DC 20005-4918
202-895-0420
www.cleanwateraction.org

Climate Crisis Coalition
P.O. Box 125
South Lee, MA 01260
413-243-5665
climatecrisiscoalition.org

The Climate Institute
1785 Massachusetts Avenue, NW
Washington, DC 20036
202-547-0104
climate.org

Climate Solutions
219 Legion Way SW, Suite 201
Olympia, WA 98501-1113
360-352-1763
climatesolutions.org

The Cousteau Society
930 West 21st Street
Norfolk, VA 23517
804-627-1144
www.cousteau.org

Earth First!
P.O. Box 5871
Tucson, AZ 85703
602-622-1371
www.earthfirst.org

Earth Island Institute
300 Broadway, Suite 28
San Francisco, CA 94133
415-788-3666
www.earthisland.org

Earthjustice Legal Defense Fund
203 Hoge Building
705 Second Avenue
Seattle, WA 98104
206-343-7340
www.earthjustice.org

Energy Action Coalition
1616 P Street NW, Suite 340
Washington, DC 20036
203-887-7225
energyaction.net

Environmental Action Foundation
333 John Carlyle Street, Suite 200
Alexandria, VA 22314
703-837-5360
www.eafonline.org

Environmental Defense Fund
257 Park Avenue S
New York, NY 10010
212-505-2100 or 800-684-3322
www.edf.org

Environmental Information Center (EIC)
1400 16th Street NW, Suite 330, Box 5
Washington, DC 20036-2266
202-797-6500
EICInfo@acpa.com

US Climate Action Network
1326 14th Street NW
Washington, DC 20005
202-609-9846
usclimatenetwork.org

Environmental Opportunities

The Brubach Corporation, Publishers of Environmental Career Opportunities
P.O. Box 678
Standardsville, VA 22973
800-315-9777

Friends of the Earth
1025 Vermont Avenue NW, 3rd Floor
Washington, DC 20005
202-783-7400
www.foe.org

Global Ecovillage Network
560 Farm Road
P.O. Box 90
Summertown, TN 38483
931-964-3992
www.gaia.org

Green Seal
1730 Rhode Island Avenue NW, Suite 1050
Washington, DC 20036
202-331-7337
www.greenseal.org

Greenpeace USA
702 H Street NW, Suite 300
Washington, DC 20001
800-326-0959
www.greenpeaceusa.org

Honor the Earth
2801 Twenty-first Avenue S
Minneapolis, MN 55407
800-327-8407
www.honorearth.com

Indigenous Environmental Network
P.O. Box 485
Bemidji, MN 56601
218-751-4967
www.alphacdc.com/ien

The Institute for Local Self Reliance (ILSR)
2425 18th Street NW
Washington, DC 20009
202-232-4108
www.ilsr.org

International Council for Local Environmental Initiatives
15 Shattuck Square, Suite 215
Berkeley, CA 94704
510-540-8843
www.iclei.org

International Society for Ecology and Culture
P.O. Box 9475
Berkeley, CA 94709
510-527-3873
www.isec.org

Izaak Walton League
707 Conservation Lane
Gaithersburg, MD 20878
301-548-0150
www.iwla.org

League of Conservation Voters
2000 L Street NW, Suite 800
Washington, DC 20036
202-785-VOTE
www.lcv.org

National Audubon Society
700 Broadway
New York, NY 10003
212-979-3000
www.audubon.org/naswww.audubon.org/nas

National Environmental Trust
1200 18th Street NW, 5th Floor
Washington, DC 20036
202-887-8800
net.org

National Parks Conservation Association
1300 Nineteenth Street NW, Suite 300
Washington, DC 20036
800-628-7275
www.npca.org

National Recycling Coalition
1527 King Street, Suite 105
Alexandria, VA 22314
703-683-9025
www.nrc-recycle.org

National Resources Council of America
801 Pennsylvania Avenue SE, Suite 410
Washington, DC 20003
202-547-7553
www.nau.edu

Natural Resources Defense Council
40 West 20th Street
New York, NY 10011
212-727-2700
www.nrdc.org/nrdc

The National Toxics Campaign
1168 Commonwealth Avenue
Boston, MA 02134
617-232-0327

National Wildlife Federation
11100 Wildlife Center Drive
Reston, VA 20190
800-822-9919
www.nwf.org

The Nature Conservancy
1815 North Lynn Street
Arlington, VA 22209
703-841-5300
www.tnc.org

Northwest Ecosystem Alliance
1421 Cornwall Avenue, Suite 201
Bellingham, WA 98225
360-671-9950
www.ecosystem.org

Northwest Environment Watch
1402 Third Avenue, Suite 500
Seattle, WA 98101
206-447-1880
www.northwestwatch.org

Pesticide Action Network
965 Mission Street
San Francisco, CA 94103
415-541-9140
www.pesticideinfo.org

Rainforest Action Network
221 Pine Street, Suite 500
San Francisco, CA 94104
415-398-4404
www.ran.org

Rocky Mountain Institute
1739 Snowmass Creek Road
Old Snowmass, CO 81654-9199
303-927-3128
www.rmi.org

Sea Shepherd Conservation Society
Box 7000-S
Redondo Beach, CA 90277
213-373-6979
www.seashepherd.org

Sierra Club
85 Second Street, 2nd Floor
San Francisco, CA 94105
415-977-5500
www.sierraclub.org

Sierra Student Coalition
P.O. Box 2402
Providence, RI 02906
800-JOIN-SEC
www.ssc.org

Southern Environmental Law Center
The Candler Building
127 Peachtree Street, Suite 605
Atlanta, GA 30303
404-521-9900
www.selcge.org

Southern Organizing Committee Youth
Task Force
P.O. Box 10510
Atlanta, GA 30310
404-876-5443

Student Conservation Association, Inc.
P.O. Box 550
Charlestown, NH 03603
603-543-1700
www.sca.inc.org

Student Environmental Action
Coalition (SEAC)
P.O. Box 31909
Philadelphia, PA 19104-0609
215-222-4711
www.seac.org

Student Pugwash USA
815 15th Street NW, Suite 814
Washington, DC 20005
800-WOW-A-PUG
www.spusa.org/pugwash

Sustainable Northwest
620 SW Main Street, Suite 112
Portland, OR 97205
503-221-6911
www.sustainablenorthwest.org

Union of Concerned Scientists
2 Brattle Square
Cambridge, MA 02238
617-547-5552
www.ucsusa.org

U.S. Public Interest Research Group (USPIRG)
218 D Street SE
Washington, DC 20003
202-546-9707
www.pirg.org

The Wilderness Society
1615 M Street NW
Washington, DC 20036
1-800-THE-WILD
www.wilderness.org

World Resources Institute
10 G Street NE, Suite 800
Washington, DC 20002
202-729-7600
www.igc.org/wri

Worldwatch Institute
1776 Massachusetts Avenue NW
Washington, DC 20036
202-452-1999
www.worldwatch.org

World Wildlife Fund
1250 24th Street NW
Washington, DC 20037
800-CALL-WWF
www.wwf.org

Zero Population Growth
1400 16th Street NW, Suite 320
Washington, DC 20036
202-332-2200
www.zpg.org

Human Rights Organizations

ACORN (Association of Community Organizations for Reform Now)
88 Third Avenue, 3rd Floor
Brooklyn, NY 11217
718-246-7900
www.acorn.org

Alliance for Democracy
681 Main Street
Waltham, ME 02451
888-466-8233
www.afd-online.org

Alliance for National Renewal National Civic League, ATTN: ANR
1319 F Street NW, #204
Washington, DC 20004
202-783-2961
www.ncl.org

American Civil Liberties Union
122 Maryland Avenue NE
Washington, DC 20002
202-544-1681
www.aclu.org

American Friends Service Committee
1501 Cherry Street
Philadelphia, PA 19102
215-241-7000
www.afsc.org

Amnesty International
500 Sansome Street, Suite 615
San Francisco, CA 94111
415-291-9233
www.aiusa.org
www.amnesty.org

Bank Information Center
2025 Eye Street NW, Suite 522
Washington, DC 20006
202-466-8191
www.bicusa.org

Campus Outreach Opportunity League (COOL)
411 Washington Avenue N, Suite 110
Minneapolis, MN 55108
612-333-2665
www.cool2serve.org

Center for Democratic Renewal
P.O. Box 50469
Atlanta, GA 30302
404-221-0025
www.publiceye.org/cdr

Center for Policy Alternatives
1875 Connecticut Avenue NW, Suite 710
Washington, DC 20009
202-387-6030
www.cfpa.org

**The Center to Prevent
Handgun Violence**
1225 Eye Street NW, Suite 1100
Washington, DC 20005
202-289-7319
www.cphv.org

Coalition to Stop Gun Violence
1000 16th Street NW, Suite 603
Washington, DC 20036
202-530-0340
www.CSGV.org

Community Action Network
P.O. Box 95113
Seattle, WA 98145
206-632-1656
www.seattlecan.org

Concerned Women for America
1015 Fifteenth Street NW, Suite 1100
Washington, DC 20005
202-488-7000
www.cwfa.org

Congress of Racial Equality (CORE)
817 Broadway, 3rd Floor
New York, NY 10003
212-598-4000
www.core-online.org

**Democracy Unlimited of
Humboldt County**
761 Eighth Street
Arcata, CA 95518
707-822-2242
www.monitor.net/democracyunlimited

Democratic Socialists of America
15 Dutch Street
New York, NY 10038
212-962-0390
www.dsausa.org

Disability Rights Center
2500 Q Street NW, Suite 121
Washington, DC 20007
202-337-4119
www.drcme.org

Disability Rights Education Fund
2212 Sixth Street
Berkeley, CA 94710
415-644-2555

Economic Policy Institute
1660 L Street NW, Suite 1200
Washington, DC 20036
202-775-8810
www.epinet.org

**Educational Fund to End
Handgun Violence**
1000 16th Street NW
Washington, DC 20036
202-530-5888
www.endhandgunviolence.org

**Foundation for Community
Encouragement**
P.O. Box 17210
Seattle, WA 98107
888-784-9001
www.fce-community.org

Fund for the Feminist Majority
1600 Wilson Boulevard, Suite 704
Washington, DC 22209
703-522-2214
www.feminist.org

Handgun Control, Inc.
1225 Eye Street NW, Suite 1100
Washington, DC 20005
202-898-0792
www.handguncontrol.org

Human Rights Watch
485 Fifth Avenue
New York, NY 10017
212-972-8400
www.hrw.org

Infact
46 Plympton Street
Boston, MA 02118
617-695-2525
www.infact.org

Institute for Policy Studies
733 Fifteenth Street NW, Suite 1020
Washington, DC 20005
202-234-9382
www.ips-dc.org

International Forum on Globalization
1062 Fort Cronkhite
Sausalito, CA 94965
415-229-9350
www.ifg.org

**International Law Project
for Human, Economic and
Environmental Defense (HEED)**
National Lawyers Guild
8124 West 3rd Street, Suite 201
Los Angeles, CA 90048
213-736-1094
www.heed.net

Labor/Community Strategy Center
The Wiltern Center
3780 Wilshire Boulevard, Suite 1200
Los Angeles, CA 90010
213-387-3500
www.thestrategycenter.org

Leadership Conference on Civil Rights
2027 Massachusetts Avenue NW
Washington, DC 20036
202-667-1780
www.civilrights.org

League of Women Voters
1730 M Street NW, Suite 1000
Washington, DC 20036
202-429-1965
www.lwv.org

**Martin Luther King Jr. Center for
Nonviolent Social Change**
449 Auburn Avenue NE
Atlanta, GA 30312
404-524-1956
www.thekingcenter.com

**Mexican American Legal Defense and
Education Fund (MALDEF)**
634 South Spring Street, 11th Floor
Los Angeles, CA 90014
213-629-2512
www.maldef.org

**National Abortion Rights Action
League (NARAL)**
1156 15th Street NW, Suite 700
Washington, DC 20005
202-973-3000
www.naral.org

**National Association for the
Advancement of Colored People
(NAACP)**
4805 Mt. Hope Drive
Baltimore, MD 21215
301-358-8900
www.naacp.org

National Civic League
1445 Market Street, #300
Denver, CO 80202-1728
303-571-4343

**National Coalition to Abolish the
Death Penalty**
1419 U Street NW, Suite 104
Washington, DC 20009
202-387-3890
www.ncadp.org

**National Organization for Women
(NOW)**
733 15th Street, NW, 2nd Floor
Washington, DC 20005
202-628-8669
www.now.org

National Right to Life Committee
419 7th Street NW, Suite 500
Washington, DC 20004
202-626-8800
www.nrlc.org

National Urban League
500 East 62nd Street
New York, NY 10021
212-310-9000
www.nul.org

National Women's Political Caucus
1630 Connecticut Avenue NW, #201
Washington, DC 20009
202-785-1100
www.nwpc.org

Native American Rights Fund
1506 Broadway
Boulder, CO 80302
303-447-8760
www.narf.org

Natural Capital Institute
P.O. Box 2938
Sausalito, CA 94966
415-334-6990

The Nonviolence Web
P.O. Box 30947
Philadelphia, PA 19104
215-382-4876
www.nonviolence.org

Operation Human SERVE
622 West 113th Street, Room 410
New York, NY 10025
212-854-4053

Peace Action
1819 H Street NW, Suite 420
Washington, DC 20006
202-862-9740
www.peace-action.org

People for the American Way
2000 M Street NW, Suite 400
Washington, DC 20036
202-467-4999 or 800-326-7329
www.pfaw.org

**People Link, Institute for
Mass Communications**
423 Fifty-fourth Street
Brooklyn, NY 11220
718-238-8883
www.people-link.com

Project Underground
1916A Martin Luther King Jr. Way
Berkeley, CA 94704
510-705-8981
www.moles.org

Public Citizen
1600 Twentieth Street NW
Washington, DC 20009
800-289-3787
www.citizen.org

Public Citizen's Global Trade Watch
215 Pennsylvania Avenue SE
Washington, DC 20003
202-546-4996
www.tradewatch.org

**Public Interest Research Groups
(PIRGs)**
218 D Street SE
Washington, DC 20003
202-546-9707
www.pirg.org/uspirg

Reclaim Democracy!
P.O. Box 532
Boulder, CO 80306
303-402-0105
www.reclaimdemocracy.org

RESIST
259 Elm Street, Suite 201
Somerville, MA 02144
617-623-5110
www.resistinc.org

Servenet, Youth Service America
1101 Fifteenth Street, Suite 200
Washington, DC 20005
202-296-2992
www.servenet.org

Southern Christian Leadership Conference
334 Auburn Avenue NE
Atlanta, GA 30303
404-522-1420

Southern Poverty Law Center
400 Washington Avenue
Montgomery, AL 96104
205-264-0286
www.splcenter.org

Sweatshop Watch
310 Eighth Street, Suite 309
Oakland, CA 94607
www.sweatshopwatch.org

TransAfrica Forum
1744 R Street NW
Washington, DC 20009
202-797-2301
www.transafricaforum.org

Turning Point Project
666 Pennsylvania Avenue SE, Suite 302
Washington, DC 20003
800-249-8712
www.turnpoint.org

United for a Fair Economy/ Share the Wealth
27 Temple Place, 2nd Floor
Boston, MA 02111
617-423-2148
www.stw.org

United Students Against Sweatshops (USAS)
1413 K Street NW, 9th Floor
Washington, DC 20005
202-NO-SWEAT
www.usasnet.org

Volunteermatch ImpactOnline, Inc.
385 Grove Street
San Francisco, CA 94102
415-214-6868
www.volunteermatch.org

Women's Environment and Development Organization (WEDO)
355 Lexington Avenue
New York, NY 10017
212-973-0325
www.wedo.org

Women's International League for Peace and Freedom
1213 Race Street
Philadelphia, PA 19107
215-563-7110
www.wilpf.org

Women's Legal Defense Fund
2000 P Street NW
Washington, DC 20036
202-887-0364

WTO History Project
Center for Labor Studies
University of Washington
Box 353530
Seattle, WA 98195
206-543-7946
www.depts.washington.edu/pcls

Human Welfare Organizations

Big Brothers/Big Sisters of America
230 North 13th Street
Philadelphia, PA 19107
215-567-7000
www.bbbsa.org

Campus Compact— The Project for Public and Community Service Brown University
P.O. Box 1975
Providence, RI 02912
401-863-1119

CARE
151 Ellis Street NE
Atlanta, GA 30303-2439
800-521-CARE, ext. 999
www.care.org

Children's Defense Fund
122 C Street NW
Washington, DC 20001
202-628-8787
www.childrensdefense.org

City Year, Inc.
11 Stillings Street
Boston, MA 02210
617-350-0700

Coalition for the Homeless
500 8th Avenue, Room 910
New York, NY 10018
212-695-8700

FARM AID
P.O. Box 228
Champaign, IL 61824
800-FARM-AID or 617-354-2922
www.farmaid.org

Food Research and Action Center
1875 Connecticut Avenue NW, Suite 540
Washington, DC 20009
202-986-2200
www.frac.org

Habitat for Humanity
Habitat and Church Streets
Americus, GA 31709-3498
800-422-4828
www.habitat.org

Institute for Community Economics
57 School Street
Springfield, MA 01105-1311
413-746-8660
www.icelt.org

Literacy Volunteers of America
5795 Widewaters Parkway
Syracuse, NY 10038
212-445-8000
www.literacyvolunteers.org

National Coalition for the Homeless
1012 Fourteenth Street NW, Suite 600
Washington, DC 20005
202-737-6444
http://nch.ari.net

National Law Center on Homelessness and Poverty
1411 K Street NW, Suite 1400
Washington, DC 20005
202-638-2535
www.nlchp.org

National Low Income Housing Coalition
1012 14th Street NW, Suite 1006
Washington, DC 20005
202-662-1530
www.nlihc.org

National Student Campaign Against Hunger and Homelessness
29 Temple Place
Boston, MA 02111
617-292-4823

Overseas Development Network (ODN)
333 Valencia Street, Suite 330
San Francisco, CA 94103
415-431-4204
www.nonprofits.org/gallery/alpha/odn

Oxfam America
26 West Street
Boston, MA 02111-1206
617-482-1211 or 800-776-9326
www.oxfamamerica.org

Peace Corps
P-301
Washington, DC 20526
800-424-8580
www.peacecorps.gov

Public Allies
633 W Wisconsin Avenue, Suite 610
Milwaukee, WI 53203
414-273-0533
www.publicallies.org

Save the Children
50 Wilton Rd.
Westport, CT 06880
203-226-7272 or 800-243-5075
www.savethechildren.org

Student Coalition for Action at Literacy Education (SCALE)
University of North Carolina at Chapel Hill, CB# 3505
140H East Franklin Street
Chapel Hill, NC 27599-3505
919-962-1542
www.unc.edu/depts/scale

Wellstone Action
821 Raymond Avenue, Suite 260
St. Paul, MN 55114
651-645-3939
www.wellstone.org

Youth on Board
58 Day Street, 3rd Floor
P.O. Box 440322
Somerville, MA 02144
617-623-9900
www.youthonboard.org

Lesbian and Gay Organizations

ACLU National Gay Rights Project
6333 South Shatto Street, Suite 207
Los Angeles, CA 90048
213-487-1720

Basic Rights Oregon
P.O. Box 40625
Portland, OR 97240
503-222-6151
www.basicrights.org

Gay and Lesbian Advocates and Defenders
294 Washington Street, Suite 740
Boston, MA 02108
617-426-2020

Gay and Lesbian Alliance Against Defamation (GLADD)
8455 Beverly Boulevard, Suite 305
Los Angeles, CA 90048
800-GAY-MEDIA
www.gladd.org

The Gay and Lesbian Victory Fund
1012 14th Street NW, Suite 1000
Washington, DC 20005
202-842-8679
www.victoryfund.org

Human Rights Campaign (HRC)
1640 Rhode Island Avenue, NW
Washington, DC 20036
202-628-4160
www.hrc.org

Lambda Legal Defense and Education Fund, Inc.
120 Wall Street, Suite 1500
New York, NY 10005
212-809-8585
www.lambda.legal.org

Log Cabin Republicans
1633 Q Street NW, #210
Washington, DC 20009
202-347-5306
www.lcr.org

National Gay and Lesbian Task Force
1700 Kalorama Road NW
Washington, DC 20009
202-332-6483
www.ngltf.org

National Youth Advocacy Coalition
1638 R Street NW, Suite 300
Washington, DC 20009
202-719-7596
www.nyacyouth.org

Parents, Families, and Friends of Lesbians and Gays (PFLAG)
1726 M Street NW, Suite 400
Washington, DC 20036
202-467-8180
www.pflag.org

Servicemembers Legal Defense Network (SLDN)
P.O. Box 63013
Washington, DC 20009
202-328-3244
www.sldn.org

Democracy Web Sites on the Internet

Brennan Center for Justice:
http://breannancenter.org

Center for Responsive Politics:
www.opensecrets.org

Change-Congress.org:
http://change-congress.org

Common Cause:
www.commoncause.org

DC Vote: www.dcvote.org

Demos.org: http://demos.org

FairVote: http://fairvote.org

Free Press: www.freepress.net

New America Foundation:
www.newamerica.net/programs/political_reform

New Voters Project:
www.newvotersproject.org

Public Campaign:
www.publicampaign.org

Sentencing Project:
www.sentencingproject.org

WhyTuesday.org:
www.whytuesday.org

Discussion Questions

Chapter 2

1. How did the constitutional framers attempt to prevent factions and provide for overall system stability?

2. What are the central elements of the participatory democratic model? In what specific ways can participatory citizen politics be distinguished from conventional politics?

3. What are the central arguments associated with the critique of the participatory model?

4. According to those who support the democratic theory of elitism, what role should the citizenry play in the American political system? How do supporters of the democratic theory of elitism justify their conclusions? In answering these questions, be sure to discuss the critique of the participatory model.

5. In what specific ways does the thinking of the framers of the Constitution support the democratic theory of elitism? What specific roles did the framers perceive that citizens should play in their newly created political and economic system?

6. To what extent does the day-to-day operation of the American political system discourage citizens from participating meaningfully in politics? Can this be overcome? If so, how?

7. What are the consequences of the American radical individualistic impulse for developing a more public and participatory citizenry?

8. In what specific ways is the American political socialization process a significant barrier to developing the kind of critical citizenry that is at the core of the New Citizenship and the participatory democratic tradition? If political socialization is a barrier, can it be overcome? If so, how?

Chapter 3

1. What empirical evidence supports the claim that Americans are increasingly displaying civic indifference?

2. In what specific ways does voter turnout in presidential and off-year elections reflect a detached and apathetic citizenry?

3. What specific factors account for low voter turnout in both presidential and off-year elections? As you answer this question, be sure to incorporate individual and structural explanations.

4. What do the qualitative surveys of voters' attitudes concerning politics and political participation discussed in Chapter 3 suggest regarding civic indifference?

5. In what ways have citizens been displaying their anger toward politicians and politics?

6. What evidence exists to suggest that young people are largely apathetic, uninterested, and indifferent when it comes to politics? What evidence is there to suggest that this negative claim about young people is untrue?

7. What explanations might account for the indifference of some college students toward politics?

8. What evidence suggests that college students might become more actively involved in politics, provided that politics is reconceptualized?

9. What specific contributions have members of the Millennial Generation offered to American politics? What contributions might this generation offer in future?

10. In what ways does the Millennial Generation reinforce and challenge previous assumptions regarding civic indifference?

11. To what extent does the American political system need a significant amount of civic indifference for it to survive and thrive?

Chapter 4

1. What is the connection between the civil rights movement of the 1950s and 1960s and unconventional politics in the 1980s and 1990s?

2. How does the civil rights movement provide a concrete and useful example of a way to achieve a renewal of democratic citizenship at the national level?

3. What were the central goals of the civil rights movement? How did the movement attempt to accomplish these goals?

4. Why are the citizenship schools important for understanding the civil rights movement and its connection to the New Citizenship? What was the central goal of the Crusade for Citizenship program?

5. In what specific ways did the efforts of SCLC (Southern Christian Leadership Conference) in the 1950s provide a foundation for political, educational, and social change?

6. In what ways did the sit-ins and the emergence of SNCC (Student Nonviolent Coordinating Committee) have a profound national impact on activist-oriented students at predominantly white northern colleges and universities?

7. Just what is the enduring legacy of the civil rights movement?

8. In what ways are the consequences of the civil rights movement still being felt today in the larger society and on college campuses? What are the connections that can be made between the civil rights movement and the development of the New Citizenship?

9. How do organizations such as ACT UP, Earth First!, Operation Rescue, and the militias potentially undermine civility and overall system stability? Are there parallels between these organizations and Shays's Rebellion of the eighteenth century?

Chapter 5

1. What are the sources of the Me Generation? To what extent is the term an accurate description of young people who came of age during the 1970s and 1980s? How do we even know that a Me Generation even existed?

2. Outline the central components of the New Citizenship, as described in Chapter 5. What are the sources of each of these components? To what extent do each of them challenge the civic indifference dilemma?

3. What constitutes the "new populism"?

4. In what ways do Alinsky-style neighborhood organizations embrace elements of the "new populism"?

5. Provide an overview of the various neighborhood organizations discussed in Chapter 5. In what ways are these organizations similar to one another? How do they differ from one another?

6. In what specific ways do the student organizations discussed in Chapter 5 challenge civic indifference? What are the strengths of these organizations? What are their limitations?

7. Why might the Internet be considered a key element of the New Citizenship? What connections can be made between the Internet and expanding democracy? What are the limitations and weaknesses of the Internet?

8. How are we going to live in a society that encourages people to assert their identities and celebrate their differences, while maintaining the community, stability, and civility of that society?

Chapter 6

1. What role do you think that the citizenry *should* play in the American political system? What role *can* the citizenry play, according to the analysis provided in this book?

2. What are the characteristics of "critical education for citizenship"?

3. Outline the four models of citizenship education discussed in Chapter 6. What do you perceive to be the strengths and weaknesses associated with each of them?

4. How can service learning on college campuses be connected to the New Citizenship?

5. What is the connection between service learning and politics?

6. Outline the basic elements of President Clinton's national service plan. What do you perceive to be the strengths and weaknesses of his plan?

7. What is President Barack Obama's approach to national service? In what ways is his approach similar to or different from those of President Clinton and President Bush?

8. Outline the critique of service. How might proponents of service-based learning respond to this critique?

9. What are the connections between service learning and a liberal arts education?

10. How is civic indifference being challenged by the elements of the New Citizenship, as described in this book? What are the barriers to the continued development of the New Citizenship as we head into the twenty-first century? Can those barriers be overcome? If so, how?

11. In what specific ways does the New Citizenship support the participatory democratic model outlined in Chapter 2?

12. How does civic indifference support the democratic theory of elitism, as discussed in Chapter 2?

13. How can educators inspire their students to transcend their narrow self-interests within the context of a political and economic framework that often reinforces the politics of privatism? What role might service learning play in helping educators to accomplish this goal?

Glossary

Boycott. A refusal to engage in business with or buy the products or services of a person or company or even a public utility. This nonviolent method of protest, a kind of unconventional politics, was used to great success during the civil rights movement in the 1950s and 1960s. One of the most famous boycotts was the Montgomery Bus Boycott of 1957, which evolved after Rosa Parks was arrested for refusing to give up her seat in the white section of a public bus. After her arrest, Montgomery African Americans called a mass meeting and voted to boycott all city buses. Car pools were formed to transport African Americans throughout Montgomery and many people walked long distances. See also **unconventional politics**.

Brown v. Board of Education. Landmark case in which the Supreme Court in 1954 unanimously declared that schools segregated by race were unconstitutional. The court thereby overturned the *Plessy v. Ferguson* decision (1896), which had established the separate but equal doctrine.

Citizenship schools. Central components of the Southern Christian Leadership Conference's (SCLC's) Citizenship Education Program, citizenship schools taught many illiterate rural African Americans to read and write, skills that were needed for them to pass difficult literacy tests that authorities used to prevent poorer citizens of both races from voting. The schools formed a foundation for the entire civil rights movement in the Deep South during the late 1950s.

Civil society. The middle ground between the private sector and the government. Rather than where people buy or sell or vote in elections, civil society is where they meet with their neighbors to plan community events and to organize community block-watch programs. People work there voluntarily and share a concern for the larger public, rather than private, interests. See also **private sphere**.

Classical liberalism. The underlying ideology in America, promoting such values as individualism, equality of opportunity, liberty and freedom, the rule of law, and limited government. The constitutional framers, influenced by eighteenth-century theorists John Locke and Adam Smith, embraced classical liberal principles from the outset. See also **liberal democracy**.

Critical education for citizenship. Education aimed at training citizens to participate in public problem-solving and political action. This broad approach to democracy and citizenship is rooted in the participatory democratic vision.

Crusade for Citizenship program. The portion of the civil rights movement that embraced citizenship schools throughout the South and attempted to empower African American citizens through education.

Deindustrialization of America. The process that has occurred since the 1970s whereby factories in the Northeast and Midwest shut down or reduce production, eliminating blue-collar jobs, whereas new jobs are created primarily in the West and Southwest. The new jobs often require more highly skilled and educated people, particularly people with computer skills.

Democratic theory of elitism. Proponents of this theory believe that elites in power should make the crucial decisions facing society and that citizens should be rather passive in politics, generally participating by voting for competing elites in periodic elections. Democratic elitists argue that the role expected of the citizen in a participatory setting is unrealistic and that too much participation will contribute to the instability of the political and economic system. See also **participatory democracy.**

Democratic Leadership Council (DLC). The goal of the council was to overhaul the Democratic party's liberal image and move the party to the center of the ideological spectrum, especially on social issues. The DLC was formed in 1985 by a group of elected officials, including Senator Charles Robb of Virginia, Representative Dick Gephardt of Missouri, then-governor Bruce Babbitt of Arizona, and Senator Sam Nunn of Georgia as well as several political operatives. Bill Clinton was also an early member.

End of ideology. A phrase coined in the late 1950s by sociologist Daniel Bell, referring to an America characterized by widespread consensus on basic American values, including individualism, equality of opportunity, and limited government.

Focus group. A group of citizens representing a cross section of the United States, brought together by professional pollsters to respond to a candidate's or political officeholder's policies or views. Focus groups have long been used in advertising as a way to gauge the public's response to advertising slogans and commercials.

Freedom rides. In 1961 black and white volunteers rode buses in the South in a challenge to the refusal to desegregate bus stations and interstate buses. Those who engaged in these acts of **nonviolent civil disobedience** were called "freedom riders"; they were beaten and stoned by whites for attempting to sit in the "whites-only" sections of interstate buses and terminals.

Gerrymandering. The act of manipulating the shape of legislative districts to produce a majority of votes for the political party in control of the state legislature. The term is derived from the legislative redistricting efforts of Governor Elbridge Gerry of Massachusetts in 1812, who drew wildly shaped districts for political purposes.

Grandfather clause. Denial of the right to vote to all whose grandfathers were slaves, a device used in the late nineteenth and early twentieth centuries by the southern states in an effort to prevent black suffrage. The grandfather clause is one of many examples of how the South avoided the racial changes ushered in by Reconstruction. In *Guinn v. United States* (1915), the Supreme Court declared the grandfather clause unconstitutional.

Great Society. Term that President Lyndon Johnson used to describe his policies, including the War on Poverty, Model Cities, Medicare and Medicaid, the Civil Rights Act of 1964, and the Voting Rights Act of 1965.

Hobbesian. Adjective referring to the ideas of Thomas Hobbes (1588–1679), the political philosopher whose most famous work was *The Leviathan* (1651). In this work Hobbes outlined a negative conception of humanity and a society characterized by "warre of every one against every one." In addition, he claimed that life is "solitary, poore, nasty, brutish, and short." Some of the constitutional framers embraced a Hobbesian conception of human nature.

Initiative. A proposal for a law, initiated by citizens and placed on the ballot through a petition with the signatures of a specified number of voters. The increased use of the initiative is an example of the attempt by citizens to challenge the existing political system to be more open to citizen concerns.

Liberal democracy. A political and economic framework that rejects excessive interference from the federal government in the private sphere and promotes the right of the individual to pursue his/her own interests in the economic marketplace. Those who embrace liberal democracy believe that political elites chosen by the citizenry in periodic elections should be the principal decision makers. See also **classical liberalism.**

Literacy tests. Voter-qualification tests imposed by some states, largely in the South, used to deny African Americans the right to vote. The Civil Rights Act of 1964 was designed to end all racial discrimination, including the imposition of literacy tests as a barrier to voting.

Millennial Generation. Those citizens born between 1985 and 2004, whose most defining characteristic is an ability to use the Internet and other forms of technology to engage politics and organizing in interesting and sophisticated ways. The 2008 presidential election is the first election in which these citizens were galvanized to participate in the political process.

Mississippi Freedom Summer. The summer of 1964, when one thousand college student volunteers, many from prominent northern white families, went to Mississippi in an organized effort to highlight white violence against blacks. Civil rights activists, including Robert Moses, felt that attacks on white college students would receive national attention and more likely prompt federal action than the continuing and long-standing beatings of African Americans in Mississippi and elsewhere in the South.

New Democrat. Term used to describe those Democrats who have rejected the tenets of modern liberalism and have attempted to change their image and steer their party in a more "moderate" direction. Those who adhere to the New Democrat label generally reject an activist federal government role in social policy and tend to endorse "workfare," tougher sanctions on criminals, and public/private partnerships in dealing with urban problems. See also the **Democratic Leadership Council (DLC).**

New populism. Movement that challenges the inordinate influence of policy elites and seeks to win power and build organizations that are controlled by working-class people.

NIMBY. Acronym of "not in my backyard," the slogan of citizens who organize to protest the siting of dangers to the environment, such as nuclear waste repositories, mass burn incinerators, and toxic waste treatment plants, in their communities. NIMBY warns businesses and politicians that products must be made to produce the least waste possible and that factories must be environmentally sound and non-polluting. Some have argued that people who act on the basis of NIMBY are destructive because they put the interests of individual neighborhoods ahead of the interests of the larger society.

Nonviolent civil disobedience. The deliberate breaking of an "unjust" law, combined with the willingness to accept the legal consequences of that action. Martin Luther King Jr., a follower of the practices of Gandhi, argued that nonviolent civil disobedience had to be a central component of the civil rights movement. It was a successful vehicle for attracting media coverage, for helping to dramatize the grievances of African Americans, and for highlighting racial injustices. It has been used with great success by other groups in recent years, including ACT UP and Earth First!

Off-year elections. Elections at a time when a presidential election is not taking place. Voter-turnout figures in such elections are generally quite low, often well below 40 percent of the eligible voting electorate.

Participatory democracy. A political theory that embraces active participation by the citizenry in community and workplace decision making at the local level. It is rooted in the notion that "whatever touches all should be judged by all." To participatory democrats, democracy means much more than voting for competing elites in periodic elections. They believe that active participation in politics will lead to the development of the individual and the individual's realization of citizenship, one that is rooted in a positive conception of liberty. In a true participatory setting, citizens do not merely act as autonomous individuals pursuing their own interests. Instead, through a process of decision, debate, and compromise, they link their concerns with the needs of the community. See also **democratic theory of elitism**.

Partisan attachment. The strong relationship that some citizens have to political parties, policies, candidates, and/or elected officials. Partisan attachment holds political parties together. In recent years it has been declining along with the decline of political parties and the rise of independent voters and split electoral outcomes.

Political alienation. The distancing from the political system characteristic of citizens who are so frustrated, angry, or cynical about the government that they do not vote or participate in any form of political activity.

Political efficacy. The ability of a citizen to understand and to participate in politics as well as the sense that one's participation in politics can make a difference in influencing governmental responses.

Political mobilization. The process by which citizens are galvanized to participate in politics. Political mobilization strategies are embraced by political and social movements and organizations as well as by political elites.

Political socialization. The process by which citizens acquire their attitudes and beliefs regarding the political system in which they live and their roles within that system. Key political socialization agents are the family, schools, peers, the media, religious institutions, and the workplace.

Poll tax. A state-imposed tax on voters. Generally between $1 and $5, it was widely used in the South as one of several ways to prevent African Americans from exercising the franchise. The Twenty-fourth Amendment (1964) rendered the poll tax unconstitutional in national elections. See also **grandfather clause**.

Private sphere. That which relates to an individual's interest and life, as opposed to the **public sphere**. See also **liberal democracy** and **classical liberalism**.

Public good. The good that we seek in common and that attempts to link individual interests with larger community concerns. It aims to forge common ground, consensus, and collaborative forms of decision making.

Public sphere. The arena of intersection between an individual's interests and those of the larger community.

Redlining. The process by which urban financial institutions refuse to grant home mortgage loans in areas that are thought to be poor risks regardless of the financial situations of the people who apply for such loans. As a result, the areas in question suffer economic decline, as houses cannot be updated or improved. Financial institutions literally draw red lines around these areas on a map; hence, the label *redlining*.

Referendum. System by which a law previously approved by elected officials is referred to the ballot either by the officials or by citizen petition. The referendum is an increasingly popular mechanism for citizens to challenge existing policies.

Southern Christian Leadership Conference (SCLC). Organization founded by Rev. Martin Luther King Jr. in 1957; its goal was to achieve full civil rights for African Americans. An integral part of the civil rights movement, the SCLC had a strong religious base and was steeped in the principles of nonviolent civil disobedience. It continues to have influence in civil rights matters, largely in the South.

Term limits. Legislation prohibiting elected officials from serving in any one office for more than a specified number of terms, thus ensuring rotation. Term limits have gained in popularity in recent years as voters perceive that some elected officials have lost touch with their constituencies. Recognizing the anti-incumbency mood and the popularity of term limits, some candidates for election have embraced them as central elements of their campaigns.

Unconventional politics. A form of politics that requires participants to go outside the formal channels of the American political system (voting, interest group politics) and embrace the politics of protest and mass involvement. Unconventional politics was employed with great success by the civil rights movement and has been used in contemporary American politics by groups across the ideological spectrum, including Earth First!, ACT UP, Operation Rescue, and the militias.

Notes

Chapter 1

1. Howell Raines, *My Soul Is Rested: The Story of the Civil Rights Movement in the Deep South* (New York: Penguin, 1977).
2. Theda Skocpol, *Diminished Democracy: From Membership to Management in American Civic Life* (Norman: University of Oklahoma Press, 2003), 247.
3. Lester W. Milbrath, *Political Participation* (Chicago: Rand McNally,1965), 20.
4. Lizzy Ratner, "Generation Recession," *The Nation* (November 23, 2009): 23.

Chapter 2

1. Craig A. Rimmerman, *Presidency by Plebiscite* (Boulder: Westview Press, 1993).
2. Seymour Martin Lipset, *The First New Nation* (New York: Norton, 1979).
3. Richard Hofstadter, "The Founding Fathers: An Age of Realism," in *The Moral Foundations of the American Republic,* 3rd ed., ed. Robert Horwitz, 63 (Charlottesville: University of Virginia Press, 1986).
4. James MacGregor Burns, *The Power to Lead: The Crisis of the American Presidency* (New York: Simon & Schuster, 1984), 105–106.
5. Ibid., 106.
6. John Patrick Diggins, *The Lost Soul of American Politics: Virtue, Self-Interest, and the Foundations of Liberalism* (Chicago: University of Chicago Press, 1984), 53.
7. Benjamin R. Barber, *Strong Democracy: Participatory Politics for a New Age* (Berkeley: University of California Press, 1984), 48.
8. David Mathews, *Politics for People: Finding a Responsible Public Voice* (Urbana: University of Illinois Press, 1994), 51.
9. John F. Manley and Kenneth M. Dolbeare, *The Case Against the Constitution* (Armonk, N.Y.: M. E. Sharpe, 1987), x.
10. Jackson Turner Main, *The Antifederalists: Critics of the Constitution, 1781–1788* (Chicago: University of Chicago Press, 1961), 52.
11. Lawrence J. R. Herson, *The Politics of Ideas: Political Theory and American Public Policy* (Homewood, Ill.: Dorsey Press, 1984).
12. Robert N. Bellah et al., *Habits of the Heart: Individualism and Commitment in American Life* (New York: Harper & Row, 1985), 204.
13. Ibid., 294.
14. Sheldon Wolin, *The Presence of the Past: Essays on the State and the Constitution* (Baltimore, Md.: Johns Hopkins University Press, 1989), 5.
15. Lipset, *First New Nation,* 208.

16. Suzanne W. Morse, ed., *Politics for the Twenty-First Century: What Should Be Done on Campus?* (Dubuque, Iowa: Kettering Foundation, 1992), 3.

17. Bellah et al., *Habits of the Heart*, 112.

18. Richard Flacks, *Making History* (New York: Columbia University Press, 1988), 51.

19. William E. Hudson, *American Democracy in Peril: Seven Challenges to America's Future* (Chatham, N.J.: Chatham House, 1995), 31.

20. Michael Kammen, *A Machine That Would Go by Itself: The Constitution in American Culture* (New York: Alfred A. Knopf, 1986).

21. Alexis de Tocqueville, *Democracy in America,* ed. Richard Heffner. (New York: Mentor Books, 1956), 61.

22. Hudson, *American Democracy in Peril,* 19.

23. Rimmerman, *Presidency by Plebiscite*, esp. 126–132.

24. Carole Pateman, *Participation and Democratic Theory* (Cambridge: Cambridge University Press, 1970); C. B. Macpherson, *The Life and Times of Liberal Democracy* (Oxford: Oxford University Press, 1976); and Ronald M. Mason, *Participatory and Workplace Democracy: A Theoretical Development in the Critique of Liberalism* (Carbondale: Southern Illinois University Press, 1982).

25. Isaiah Berlin, *Four Essays on Liberty* (Oxford: Oxford University Press, 1969).

26. Pateman, *Participation and Democratic Theory.*

27. Barber, *Strong Democracy.*

28. Mathews, *Politics for People,* 111.

29. Ibid., 112.

30. Hudson, *American Democracy in Peril,* 20.

31. Mathews, *Politics for People,* 125.

32. Ibid., 125–126.

33. Ibid., 136–137.

34. Peter Bachrach, *The Theory of Democratic Elitism: A Critique* (Boston: Little, Brown, 1971), 8.

35. Daniel C. Kramer, *Participatory Democracy: Developing Ideals of the Political Left* (Cambridge, Mass.: Schenkman, 1972), 128.

36. Martin Oppenheimer, "The Limitations of Socialism: Some Sociological Observations on Participatory Democracy," in *The Case for Participatory Democracy,* ed. C. George Benello and Dimitrios Roussopoulos (New York: Viking, 1971), 281.

37. Jane J. Mansbridge, *Beyond Adversary Democracy* (New York: Basic Books, 1980), 302.

38. Ibid., 100.

39. Michael Peter Smith, *The City and Social Theory* (New York: St. Martin's Press, 1979), 263.

40. Hudson, *American Democracy in Peril,* 15.

41. Bernard Berelson, Paul Lazarsfeld, and William McPhee, *Voting* (Chicago: University of Chicago Press, 1954), 314.

42. Ibid., 29.

43. Joseph Schumpeter, *Capitalism, Socialism, and Democracy.* 3rd ed. (New York: Harper & Row, 1950), 269.

44. Samuel P. Huntington, "The United States," in *The Crisis of Democracy,* ed. Michel Crozier, Samuel P. Huntington, and Joji Watnanuki, 113 (New York: New York University Press, 1975).

45. Theodore J. Lowi, *The End of Liberalism: The Second Republic of the United States,* 2nd ed. (New York: Norton, 1979), 56.

46. Ibid., 311–312.

47. Robert D. Putnam, *Making Democracy Work: Civic Traditions in Modern Italy* (Princeton, N.J.: Princeton University Press, 1993), 87–91.

48. Berlin, *Four Essays on Liberty.*

49. Mathews, *Politics for People,* 114.

Chapter 3

1. E. J. Dionne Jr., *Why Americans Hate Politics* (New York: Simon & Schuster, 1991).

2. William Greider, *Who Will Tell the People?* (New York: Simon & Schuster, 1992), 13.

3. Barack Obama, *Dreams from My Father: A Story of Race and Inheritance,* rev. ed. (New York: Three Rivers Press, 2004), 454.

4. Robert D. Putnam, *Bowling Alone: The Collapse and Revival of American Community* (New York: Simon & Schuster, 2000), 31.

5. Abby Kiesa et al., *Millennials Talk Politics: A Study of College Student Political Engagement* (College Park, Md.: CIRCLE, 2007), 4.

6. Morley Winograd and Michael D. Hais, *Millennial Makeover: MySpace, You Tube, and the Future of American Politics* (New Brunswick, N.J.: Rutgers University Press, 2008), 1.

7. Russell J. Dalton, *The Good Citizen: How a Younger Generation Is Reshaping American Politics* (Washington, D.C.: CQ Press, 2008), 171.

8. William E. Hudson, *American Democracy in Peril: Seven Challenges to America's Future* (Chatham, N.J.: Chatham House, 1995), 112.

9. Ibid.

10. David Mathews, *Politics for People: Finding a Responsible Public Voice* (Urbana: University of Illinois Press, 1994), 29.

11. Steven J. Rosenstone and John Mark Hansen, *Mobilization, Participation, and Democracy in America* (New York: Macmillan, 1993), 58.

12. Ibid., 4–5.

13. Frances Fox Piven and Richard A. Cloward, *Why Americans Don't Vote* (New York: Pantheon, 1988), 113.

14. Rosenstone and Hansen, *Mobilization, Participation, and Democracy in America,* 15.

15. Ibid., 14.

16. Ibid., 229.

17. Putnam, *Bowling Alone,* 33.

18. Martin P. Wattenberg, *Where Have All the Voters Gone?* (Cambridge: Harvard University Press, 2002), 2.

19. Piven and Cloward, *Why Americans Don't Vote,* 113.

20. Ibid., 119.

21. Ibid., 209.

22. Frances Fox Piven and Richard A. Cloward, *Why Americans Still Don't Vote: And Why Politicians Want It That Way* (Boston: Beacon Press, 2000).

23. Peter Dreier, "Detouring the Motor-Voter Law," *The Nation* (October 1994): 490.

24. Frances Fox Piven and Richard A. Cloward, "Northern Bourbons: A Preliminary Report on the National Voter Registration Act," *PS: Political Science and Politics* (March 1996): 39–42.

25. Piven and Cloward, *Why Americans Still Don't Vote,* viii.

26. Alexander Keyssar, *The Right to Vote: The Contested History of Democracy in the United States* (New York: Basic Books, 2000), 315.

27. Thomas E. Patterson, *The Vanishing Voter: Public Involvement in an Age of Uncertainty* (New York: Knopf, 2002), 132.

28. Ibid., 58.

29. Hudson, *American Democracy in Peril,* 121.

30. Robert D. Putnam, "Bowling Alone: America's Declining Social Capital," *Journal of Democracy* 6, no. 1 (January 1995): 66.

31. Ibid.

32. Putnam, *Bowling Alone,* 41.

33. Robert D. Putnam, "The Strange Disappearance of Civic America," *American Prospect,* no. 24 (Winter 1996): 34.

34. Putnam, *Bowling Alone,* 19.

35. Putnam, "Bowling Alone," 75.

36. Putnam, *Bowling Alone,* 231.

37. Putnam, "Bowling Alone," 65.

38. Robert D. Putnam, "A Better Society in a Time of War," *New York Times,* October 19, 2001, A19.

39. Matthew A. Crenson and Benjamin Ginsberg, *Downsizing Democracy: How America Sidelined Its Citizens and Privatized Its Public* (Baltimore, Md.: Johns Hopkins University Press, 2002), 2.

40. Theda Skocpol, *Diminished Democracy: From Membership to Management in American Civic Life* (Norman: University of Oklahoma Press, 2003), 10.

41. Mathews, *Politics for People,* 34.

42. Harwood Group, *Citizens and Politics: A View from Main Street America* (Dayton, Ohio: Kettering Foundation, 1991); Mathews, *Politics for People,* 11.

43. Hudson, *American Democracy in Peril,* 131.

44. Harwood Group, *Citizens and Politics.*

45. Mathews, *Politics for People,* 12.

46. www.pew-partnership.org/pubs/rwa/printable/summary.html.

47. Susan Tolchin, *The Angry American: How Voter Rage Is Changing the Nation* (Boulder, Colo.: Westview Press, 1996), 4–5.

48. Katherine Isaac, *Civics for Democracy: A Journey for Teachers and Students* (Washington, D.C.: Essential Books, 1992), 171.

49. Mathews, *Politics for People,* 12.

50. Sean Wilentz, "Pox Populi," *New Republic* (August 9, 1993): 33.

51. Ibid., 29.

52. Stanley B. Greenberg, Al From, and Will Marshall, *The Road to Realignment: The Democrats and the Perot Voters* (Washington, D.C.: Democratic Leadership Council, 1993), II-2.

53. George Dance, "Ron Paul Helps Launch Young Americans for Liberty" (December 7, 2008); available at www.nolanchart.com/article5610.html.

54. Ibid.

55. Howard Fineman, "The Power of Talk," *Newsweek* (February 8, 1993): 25.

56. Ibid., 27.

57. Patterson, *Vanishing Voter,* 21.

58. Suzanne W. Morse, ed., *Politics for the Twenty-First Century: What Should Be Done on Campus?* (Dubuque, Iowa: Kettering Foundation, 1992), 2.

59. Damien Cave, "Mock the Vote," *Rolling Stone* (May 27, 2004): 47.

60. Richard Morin and Dan Balz, "Children of the Tuned-in Find Politics a Turnoff: Offspring of '60's Generation Bored by Process," *Washington Post,* June 17, 1992, A1.

61. www.neglection2000.org/voting/behavior.html.

62. www.childtrendsdatabank.org/figures/83-Figure-3.gif.

63. Stephen E. Frantzich, *Citizen Democracy: Political Activists in a Cynical Age* (Lanham, Md.: Rowman & Littlefield, 1999), 89.

64. David Mathews, "Introduction," in Harwood Group, *College Students Talk Politics* (Dayton, Ohio: Kettering Foundation, 1993), iii.

65. newvotersproject.org.

66. Ibid.

67. Ibid.

68. Ibid.

69. Tommy Denton, "Young Voters Had Better Enter the Fray," *Roanoke Times and World News,* August 18, 2002, 1.

70. Bennett Drake, "Doing Disservice," *American Prospect* 14, no. 9 (2003): A20.

71. Anne Colby et al., *Educating Citizens: Preparing America's Undergraduates for Lives of Moral and Civic Responsibility* (San Francisco: Jossey-Bass, 2003), 7–8.

72. Higher Education Research Institute, *The American Freshman: National Norms for Fall 1994* (Los Angeles: Higher Education Research Institute, UCLA, 1995), 1.

73. Higher Education Research Institute, *The American Freshman: National Norms for Fall 2001* (Los Angeles: Higher Education Research Institute, UCLA, 2001); Higher Education Research Institute, *The American Freshman: National Norms for Fall 2002* (Los Angeles: Higher Education Research Institute, UCLA, 2002); Higher Education Research Institute, *The American Freshman: National Norms for Fall 2003* (Los Angeles: Higher Education Research Institute, UCLA, 2003).

74. Higher Education Research Institute, *The American Freshman: National Norms for Fall 2008* (Los Angeles: Higher Education Research Institute, UCLA, 2008).

75. Michael Connery, *Youth to Power: How Today's Young Voters Are Building Tomorrow's Progressive Majority* (Brooklyn, N.Y.: ig publishing, 2008), 10.

76. Ronald Brownstein, "Millennial Tremors," *National Journal* (February 14, 2009): 60.

77. www.civicyouth.org.

78. Marjorie Connelly, "Dissecting the Changing Electorate," *New York Times,* November 9, 2008; available at http://wwww.nytimes.com/2008/11/09/weekinreview/09connelly.html?ei=5070@emc=eta1.

79. Zukin et al., *A New Engagement? Political Participation, Civic Life, and the Changing American Citizen* (Oxford: Oxford University Press, 2006), 5.

80. Peter Levine, *The Future of Democracy: The Next Generation of American Citizens* (Lebanon, N.H.: University Press of New England, 2007), 50.

81. Gregory Markus, "America's Politically Inert Youth," *Christian Science Monitor* (March 16, 1992): 18.

82. People for the American Way, *Democracy's Next Generation: American Youth Attitudes on Citizenship, Government, and Politics* (Washington, D.C.: People for the American Way, 1989), 12–13.

83. Times Mirror Center for the People and the Press, press release, Washington, D.C., June 28, 1990, 1.

84. Ruth Sidel, *Battling Bias: The Struggle for Identity and Community on College Campuses* (New York: Viking, 1994), 52.

85. Sara Murray, "The Curse of the Class of 2009," *The Wall Street Journal,* May 9–10, 2009, A1.

86. Harwood Group, *College Students Talk Politics* (Dayton, Ohio: Kettering Foundation, 1993), xvi.

87. Ibid., 2.

88. Ibid.

89. Ibid., vii.

90. Ibid., 3.

91. Ibid.

92. Ibid.

93. Ibid.

94. Ibid.

95. Ibid.

96. Ibid.

97. Kiesa et al., *Millennials Talk Politics,* 4.

98. Ibid.

99. Ibid., 4–5.

100. Sarah E. Long, *The New Student Politics: The Wingspread Statement on Student Civic Engagement,* 2nd ed. (Providence, R.I.: Campus Compact, 2002), v.

101. Ibid., 1.

102. Harwood Group, *Citizens and Politics,* 53.

103. Ibid.

104. Mathews, *Politics for People,* 36.

105. Ibid., 43.

106. Harwood Group, *Citizens and Politics.*

Chapter 4

1. Leonard Zeskind, *Blood and Politics: The History of the White Nationalist Movement from the Margins to the Mainstream* (New York: Farrar, Straus & Giroux, 2009), 400–401.

2. Doug McAdam, *Freedom Summer* (New York: Oxford University Press, 1988), 12.

3. C. Vann Woodward, quoted in Charles W. Eagles, *Introduction to the Civil Rights Movement in America* (Jackson: University Press of Mississippi, 1986), ix.

4. Aldon D. Morris, *The Origins of the Civil Rights Movement: Black Communities Organizing for Change* (New York: Free Press, 1984), 286.

5. Ibid., 286–287.

6. Harrell R. Rogers and Michael Harrington, *Unfinished Democracy: The American Political System* (Glenview, Ill.: Scott, Foresman, 1981), 146.

7. Morris, *Origins of the Civil Rights Movement*, 104–105.

8. Taylor Branch, *Parting the Waters: America in the King Years: 1954–63* (New York: Simon & Schuster, 1988).

9. Sidney Tarrow, *Power in Movement: Social Movements, Collective Action and Politics* (Cambridge: Cambridge University Press, 1994), 109.

10. John Dittmer, *Local People: The Struggle for Civil Rights in Mississippi* (Urbana: University of Illinois Press, 1994), 77.

11. Myles Horton, *The Long Haul* (New York: Anchor, 1990), 115.

12. Morris, *Origins of the Civil Rights Movement*, 112.

13. Ibid., 111.

14. McAdam, *Freedom Summer*, 236.

15. Morris, *Origins of the Civil Rights Movement*, 219.

16. Clayborne Carson, *In Struggle: SNCC and the Black Awakening of the 1960s* (Cambridge: Harvard University Press, 1981), 19.

17. Clayborne Carson, in *The Civil Rights Movement in America*, ed. Charles W. Eagles, 25 (Jackson: University Press of Mississippi, 1986).

18. Howell Raines, ed., *My Soul Is Rested: The Story of the Civil Rights Movement in the Deep South* (New York: Penguin, 1977), 75.

19. Carson, *In Struggle*, 9.

20. Raines, *My Soul Is Rested*, 76.

21. Carson, *In Struggle*, 11.

22. John Lewis, with Michael D'Orso, *Walking with the Wind: A Memoir of the Movement* (New York: Simon & Schuster, 1998), 85–86.

23. Carson, *In Struggle*, 11.

24. Kirkpatrick Sale, *SDS* (New York: Random House, 1973), 23.

25. Morris, *Origins of the Civil Rights Movement*, 222.

26. Robert Weisbrot, *Freedom Bound: A History of America's Civil Rights Movement* (New York: Plume, 1990), 42.

27. Carson, *In Struggle*, 37.

28. Weisbrot, *Freedom Bound*, 55.

29. Morris, *Origins of the Civil Rights Movement*, 231.

30. Weisbrot, *Freedom Bound*, 62–63.

31. McAdam, *Freedom Summer*, 4.

32. Sara M. Evans, *Personal Politics* (New York: Alfred A. Knopf, 1979), 71.

33. Carson, *In Struggle*, 96.

34. Ibid., 112.

35. John Dittmer, "The Politics of the Mississippi Movement, 1954–1964," in *The Civil Rights Movement in America*, ed. Charles W. Eagles, 82–83 (Jackson: University Press of Mississippi, 1986).

36. Evans, *Personal Politics*, 42.

37. Dittmer, "Politics of the Mississippi Movement," 83.

38. Jill Quadagno, *The Color of Welfare: How Racism Undermined the War on Poverty* (New York: Oxford University Press, 1994), 39.

39. McAdam, *Freedom Summer*, 5.

40. Ibid., 138.

41. Ibid., 139.

42. Evans, *Personal Politics*, 125.

43. William H. Chafe, "The End of One Struggle, the Beginning of Another," in *The Civil Rights Movement in America*, ed. Charles W. Eagles, 127–128 (Jackson: University Press of Mississippi, 1986).

44. Quadagno, *Color of Welfare*, 29.

45. T.V. Reed, *The Art of Protest: Culture and Activism from the Civil Rights Movement to the Streets of Seattle* (Minneapolis: University of Minnesota Press, 2005), 180.

46. Urvashi Vaid, *Virtual Equality: The Mainstreaming of Gay and Lesbian Liberation* (New York: Anchor Books, 1995), 100–101.

47. Ibid.

48. Stanley Aronowitz, *The Death and Rebirth of American Radicalism* (New York: Routledge, 1996), 131.

49. Robert Gottlieb, *Forcing the Spring: The Transformation of the American Environmental Movement* (Washington, D.C.: Island Press, 1993), 197.

50. James William Gibson, *A Reenchanted World: The Quest for a New Kinship with Nature* (New York: Metropolitan Books, 2009), 130.

51. Philip Shabecoff, *A Fierce Green Fire: The American Environmental Movement* (New York: Hill and Wang, 1993), 123.

52. Gibson, *Reenchanted World*, 132.

53. Dave Foreman, *Confessions of an Eco-Warrior* (New York: Harmony Books, 1991), 82.

54. Gottlieb, *Forcing the Spring*, 197.

55. Shabecoff, *Fierce Green Fire*, 124.

56. Gibson, *Reenchanted World*, 137.

57. http://earthliberationfront.com/about.

58. Ibid.

59. Ibid.

60. Nick Madigan, "Cries of Activism and Terrorism in S.U.V. Torching," *New York Times*, August 31, 2003, 20.

61. Gibson, *Reenchanted World*, 137.

62. Ibid.

63. Ibid., 138.

64. Ibid.

65. Joe Stumpe and Monica Davey, "Abortion Doctor Shot to Death in Kansas Church," *New York Times*, June 1, 2009; available at www.nytimes.com/2009/06/01/us/o1tiller.html?emc+eta1.

66. Ibid.

67. Ibid.

68. Barbara Hinkson Craig and David M. O'Brien, *Abortion and American Politics* (Chatham, N.J.: Chatham House, 1993), 57–58.

69. Kenneth Stern, *A Force upon the Plain* (New York: Simon & Schuster, 1996), 50.

70. Zeskind, *Blood and Politics,* 72.

71. Stern, *Force Upon the Plain,* 97.

72. Ibid., 64.

73. Alex Ogle, "Report: Right-Wing Militias on the Rise in US" (August 13, 2009); available at www.truthout.org/081409H.

74. Ibid.

75. Ibid.

76. Ibid.

Chapter 5

1. Doug McAdam, *Freedom Summer* (New York: Oxford University Press, 1988), 201.

2. Robert Fisher, *Let the People Decide: Neighborhood Organizing in America* (Boston: Twayne, 1984), 126.

3. Ibid., 128.

4. Harry C. Boyte, *Commonwealth: A Return to Citizen Politics* (New York: Free Press, 1989), 12.

5. Fisher, *Let the People Decide,* 142.

6. Ibid.

7. Ibid., 135.

8. Ibid., 133.

9. Ibid., 134.

10. Ibid., 135.

11. Ibid., 135–136.

12. Peter Dreier, "ACORN Under the Microscope," *The Huffington Post,* July 14, 2008; available at www.huffingtonpost.com/peter-dreier/acorn-under-the-microscope.

13. Stephanie Strom, "Funds Misappropriated at 2 Nonprofit Groups," *New York Times,* July 9, 2008; available at www.nytimes.com/2008/07/09/us/09embezzle.html.

14. Dreier, "ACORN Under the Microscope."

15. "Obama and ACORN," *The Wall Street Journal,* October 14, 2008; available at http://online.wsj.com/article/SB/223940510712307.html.

16. Christopher Hayes, "ACORN and Accountability," *The Nation* (October 12, 2009): 4.

17. Ibid., 6.

18. Fisher, *Let the People Decide,* 142).

19. www.picced.org/lowres/seco.htm.

20. www.jhsph.edu/Student-Life/InterAction/VolunteerAgencies/NeighOrgs/Southeast Commorg.html.

21. Fisher, *Let the People Decide,* 143–144.

22. Ibid., 144.

23. Ibid., 145.

24. Ibid., 145–146.

25. www.buildiaf.org.

26. Boyte, *Commonwealth,* 101–102.

27. Ibid., 112.

28. www.buildiaf.org.

29. Ibid.

30. Boyte, *Commonwealth,* 124–125.

31. Ibid., 125–126.

32. Robert N. Bellah et al., *Habits of the Heart: Individualism and Commitment in American Life* (New York: Harper & Row, 1985), 215.

33. www.iscv.org/.

34. Bellah et al., *Habits of the Heart,* 214.

35. Ibid., 215–216.

36. Ibid., 217.

37. www.iscv.org/.

38. Ibid.

39. Eric Mann, *L.A.'s Lethal Air: New Strategies for Policy, Organizing, and Action* (Los Angeles: Labor/Community Watchdog, 1991), 56.

40. Ibid., 35.

41. Ibid., 58.

42. www.thestrategycenter.org.

43. Ibid.

44. Mann, *L.A.'s Lethal Air,* 65–71.

45. Ibid., 72.

46. Richard Zimmerman, *What Can I Do to Make a Difference?* (New York: Plume, 1991), 59.

47. William Greider, *Who Will Tell the People?* (New York: Simon & Schuster, 1992), 167.

48. www.chej.org/missions@staff.html.

49. www.chej.org.

50. Ibid.

51. Greider, *Who Will Tell the People?,* 169.

52. Karen Paget, "Resurgence at the Grassroots?" *American Prospect,* no. 2 (Summer 1990): 115–116.

53. www.horizonmag.com/9/public-allies.asp.

54. www.publicallies.org/au_vision.html.

55. www.horizonmag.com/9/public-allies.asp.

56. www.publicallies.org/au_vision.html.

57. www.publicallies.org/au_future.html.

58. www.publicallies.org.

59. Campus Green Vote, "Campus Green Vote Fact Sheet" (Washington, D.C.: Campus Green Vote, 1993).

60. Campus Green Vote, *The Green Voter. A Newsletter for Eco-Activists Working Towards a Green Congress* 1, no. 6 (February 21, 1995).

61. Campus Green Vote, "Campus Green Vote Fact Sheet."

62. www.emagazine.com/november-december-1999/1199curr_seeds.html.

63. www.cvef.org/press-releases/page.jsp?itemid=28550502.

64. Ibid.

65. Suzanne W. Morse, ed., *Politics for the Twenty-First Century: What Should Be Done on Campus?* (Dubuque, Iowa: Kettering Foundation, 1992), 9.

66. www.cool2serve.org.

67. www.cool2serve.org/about/merger.htm.

68. www.centerforcivicparticipation.org/organizingvoterprojectsleaguecool.html.

69. Paul Rogat Loeb, *Generation at the Crossroads: Apathy and Action on the College Campus* (New Brunswick, N.J.: Rutgers University Press, 1994), 239.

70. Ibid., 232.

71. http://usas.org/.

72. Arthur Levine, "A New Generation of Student Protesters Arises," *Chronicle of Higher Education* (February 26, 1999): A72.

73. Yasmin Madadi, "USAS Kicks Ass," *The Nation* (May 12, 2009): 5.

74. Ibid.

75. Steven Greenhouse, "Labor Fight Ends in Win for Students," *New York Times,* November 18, 2009; available at www.nytimes.com/2009/11/18/business/18labor.html.

76. Ibid.

77. Ibid.

78. Ibid.

79. Steven Greenhouse, "Activism Surges at Campuses Nationwide, and Labor Is at Issue," *New York Times,* March 29, 1999, B1.

80. Alexander Cockburn, "The Way the World Works," *The Nation* (July 3, 2000): 8.

81. John Nichols, "The Beat," *The Nation* (August 21/28, 2000): 9.

82. Joel Lefkowitz, "Students, Sweatshops, and Local Power," in *From ACT UP to the WTO,* ed. Benjamin Shepard and Ronald Hayduk, 74 (New York: Verso, 2002).

83. Eric Schlosser, *Fast Food Nation: The Dark Side of the All-American Meal* (Boston: Houghton Mifflin, 2001), 267–268.

84. Christine Kelly and Joel Lefkowitz, "Radical and Pragmatic: United Students against Sweatshops," in *Teamsters and Turtles? U.S. Progressive Political Movements in the 21st Century,* 90 (Lanham, Md.: Rowman & Littlefield, 2003).

85. Michael Connery, *Youth to Power: How Today's Young Voters Are Building Tomorrow's Progressive Majority* (Brooklyn, N.Y.: ig publishing, 2008), 58–59.

86. ww.usstudents.org/who-we-are.

87. Te-Ping Chen, "Back to the USSA," *The Nation* (November 23, 2009): 20.

88. www.usstudents.org/who-we-are.

89. Connery, *Youth to Power,* 60.

90. Tim Dickinson, "Obama's Real Reform," *Rolling Stone* (August 6, 2009): 41.

91. Kay Steiger, "Democracy Versus Debt," *The American Prospect* (March 2008): A19.

92. Chen, "Back to the USSA," 22.

93. Howard Rheingold, *The Virtual Reality* (Reading, Mass.: Addison-Wesley, 1993), 13–14.

94. Ibid., 91.

95. David M. Herszenhorn, "Students Turn to Internet for Nationwide Protest Planning," *New York Times,* March 29, 1995, A20.

96. Stephen E. Frantzich, *Citizen Democracy: Political Activists in a Cynical Age* (Lanham, Md.: Rowman & Littlefield, 1999), 59.

97. Lesley J. Wood and Kelly Moore, "Target Practice: Community Activism in a Global Era," in *From ACT UP to the WTO,* ed. Benjamin Shepard and Ronald Hayduk, 26 (New York: Verso, 2002).

98. Jane Spencer, "Raising a Ruckus: Students Take the Bus to DC," *The Nation* (April 24, 2000): 22.

99. Morley Winograd and Michael D. Hais, *Millennial Makeover: MySpace, You Tube, and the Future of American Politics* (New Brunswick, N.J.: Rutgers University Press, 2008), xi.

100. Andrew Boyd, "The Web Rewires the Movement," *The Nation* (August 4 and 11, 2003): 14.

101. Ben Winters, "You Make the Call," *In These Times.* (March 31, 2003): 8.

102. Boyd, "The Web Rewires the Movement," 14.

103. Lowell Feld and Nate Wilcox, *Netroots Rising: How a Citizen Army of Bloggers and Online Activists is Changing American Politics* (Westport, Conn.: Praeger, 2008), 36.

104. Jake Sherman, "Conservatives Take a Page from Left's Online Playbook," *Wall Street Journal,* August 20, 2009, A4.

105. Ibid.

106. Michael Janofsky, "Internet Helps Make Dean a Contender," *New York Times,* July 5, 2003, A1.

107. Tim Dickinson, "Obama's Brain Trust." *Rolling Stone* (July 10–24, 2008): 78.

108. Ari Melber, "Obama's iSuccess," *The Nation* (October 27, 2008): 8.

109. Jim Rutenberg and Christopher Drew, "Obama Plans National Push on Ads and Turnout," *New York Times,* June 22, 2008.

110. Ibid.

111. Claire Cain Miller, "How Obama's Internet Campaign Changed Politics," *New York Times,* November 7, 2008.

112. Ibid.

113. Christopher Rhoads, "Going Back to Grass Roots for Obama Stimulus Push," *Wall Street Journal,* January 31 and February 1, 2009, A3.

114. Ibid.

115. Karen Mossberger, Caroline J. Tolbert, and Mary Stansbury, *Virtual Inequality: Beyond the Digital Divide* (Washington, D.C.: Georgetown University Press, 2003), 2.

116. Anand Giridharadas, "'Athens' on the Net" ("Week in Review"), *New York Times,* September 13, 2009, 5.

117. Edmund Andrews, "Mr. Smith Goes to Cyberspace," *New York Times,* January 6, 1995, A22.

118. George Monbiot, *Heat: How to Stop the Planet from Burning* (Cambridge, Mass.: South End Press, 2007), 214.

119. John Markhoff, "A Newer, Lonelier Crowd Emerges in Internet Study," *New York Times,* February 16, 2000, A1, A8.

120. Frantzich, *Citizen Democracy,* 59.

121. Peter Levine, *The Future of Democracy: The Next Generation of American Citizens* (Lebanon, N.H.: University Press of New England, 2007), 96.

Chapter 6

1. Anne Colby, Thomas Ehrlich, Elizabeth Beaumont, and Jason Stephens, *Educating Citizens: Preparing America's Undergraduates for Lives of Moral and Civic Responsibility* (San Francisco: Jossey-Bass, 2003), xii.

2. Richard Guarasci and Craig A. Rimmerman, "Applying Democratic Theory in Community Organizations," in *Teaching Democracy by Being Democratic,* ed. Ted Becker and Richard Couto (Westport, Conn.: Praeger, 1996).

3. Suzanne W. Morse, ed., *Politics for the Twenty-First Century: What Should Be Done on Campus?* (Dubuque, Iowa: Kettering Foundation, 1992).

4. Ibid., 5.

5. Ibid., 5–6.

6. Ibid., 6.

7. Ibid.

8. Doug Bandow, "National Service: Utopias Revisited," *Policy Analysis,* no. 190 (March 15, 1993): 4.

9. Steven Waldman, *The Bill* (New York: Viking, 1995), 5.

10. Ibid., 8.

11. Ibid., 19.

12. Harris Wofford, *1999 Highlights: Corporation for National Service* (Washington, D.C.: Corporation for National Service, 1999), 2.

13. Ibid., 3.

14. Ibid., 4.

15. *USA Freedom Corps 2003 Annual Report: Building a Culture of Service* (Washington, D.C.: The White House, 2004).

16. Jonathan Alter, "Lip Service vs. National Service," *Newsweek* (June 30, 2003): 29.

17. "National Service," *Rolling Stone* (April 2, 2009): 63.

18. David M. Herszenhorn, "National Service Corps Set to Become Law," *New York Times,* March 31, 2009; available at http://thecaucus.blogs.nytimes.com/2009/03/31/national-service-corps-set-to-become-law.

19. Morse, *Politics for the Twenty-First Century,* 9.

20. Benjamin R. Barber and Richard Battistoni, "A Season of Service: Introducing Service Learning into the Liberal Arts Curriculum," *PS: Political Science and Politics* 26, no. 2 (June 1993): 239.

21. Guarasci and Rimmerman, "Applying Democratic Theory in Community Organizations."

22. Jean Bethke Elshtain, "The Decline of Democratic Faith," in *Experiencing Citizenship: Concepts and Models for Service-Learning in Political Science,* ed. Richard M. Battistoni and William E. Hudson, 13 (Washington, D.C.: American Association for Higher Education, 1997).

23. David Eggers, "Serve or Fail," *New York Times,* June 13, 2004, 17.

24. Jodi Wilgoren, "Public Service's Profile Is Rising in Many College Curriculums," *New York Times,* April 24, 2000, A18.

25. www.slcc.edu/student/serv.center/asb2001.html.

26. Robert D. Putnam, "AmeriCorpse?" *New York Times,* March 24, 1995, A31.

27. Harry C. Boyte, "Community Service and Civic Education," *Phi Beta Kappan* (June 1991): 765.

28. Ibid., 766.

29. Nina Eliasoph, *Avoiding Politics: How Americans Produce Apathy in Everyday Life* (Cambridge: Cambridge University Press, 1998), 61.

30. Boyte, "Community Service and Civic Education," 766.

31. Kettering Foundation, "Public Work: An Interview with Harry Boyte," *Higher Education Exchange* (2000): 43.

32. Matthew A. Crenson and Benjamin Ginsberg, *Downsizing Democracy: How America Sidelined Its Citizens and Privatized Its Public* (Baltimore, Md.: Johns Hopkins University Press, 2002), 9.

33. Eric B. Gorham, *National Service, Citizenship, and Political Education* (Albany: State University of New York Press, 1992), 1.

34. Guarasci and Rimmerman, "Applying Democratic Theory in Community Organizations."

35. Gorham, *National Service, Citizenship, and Political Education*, 10.

36. Bandow, "National Service: Utopias Revisited."

37. Guarasci and Rimmerman, "Applying Democratic Theory in Community Organizations."

38. Craig A. Rimmerman, ed., *Service-Learning and the Liberal Arts* (Lanham, Md.: Rowman & Littlefield, 2009).

39. Guarasci and Rimmerman, "Applying Democratic Theory in Community Organizations."

40. Ibid.

41. Ibid.

42. Ibid.

43. Rimmerman, *Service-Learning and the Liberal Arts,* 80.

44. Guarasci and Rimmerman, "Applying Democratic Theory in Community Organizations."

45. Boyte, "Community Service and Civic Education."

46. www.actionforchange.org/getinformed/about-ryv.html.

47. www.nytimes.com/ref/college/collegesspecial2/collaascu.html.

48. Robert D. Putnam, *Bowling Alone: The Collapse and Revival of American Community* (New York: Simon & Schuster, 2000), 133.

49. Stewart Burns, *Social Movements of the 1960s: Searching for Democracy* (Boston: Twayne, 1990), 187–188.

50. Christopher Gunn and Hazel Dayton Gunn, *Reclaiming Capital: Democratic Initiatives and Community Development* (Ithaca, N.Y.: Cornell University Press, 1991), 150.

Bibliography

Alter, Jonathan. "Lip Service vs. National Service." *Newsweek* (June 30, 2003): 29.

Andrews, Edmund. "Mr. Smith Goes to Cyberspace." *New York Times,* January 6, 1995, A22.

Aronowitz, Stanley. *The Death and Rebirth of American Radicalism.* New York: Routledge, 1996.

Bachrach, Peter. *The Theory of Democratic Elitism: A Critique.* Boston: Little, Brown, 1971.

Bandow, Doug. "National Service: Utopias Revisited." *Policy Analysis,* no. 190 (March 15, 1993): 1–20.

Barber, Benjamin R. *An Aristocracy of Everyone: The Politics of Education and the Future of America.* New York: Ballantine, 1992.

———. *Jihad v. McWorld.* New York: Times Books, 1995.

———. *Strong Democracy: Participatory Politics for a New Age.* Berkeley: University of California Press, 1984.

Barber, Benjamin R., and Richard Battistoni. "A Season of Service: Introducing Service Learning into the Liberal Arts Curriculum." *PS: Political Science and Politics* 26, no. 2 (June 1993): 235–240.

Bell, Brenda, John Gaventa, and John Peters, eds. *We Make the Road by Walking.* Philadelphia: Temple University Press, 1990.

Bellah, Robert N., Richard Madsen, William M. Sullivan, Ann Swidler, and Steven M. Tipton. *Habits of the Heart: Individualism and Commitment in American Life.* New York: Harper & Row, 1985.

Benello, C. George, and Dimitrios Roussopoulos, eds. *The Case for Participatory Democracy: Some Prospects for a Radical Society.* New York: Viking, 1971.

Berelson, Bernard, Paul Lazarsfeld, and William McPhee. *Voting.* Chicago: University of Chicago Press, 1954.

Berlin, Isaiah. *Four Essays on Liberty.* Oxford: Oxford University Press, 1969.

Berry, Jeffrey, Kent M. Portney, and Ken Thomson. *The Rebirth of Urban Democracy.* Washington, D.C.: Brookings Institution, 1993.

Boyd, Andrew. "The Web Rewires the Movement." *The Nation* (August 4 and 11, 2003): 13–22.

Boyte, Harry C. *The Backyard Revolution: Understanding the New Citizen Movement.* Philadelphia: Temple University Press, 1980.

———. *Commonwealth: A Return to Citizen Politics.* New York: Free Press, 1989.

———. "Community Service and Civic Education." *Phi Beta Kappan* (June 1991): 765–767.

———. "Reinventing Citizenship." *Kettering Review* (Winter 1994): 78–87.

Branch, Taylor. *Parting the Waters: America in the King Years: 1954–63*. New York: Simon & Schuster, 1988.

Brownstein, Ronald. "Millennial Tremors." *National Journal*. (February 14, 2009): 60.

Burner, Eric R. *And Gently He Shall Lead Them*. New York: New York University Press, 1994.

Burns, James MacGregor. *The Power to Lead: The Crisis of the American Presidency*. New York: Simon & Schuster, 1984.

Burns, Nancy, Kay Lehman Schlozman, and Sidney Verba. *The Private Roots of Public Action: Gender, Equality, and Political Participation*. Cambridge: Harvard University Press, 2001.

Burns, Stewart. *Social Movements of the 1960s: Searching for Democracy*. Boston: Twayne, 1990.

Campus Green Vote. "Campus Green Vote Fact Sheet." Washington, D.C.: Campus Green Vote, 1993.

———. *The Green Voter: A Newsletter for Eco-Activists Working Towards a Green Congress* 1, no. 6 (February 21, 1995).

Carson, Clayborne. *In Struggle: SNCC and the Black Awakening of the 1960s*. Cambridge: Harvard University Press, 1981.

Cave, Damien. "Mock the Vote." *Rolling Stone* (May 27, 2004): 47–48.

Chafe, William H. "The End of One Struggle, the Beginning of Another." In *The Civil Rights Movement in America*, edited by Charles W. Eagles. Jackson: University Press of Mississippi, 1986.

Chen, Te-Ping. "Back to the USSA." *The Nation* (November 23, 2009): 20–22.

Cockburn, Alexander. "The Way the World Works." *The Nation* (July 3, 2000): 8.

Colby, Anne, Thomas Ehrlich, Elizabeth Beaumont, and Jason Stephens. *Educating Citizens: Preparing America's Undergraduates for Lives of Moral and Civic Responsibility*. San Francisco: Jossey-Bass, 2003.

Comstock-Gay, Stuart and Joe Goldman. "More Than the Vote." *The American Prospect*. (January/February 2009): A8–A11.

Connelly, Marjorie. "Dissecting the Changing Electorate," *New York Times*, November 9, 2008; available at http://www.nytimes.com/2008/11/09/weekinreview/09connelly .html?ei=5070@emc=eta1.

Connery, Michael. *Youth to Power: How Today's Young Voters Are Building Tomorrow's Progressive Majority*. Brooklyn, New York: ig publishing, 2008.

Craig, Barbara Hinkson, and David M. O'Brien. *Abortion and American Politics*. Chatham, N.J.: Chatham House, 1993.

Crenson, Matthew A., and Benjamin Ginsberg. *Downsizing Democracy: How America Sidelined Its Citizens and Privatized Its Public*. Baltimore, Md.: Johns Hopkins University Press, 2002.

Dalton, Russell J. *The Good Citizen: How a Younger Generation Is Reshaping American Politics*. Washington, DC: CQ Press, 2008.

Dance, George. "Ron Paul Helps Launch Young Americans for Liberty." December 7, 2008; available at www.nolanchart.com/article5610.html.

"Democracy on the Net." *The Nation* (July 21/28, 2008): 40.

Denton, Tommy. "Young Voters Had Better Enter the Fray." *Roanoke Times and World News*, August 18, 2002, 1.

Dickinson, Tim. "Obama's Brain Trust." *Rolling Stone.* (July 10–24, 2008): 78.

———. "Obama's Real Reform." *Rolling Stone.* (August 6, 2009): 41–43.

Diggins, John Patrick. *The Lost Soul of American Politics: Virtue, Self-Interest, and the Foundations of Liberalism.* Chicago: University of Chicago Press, 1984.

Dionne, E. J., Jr. *Why Americans Hate Politics.* New York: Simon & Schuster, 1991.

Dittmer, John. *Local People: The Struggle for Civil Rights in Mississippi.* Urbana: University of Illinois Press, 1994.

———. "The Politics of the Mississippi Movement, 1954–1964." In *The Civil Rights Movement in America,* edited by Charles W. Eagles. Jackson: University Press of Mississippi, 1986.

Drake, Bennett. "Doing Disservice." *American Prospect* 14, no. 9 (2003): A20.

Dreier, Peter. "ACORN Under the Microscope." *The Huffington Post,* July 14, 2008; available at www.huffingtonpost.com/peter-dreier/acorn-under-the-microscope.

———. "Detouring the Motor-Voter Law." *The Nation* (October 1994): 490–493.

Eagles, Charles W. *The Civil Rights Movement in America.* Jackson: University Press of Mississippi, 1986.

———. "Introduction." In *The Civil Rights Movement in America.* Jackson: University Press of Mississippi, 1986.

Eggers, David. "Serve or Fail." *New York Times,* June 13, 2004, 17.

Eliasoph, Nina. *Avoiding Politics: How Americans Produce Apathy in Everyday Life.* Cambridge: Cambridge University Press, 1998.

Elshtain, Jean Bethke. "The Decline of Democratic Faith." In *Experiencing Citizenship: Concepts and Models for Service-Learning in Political Science,* edited by Richard M. Battistoni and William E. Hudson. Washington, D.C.: American Association for Higher Education, 1997.

Evans, Sara M. *Personal Politics.* New York: Alfred A. Knopf, 1979.

Evans, Sara M., and Harry C. Boyte. *Free Spaces: The Sources of Democratic Change in America.* New York: Harper & Row, 1986.

Featherstone, Liza. "The New Student Movement." *The Nation* (May 15, 2000): 11–18.

Feld, Lowell, and Nate Wilcox. *Netroots Rising: How a Citizen Army of Bloggers and Online Activists Is Changing American Politics.* Westport, Conn.: Praeger, 2008.

Fineman, Howard. "The Power of Talk." *Newsweek* (February 8, 1993): 24–28.

Fisher, Robert. *Let the People Decide: Neighborhood Organizing in America.* Boston: Twayne, 1984.

Flacks, Richard. *Making History.* New York: Columbia University Press, 1988.

Foreman, Dave. *Confessions of an Eco-Warrior.* New York: Harmony Books, 1991.

Frantzich, Stephen E. *Citizen Democracy: Political Activists in a Cynical Age.* Lanham, Md.: Rowman & Littlefield, 1999.

Gibbs, Lois Marie. *Dying from Dioxin.* Boston: South End Press, 1995.

Gibson, James William. *A Reenchanted World: The Quest for a New Kinship with Nature.* New York: Metropolitan Books, 2009.

Giridharadas, Anand. "'Athens' on the Net." *New York Times* ("Week in Review"), September 13, 2009, 5.

Goodwin, Richard N. *Remembering America: A Voice from the Sixties.* Boston: Little, Brown, 1988.

Gorham, Eric B. *National Service, Citizenship, and Political Education.* Albany: State University of New York Press, 1992.

Gottlieb, Robert. *Forcing the Spring: The Transformation of the American Environmental Movement.* Washington, D.C.: Island Press, 1993.

Greenberg, Stanley B., Al From, and Will Marshall. *The Road to Realignment: The Democrats and the Perot Voters.* Washington, D.C.: Democratic Leadership Council, 1993.

Greenhouse, Steven. "Activism Surges at Campuses Nationwide, and Labor Is at Issue." *New York Times,* March 29, 1999, B1.

———. "Labor Fight Ends in Win for Students." *New York Times,* November 18, 2009; available at www.nytimes.com/2009/11/18/business/18labor.html.

Greider, William. *Who Will Tell the People?* New York: Simon & Schuster, 1992.

Guarasci, Richard, and Craig A. Rimmerman. "Applying Democratic Theory in Community Organizations." In *Teaching Democracy by Being Democratic,* edited by Ted Becker and Richard Couto. Westport, Conn.: Praeger, 1996.

Gunn, Christopher, and Hazel Dayton Gunn. *Reclaiming Capital: Democratic Initiatives and Community Development.* Ithaca, N.Y.: Cornell University Press, 1991.

Harrington, Michael. *Decade of Decision: The Crisis of the American System.* New York: Simon & Schuster, 1980.

Harwood Group. *Citizens and Politics: A View from Main Street America.* Dayton, Ohio: Kettering Foundation, 1991.

———. *College Students Talk Politics.* Dayton, Ohio: Kettering Foundation, 1993.

Hayes, Christopher. "ACORN and Accountability." *The Nation* (October 12, 2009): 4 and 6.

Herson, Lawrence J. R. *The Politics of Ideas: Political Theory and American Public Policy.* Homewood, Ill.: Dorsey Press, 1984.

Herszenhorn, David M. "National Service Corps Set to Become Law." *New York Times,* March 31, 2009.

———. "Students Turn to Internet for Nationwide Protest Planning." *New York Times,* March 29, 1995, A20.

Higher Education Research Institute. *The American Freshman: National Norms for Fall 1994.* Los Angeles: Higher Education Research Institute, UCLA, 1995.

———. *The American Freshman: National Norms for Fall 1995.* Los Angeles: Higher Education Research Institute, UCLA, 1996.

———. *The American Freshman: National Norms for Fall 2000.* Los Angeles: Higher Education Research Institute, UCLA, 2000.

———. *The American Freshman: National Norms for Fall 2001.* Los Angeles: Higher Education Research Institute, UCLA, 2001.

———. *The American Freshman: National Norms for Fall 2002.* Los Angeles: Higher Education Research Institute, UCLA, 2002.

———. *The American Freshman: National Norms for Fall 2003.* Los Angeles: Higher Education Research Institute, UCLA, 2003.

———. *The American Freshman: National Norms for Fall 2008.* Los Angeles: Higher Education Research Institute, UCLA, 2008.

Hofstadter, Richard. "The Founding Fathers: An Age of Realism." In *The Moral Foundations of the American Republic,* 3rd ed., edited by Robert Horwitz. Charlottesville: University of Virginia Press, 1986.

Horton, Myles. *The Long Haul.* New York: Anchor, 1990.

Hudson, William E. *American Democracy in Peril: Seven Challenges to America's Future.* Chatham, N.J.: Chatham House, 1995.

Huntington, Samuel P. "The United States." In *The Crisis of Democracy,* edited by Michel Crozier, Samuel P. Huntington, and Joji Watanuki. New York: New York University Press, 1975.

Isaac, Katherine. *Civics for Democracy: A Journey for Teachers and Students.* Washington, D.C.: Essential Books, 1992.

Janofsky, Michael. "Internet Helps Make Dean a Contender." *New York Times,* July 5, 2003, A1.

Jones, Kathleen B. "Citizenship in a Woman-Friendly Polity: Review Essay." *Signs: Journal of Women in Culture and Society* 15, no. 4 (1990): 781–812.

Kammen, Michael. *A Machine That Would Go by Itself: The Constitution in American Culture.* New York: Alfred A. Knopf, 1986.

Kelly, Christine, and Joel Lefkowitz. "Radical and Pragmatic: United Students against Sweatshops." In *Teamsters and Turtles? U.S. Progressive Political Movements in the 21st Century.* Lanham, Md.: Rowman & Littlefield, 2003.

Kettering Foundation. "Public Work: An Interview with Harry Boyte." *Higher Education Exchange* (2000): 43–51.

Keyssar, Alexander. *The Right to Vote: The Contested History of Democracy in the United States.* New York: Basic Books, 2000.

Kiesa, Abby, Alexander P. Orlowski, Peter Levine, Deborah Both, Emily Hoban Kirby, Mark Hugo Lopez, and Karlo Barrios Marcelo. *Millennials Talk Politics: A Study of College Student Political Engagement.* College Park, Md.: CIRCLE, 2007.

Kirby, Emily Hoban, and Kei Kawashima-Ginsberg. "The Youth Vote in 2008." April 2009; available at www.civic.youth.org

Kramer, Daniel C. *Participatory Democracy: Developing Ideals of the Political Left.* Cambridge, Mass.: Schenkman, 1972.

Kramer, Larry. *Reports from the Holocaust: The Story of an AIDS Activist.* New York: St. Martin's Press, 1994.

Kramer, Ralph. *Participation of the Poor: Comparative Community Case Studies in the War on Poverty.* Englewood Cliffs, N.J.: Prentice-Hall, 1969.

LaQuey, Tracy. *The Internet Companion: A Beginner's Guide to Global Networking.* Reading, Mass.: Addison-Wesley, 1993.

Lefkowitz, Joel. "Students, Sweatshops, and Local Power." In *From ACT UP to the WTO,* edited by Benjamin Shepard and Ronald Hayduk. New York: Verso, 2002.

Levine, Arthur. "A New Generation of Student Protesters Arises." *Chronicle of Higher Education* (February 26, 1999): A72.

Levine, Peter. *The Future of Democracy: The Next Generation of American Citizens.* Lebanon, N.H.: University Press of New England, 2007.

Lewis, John, with Michael D'Orso. *Walking with the Wind: A Memoir of the Movement.* New York: Simon & Schuster, 1998.

Lipset, Seymour Martin. *The First New Nation.* New York: Norton, 1979.

Loeb, Paul Rogat. *Generation at the Crossroads: Apathy and Action on the College Campus.* New Brunswick, N.J.: Rutgers University Press, 1994.

Long, Sarah E. *The New Student Politics: The Wingspread Statement on Student Civic Engagement.* 2nd ed. Providence, R.I.: Campus Compact, 2002.

Lowi, Theodore J. *The End of Liberalism: The Second Republic of the United States.* 2nd ed. New York: Norton, 1979.

Macpherson, C. B. *The Life and Times of Liberal Democracy.* Oxford: Oxford University Press, 1976.

Madadi, Yasmin. "USAS Kicks Ass." *The Nation* (May 12, 2009): 5.

Madigan, Nick. "Cries of Activism and Terrorism in S.U.V. Torching." *New York Times,* August 31, 2003, 20.

Main, Jackson Turner. *The Antifederalists: Critics of the Constitution, 1781–1788.* Chicago: University of Chicago Press, 1961.

Manley, John F., and Kenneth M. Dolbeare, eds. *The Case Against the Constitution.* Armonk, N.Y.: M. E. Sharpe, 1987.

Mann, Eric. *L.A.'s Lethal Air: New Strategies for Policy, Organizing, and Action.* Los Angeles: Labor/Community Watchdog, 1991.

Mansbridge, Jane J. *Beyond Adversary Democracy.* New York: Basic Books, 1980.

Markhoff, John. "A Newer, Lonelier Crowd Emerges in Internet Study." *New York Times,* February 16, 2000, A1, A8.

Markus, Gregory. "America's Politically Inert Youth." *Christian Science Monitor* (March 16, 1992): 18.

Mason, Ronald M. *Participatory and Workplace Democracy: A Theoretical Development in the Critique of Liberalism.* Carbondale: Southern Illinois University Press, 1982.

Mathews, David. *Politics for People: Finding a Responsible Public Voice.* Urbana: University of Illinois Press, 1994.

McAdam, Doug. *Freedom Summer.* New York: Oxford University Press, 1988.

Melber, Ari. "Obama's iSuccess." *The Nation* (October 27, 2008): 8.

Milbrath, Lester W. *Political Participation.* Chicago: Rand McNally, 1965.

Miller, Claire Cain. "How Obama's Internet Campaign Changed Politics." *New York Times,* November 7, 2008.

Miller, James. *Democracy Is in the Streets: From Port Huron to the Siege of Chicago.* New York: Simon & Schuster, 1987.

Mills, Kay. *This Little Light of Mine: The Life of Fannie Lou Hamer.* New York: Dutton, 1993.

Monbiot, George. *Heat: How to Stop the Planet from Burning.* Cambridge, Mass.: South End Press, 2007.

Morin, Richard, and Dan Balz. "Children of the Tuned-in Find Politics a Turnoff: Offspring of '60's Generation Bored by Process." *Washington Post,* June 17, 1992, A1.

Morris, Aldon D. *The Origins of the Civil Rights Movement: Black Communities Organizing for Change.* New York: Free Press, 1984.

Morse, Suzanne W., ed. *Politics for the Twenty-First Century: What Should Be Done on Campus?* Dubuque, Iowa: Kettering Foundation, 1992.

Mossberger, Karen, Caroline J. Tolbert, and Mary Stansbury. *Virtual Inequality: Beyond the Digital Divide.* Washington, D.C.: Georgetown University Press, 2003.

Murray, Sara. "The Curse of the Class of 2009." *The Wall Street Journal,* May 9–10, 2009, A1 and A11.

"National Service." *Rolling Stone* (April 2, 2009): 63.

Nichols, John. "The Beat." *The Nation* (August 21/28, 2000): 9.

Obama, Barack. *Dreams from My Father: A Story of Race and Inheritance.* Rev. ed. New York: Three Rivers Press, 2004.

"Obama and ACORN." *The Wall Street Journal,* October 14, 2008; available at http://online.wsj.com/article/SB/223940510712307.html.

Ogle, Alex. "Report: Right-Wing Militias on the Rise in US." August 13, 2009; available at www.truthout.org/081409H.

Oppenheimer, Martin. "The Limitations of Socialism: Some Sociological Observations on Participatory Democracy." In *The Case for Participatory Democracy,* edited by C. George Benello and Dimitrios Roussopoulos. New York: Viking, 1971.

Paget, Karen. "Resurgence at the Grassroots?" *American Prospect,* no. 2 (Summer 1990): 115–128.

Pateman, Carole. *Participation and Democratic Theory.* Cambridge: Cambridge University Press, 1970.

Patterson, Thomas E. *The Vanishing Voter: Public Involvement in an Age of Uncertainty.* New York: Knopf, 2002.

People for the American Way. *Democracy's Next Generation: American Youth Attitudes on Citizenship, Government, and Politics.* Washington, D.C.: People for the American Way, 1989.

Piven, Frances Fox, and Richard A. Cloward. "Northern Bourbons: A Preliminary Report on the National Voter Registration Act." *PS: Political Science and Politics* (March 1996): 39–42.

———. *Poor People's Movements: Why They Succeed, How They Fail.* New York: Vintage, 1979.

———. *Why Americans Don't Vote.* New York: Pantheon, 1988.

———. *Why Americans Still Don't Vote: And Why Politicians Want It That Way.* Boston: Beacon Press, 2000.

Putnam, Robert D. "AmeriCorpse?" *New York Times,* March 24, 1995, A31.

———. "A Better Society in a Time of War." *New York Times,* October 19, 2001, A19.

———. "Bowling Alone: America's Declining Social Capital." *Journal of Democracy* 6, no. 1 (January 1995): 64–78.

———. *Bowling Alone: The Collapse and Revival of American Community.* New York: Simon & Schuster, 2000.

———. *Making Democracy Work: Civic Traditions in Modern Italy.* Princeton, N.J.: Princeton University Press, 1993.

———. "The Strange Disappearance of Civic America." *American Prospect,* no. 24 (Winter 1996): 34–48.

Quadagno, Jill. *The Color of Welfare: How Racism Undermined the War on Poverty.* New York: Oxford University Press, 1994.

Raines, Howell, ed. *My Soul Is Rested: The Story of the Civil Rights Movement in the Deep South.* New York: Penguin, 1977.

Ratner, Lizzy. "Generation Recession." *The Nation* (November 23, 2009): 23–26.

Reed, T.V. *The Art of Protest: Culture and Activism from the Civil Rights Movement to the Streets of Seattle.* Minneapolis: University of Minnesota Press, 2005.

Rheingold, Howard. *The Virtual Reality.* Reading, Mass.: Addison-Wesley, 1993.

Rhoads, Christopher. "Going Back to Grass Roots for Obama Stimulus Push." *Wall Street Journal,* January 31 and February 1, 2009, A3.

Rimmerman, Craig A. "Democracy and Critical Education for Citizenship." *PS: Political Science and Politics* (September 1991): 492–495.

———. *Presidency by Plebiscite.* Boulder: Westview Press, 1993.

———. *The Lesbian and Gay Movements: Assimilation or Liberation?* Boulder, Colorado: Westview Press, 2008.

———. "Service-Learning and Public Policy." In *Service-Learning and the Liberal Arts,* edited by Craig A. Rimmerman. Lanham, Md.: Rowman & Littlefield, 2009.

———., ed. *Service-Learning and the Liberal Arts.* Lanham, Md.: Rowman & Littlefield, 2009.

Rogers, Harrell R., and Michael Harrington. *Unfinished Democracy: The American Political System.* Glenview, Ill.: Scott, Foresman, 1981.

Rosenstone, Steven J., and John Mark Hansen. *Mobilization, Participation, and Democracy in America.* New York: Macmillan, 1993.

Rutenberg, Jim, and Christopher Drew. "Obama Plans National Push on Ads and Turnout." *New York Times,* June 22, 2008.

Sale, Kirkpatrick. *SDS.* New York: Random House, 1973.

Schlosser, Eric. *Fast Food Nation: The Dark Side of the All-American Meal.* Boston: Houghton Mifflin, 2001.

Schumpeter, Joseph. *Capitalism, Socialism, and Democracy.* 3rd ed. New York: Harper & Row, 1950.

Shabecoff, Philip. *A Fierce Green Fire: The American Environmental Movement.* New York: Hill and Wang, 1993.

Sherman, Jake. "Conservatives Take a Page From Left's Online Playbook." *Wall Street Journal,* August 20, 2009, A4.

Sidel, Ruth. *Battling Bias: The Struggle for Identity and Community on College Campuses.* New York: Viking, 1994.

Skocpol, Theda. *Diminished Democracy: From Membership to Management in American Civic Life.* Norman: University of Oklahoma Press, 2003.

Smith, Michael Peter. *The City and Social Theory.* New York: St. Martin's Press, 1979.

Spencer, Jane. "Raising a Ruckus: Students Take the Bus to DC." *The Nation* (April 24, 2000): 22–23.

Steiger, Kay. "Democracy Versus Debt." *The American Prospect* (March 2008): A18–A20.

Stern, Kenneth. *A Force upon the Plain.* New York: Simon & Schuster, 1996.

Stoecker, Randy, and Elizabeth A. Tryon, with Amy Hilgendorf, eds. *The Unheard Voices: Community Organizations and Service Learning.* Philadelphia: Temple University Press, 2009.

Strom, Stephanie. "Funds Misappropriated at 2 Nonprofit Groups." *New York Times,* July 9, 2008; available at www.nytimes.com/2008/07/09/us/09embezzle.html.

Stumpe, Joe, and Monica Davey. "Abortion Doctor Shot to Death in Kansas Church." *New York Times,* June 1, 2009; available at www.nytimes.com/2009/06/01/us/o1tiller.html?emc+eta1.

Tarrow, Sidney. *Power in Movement: Social Movements, Collective Action and Politics.* Cambridge: Cambridge University Press, 1994.

Times Mirror Center for the People and the Press. Press release. Washington, D.C., June 28, 1990, 1.

Tocqueville, Alexis de. *Democracy in America.* Edited by Richard Heffner. New York: Mentor Books, 1956.

Tolchin, Susan. *The Angry American: How Voter Rage Is Changing the Nation.* Boulder: Westview Press, 1996.

USA Freedom Corps 2003 Annual Report: Building a Culture of Service. Washington, D.C.: The White House, 2004.

Vaid, Urvashi. *Virtual Equality: The Mainstreaming of Gay and Lesbian Liberation.* New York: Anchor Books, 1995.

Waldman, Steven. *The Bill.* New York: Viking, 1995.

Wattenberg, Martin P. *Where Have All the Voters Gone?* Cambridge: Harvard University Press, 2002.

Weisbrot, Robert. *Freedom Bound: A History of America's Civil Rights Movement.* New York: Plume, 1990.

Wilentz, Sean. "Pox Populi." *New Republic* (August 9, 1993): 29–35.

Wilgoren, Jodi. "Public Service's Profile Is Rising in Many College Curriculums." *New York Times,* April 24, 2000, A18.

Winograd, Morley, and Michael D. Hais. *Millennial Makeover: MySpace, You Tube, and the Future of American Politics.* New Brunswick, N.J.: Rutgers University Press, 2008.

Winters, Ben. "You Make the Call." *In These Times.* (March 31, 2003): 8.

Wofford, Harris. *1999 Highlights: Corporation for National Service.* Washington, D.C.: Corporation for National Service, 1999.

Wolin, Sheldon. *The Presence of the Past: Essays on the State and the Constitution.* Baltimore, Md.: Johns Hopkins University Press, 1989.

Wood, Lesley J., and Kelly Moore. "Target Practice: Community Activism in a Global Era." In *From ACT UP to the WTO,* edited by Benjamin Shepard and Ronald Hayduk. New York: Verso, 2002.

Zeskind, Leonard. *Blood and Politics: The History of the White Nationalist Movement from the Margins to the Mainstream.* New York: Farrar, Straus & Giroux, 2009.

Zimmerman, Richard. *What Can I Do to Make a Difference?* New York: Plume, 1991.

Zukin, Cliff, Scott Keeter, Molly Andolina, Krista Jenkins, and Michael X. Delli Carpini. *A New Engagement? Political Participation, Civic Life, and the Changing American Citizen.* Oxford: Oxford University Press, 2006.

About the Book and Author

We are not born citizens but must be educated and trained to be citizens. This is the central tenet of *The New Citizenship,* which builds on the participatory democratic vision of the 1960s. Arguing that civic effort must go beyond merely voting, Craig Rimmerman examines grassroots mobilization, community activism, service learning, and the Internet as potential tools for confronting the breakdown of civility in U.S. politics.

At the heart of *The New Citizenship* are the questions, Why do so many Americans fail to participate in their communities' affairs? What role should the citizenry play in the political system? In addressing these concerns at a time when civic indifference is a national problem, the text evaluates the dilemma of participation, civility, and stability and outlines the sources of apathy toward government, suggesting ways in which Americans can conquer that apathy. Rimmerman also identifies alternative forms of participation (besides voting) utilized by the citizenry to register discontent with its representative government. Considerable attention is devoted to the attitudes and values of college students as they approach their roles within the larger political system.

Craig A. Rimmerman is professor of public policy studies and political science at Hobart and William Smith Colleges. He is the author of *Presidency by Plebiscite: The Reagan-Bush Era in Institutional Perspective* (Westview, 1993); editor of *Gay Rights, Military Wrongs: Political Perspectives on Lesbians and Gays in the Military* (1996); coeditor (with Kenneth A. Wald and Clyde Wilcox) of *The Politics of Gay Rights* (2000); author of *From Identity to Politics: The Lesbian and Gay Movements in the United States* (2001); editor of *The Politics of Same-Sex Marriage* (2007); the author of *The Lesbian and Gay Movements: Assimilation or Liberation?* (Westview, 2008), and editor of *Service-Learning and the Liberal Arts* (2009).

Index